∞∾∾

"We Only Come Here to Struggle"

"We Only Come Here to Struggle"

Stories from Berida's Life

Berida Ndambuki & Claire C. Robertson

INDIANA UNIVERSITY PRESS
Bloomington and Indianapolis

This book is a publication of

Indiana University Press
601 North Morton Street
Bloomington, IN 47404-3797 USA

http://www.indiana.edu/~iupress

Telephone orders   800-842-6796
Fax orders   812-855-7931
Orders by e-mail   iuporder@indiana.edu

The paper used in this publication meets the minimum
requirements of American National Standard for Information
Sciences—Permanence of Paper for Printed Library Materials,
ANSI Z39.48-1984.

Manufactured in the United States of America

Library of Congress Cataloging-in-Publication Data

Ndambuki, Berida, date
We only come here to struggle : stories from Berida's life / Berida
Ndambuki and Claire C. Robertson.
p.   cm.
Includes bibliographical references and index.
ISBN 0-253-33701-1 — ISBN 0-253-21366-5 (pbk.)
1. Ndambuki, Berida, date. 2. Women—Kenya—Nairobi
Region—Biography. 3. Grocers—Kenya—Nairobi Region—
Biography. 4. Nairobi Region (Kenya)—Biography.   I.
Robertson, Claire C., date.   II. Title.

DT434.N3 N35 2000
967.62'504'092—dc21
[B]   99-048576

1 2 3 4 5   05 04 03 02 01 00

Contents

Illustrations

All photographs are by Claire Robertson.

Glossary of Frequently Used Terms

aimu   ancestral spirit

askari   police (singular or plural)

atta   flour

bhang   marijuana

harambee   fund-raiser conducted for a cause or an individual

jembe   short-handled hoe

kanga   cloth used by women wrapped over skirt

KANU   Kenya African National Union, dominant political party

kithitu   curse

kuashia   to give bridewealth

kyondo   sisal basket/s

matatu   minibus people and goods transporter

NCC   Nairobi City Council

ndengu   mung beans

ndetema   fever

ngashia   bridewealth

nthoko   cowpeas

nyayo   popular kidney bean

Nyayo   President Moi

panga   machete

shamba   farm

sufuria   metal hibachi

sukuma wiki   kale

ukimwi   AIDS

Note on currency: Beginning in the 1920s a modified British currency was used, with 20 shillings equal to a pound. In 1971 a Kenyan pound was worth about $2.80. By 1987 about 17 shillings were equal to $1; in 1997 about 60 shillings equaled $1.

Introduction

Life Histories

Life histories are one of the best ways to learn about the lives of women in cultures other than one's own. What is a life history and what value does it have? A life history is a life story or stories told to another person by its primary author, whose life it represents. Magdalene Ngaiza and Bertha Koda defined it as "an extensive record of a person's life told to and recorded by another, who then edits and writes the life as though it were an autobiography."[1] The secondary author transcribes and publishes it; many life histories have women as both primary and secondary authors. They are a way to restore women to history, to understand change, and to look at the experiences of women other than elite women, who can write their own autobiographies. Thus, a life history can give us a view from the bottom of the socioeconomic structure in societies where the vast majority of people are literate or from ordinary people in societies where relatively few people are literate. As Fran Leeper Buss has said, "oral documents . . . provide a deep evocation of the thoughts and belief systems of people generally disenfranchised from historical memory."[2] *history from below approach*

The particular form of life history used and the purposes involved in the project may vary and should be taken into account to refine our perceptions of that history and inform our use of its content. Some critics have dismissed such work as irremediably flawed because it only represents the viewpoint and experiences of the secondary author.[3] This is, I believe, too pessimistic a declaration of lack of faith in the capacity of the human imagination to bridge cultural and ego boundaries. Women scholars by their training and inclinations have perhaps been better suited to life history work than most men, and have excelled as primary and secondary authors. Although she is not literate, Berida Ndambuki, whose story this narrative is, made a scholarly attempt in her oral narrative to convey her meaning with accuracy and seriousness. She regarded our sessions as a form of white collar work at our "offisi" (office),

---

1. Magdalene K. Ngaiza and Bertha Koda, eds., *The Unsung Heroines* (Dar es Salaam, Tanzania: WRDP Publications, 1991), p. 1.

2. Fran Leeper Buss, ed. *Forged under the Sun/Forjada bajo el sol: The Life of Maria Elena Lucas* (Ann Arbor: University of Michigan Press, 1993), p. 34.

3. For thoughtful discussions of the ethical and political issues involved in life history work see Daphne Patai's introduction to her *Brazilian Women Speak: Contemporary Life Stories* (New Brunswick, N.J.: Rutgers University Press, 1988) and the various essays in Sherna Berger Gluck and Daphne Patai, eds., *Women's Words: The Feminist Practice of Oral History* (New York: Routledge, 1991). See also Kirk Hoppe, "Whose Life Is It Anyway? Issues of Representation in Life Narrative Texts of African Women," *International Journal of African Historical Studies* 26, no. 3 (1993): 623–36, and Heidi Gengenbach's reply, "Truth-Telling and the Politics of Women's Life History Research in Africa: A Reply to Kirk Hoppe," *International Journal of African Historical Studies* 27, no. 3 (1994): 619–27.

which gave it high status, in contrast to her ordinary trade in poor to working-class conditions. Her story is irreplaceable and should be heard.

Life histories have also been questioned because of their subjectivity, their lack of representativeness, and their intense focus on one person. This criticism requires two observations in rebuttal. First, the secondary author can provide context that helps readers understand where the narrator fits within her society and what aspects of her experiences are common or unusual for her age, class, gender, ethnicity, etc. Second, the subjectivity of her experiences can be seen, in Ngaiza and Koda's words, "as an asset in the search to reveal changing and varied patterns in social relations and consciousness."[4]

Are life histories fatally compromised by their oral origins and hidden agendas? How do life histories work as history, as historical documents? Historians have been recording the memoirs of others and critiquing sources for a long time. All historical sources, written and oral, reflect the agendas of their authors. Good historians take that agenda into account when they analyze a source. Part of writing good history is the effort to analyze sources critically as much as possible and to avoid biased selection of evidence—to present a balanced view that neither edits out minority viewpoints nor overgeneralizes from them.[5] Life histories reflect the agendas of both the primary and the secondary authors and are more interesting in some ways because of that complication. If historians were to remove from consideration sources in which the agenda is not openly stated, then we would have to eliminate almost all documents from use as well as all of oral history, which by definition is not recorded by the person whose account is being recorded.[6] If we were to avoid doing life histories because we are afraid of being accused of bias, then we would lose one of the best ways of understanding other cultures. It is precisely because the life history is a mediated product of interchange between members of different cultures that those in both cultures can begin to understand each other. We can and should, however, pay attention to the agendas and needs of our subjects when we solicit, edit, and publish their stories.

To illustrate how life histories may vary in purpose and execution, I will critique a less-developed example of my own work. The change in my life history work involved, as Kathryn Anderson and Dana Jack put it, a shift "from information (data) gathering to interactive process, [which] requires new skills on the researcher's part."[7] In *Women and Slavery in Africa* I published a brief history of a Ga woman from Ghana named Adukwe, which I solicited from her in order to teach us something about slavery as practiced in

4. Ngaiza and Koda, *Unsung Heroines*, p. 6.

5. Minorities can be defined by ethnicity or race, by class status or gender, by sexual or religious preference, by nationality, and otherwise.

6. We would also have to eliminate most secondary sources, since self-reflexivity and openness about personal and political agendas have not characterized most historical analyses, in which "objectivity" and authorial omniscience have been customary.

7. Kathryn Anderson and Dana C. Jack, "Learning to Listen: Interviewing Techniques and Analyses," in *Women's Words: The Feminist Practice of Oral History,* edited by Sherna Berger Gluck and Daphne Patai (New York: Routledge), p. 23.

late-nineteenth-century Ga society on the Gold Coast.[8] Her story provided a
much-needed alternative view to that of the British colonialists, who claimed
to have abolished slavery in that area by the time she was sold in downtown
Accra in broad daylight in the main market; to that of local apologists who
claimed that Ga were never slaveholders to any extent; and to the predominantly male view of slavery that prevailed across the scholarly literature of
many nationalities, which discounted or ignored peculiarly female experiences of slavery. In her story I neither aimed for a purely literary narrative
account nor did I presume to speak in Adukwe's own voice; I used the third
person. At the time I did not think of the account as being a life history, but
rather as data from one source that was pertinent to the topic of the accompanying article. Her experiences problematized the view of women as unre-
sisting victims of slavery. If I had not taped her stories, tapes that are available
to other researchers for further analysis in the Indiana University Language
Archives, a valuable perspective would have been lost with her death at age
ninety-nine soon after we completed our work. To that point no researcher
had bothered to analyze African women's experiences of slavery because of
overwhelming male bias in research combined with neo-colonialism, which
diverted research dollars away from researchers interested in issues of gender.
My nascent life history effort was therefore specifically anti-colonial and anti-
patriarchal in stance, cutting across received wisdom at that time in many
areas. Thus, my goal in conveying Adukwe's story was paradoxical in that I
deplored colonial exploitation and yet was exploitative in that the life history
served a scholarly purpose but did not prioritize her interests. In fact, she had
initially disguised her slave origins, although she gave permission to record
her story later. My agenda subordinated hers.

Do life histories invariably involve exploitation? There are potential problems with life histories stemming from their secondary authors connected to
the following issues: not providing a socioeconomic context for the story/ies
and so perhaps giving a false impression of the typicality or atypicality of the
life presented; not providing a historical or real time frame as a context, thereby giving the story a mythical feel; and not providing these same contexts for
the secondary author so that the readers can better appreciate what sorts of
intersections are occurring in the story. The interviewing may and often does
involve unequal exchanges; that is, the researcher wants and encourages personal revelations from the primary author or narrator but does not offer the
same in exchange. This inequality of the exchange is made more likely by the
status differences between the primary and the secondary authors.[9] Proper
credit and profits are not always given to the primary author. The priorities of
the primary and secondary authors may differ.

However, if the secondary author is careful there should only be positive
consequences for the primary author, especially if the narrative teaches its

---

8. Claire C. Robertson, "Post-Proclamation Slavery in Accra: A Female Affair?" in *Women and Slavery
in Africa,* edited by C. C. Robertson and M. A. Klein (Madison: University of Wisconsin Press, 1983), pp.
230–38.

9. Patai noted this problem also. *Brazilian Women Speak,* p. 6.

readers and is taught in non-exploitative ways. Authorial credit and rewards should be given where due. The ideal relationship between the primary and secondary authors may be what could be called a reassuring friendship, in which the secondary author is open, honest, and reciprocal in revelations, while creating opportunities to be questioned herself if no questions are volunteered. Some of the tape transcript excerpts included in the Postscript are examples of times when Berida became the interviewer and questioned me and my research assistants. Fieldwork can offer, as Judith Stacey has said, "loving attention and nonjudgmental acceptance."[10] The best way to avoid exploitation in the narrative itself may be a high degree of transparency in the process of creating the work so that the primary author has ultimate veto power over the final product. I have tried for as much transparency as possible here, given time and monetary constraints. Aside from a token amount to recoup expenses, immediate and future monetary rewards went and will go to Berida and to the groups in which she is active who cooperated in the project, especially those who helped to make the videotape. These rewards formed one motivation for cooperation, but the trouble involved made their work more intensive than I believe the initial rewards justified. Everyone threw themselves into the project, even those who provided logistical support, so that it became a group effort. In that context it would be a gross betrayal of all participants if the result was harmful to them in any way. I have tried my best to see to it that it is not.

Life histories remain one of the best and most effective ways of expanding the horizons of their readers and challenging their assumptions if the secondary author does not compromise the material by deleting the controversial, abandoning contradictions, imposing foreign priorities, or grossly mistranslating. To abandon life history attempts would be to silence the voices of many women whose stories would otherwise not be heard, however imperfectly. I believe these efforts are worth pursuing and perfecting.

When beginning work on this life history I asked Berida to explain her life story to her American and Kenyan audiences and to be sure to include what she thinks is important for them to know. Berida's reasons for agreeing to this project were various and included more than the personal ones I shall discuss shortly. She wants others to learn from her experiences and she wants teachers like myself to inculcate courage in students so that they may deal with life's problems. Her lively mind appreciated the opportunity to reflect on her life and assert her own value, to discover patterns in structuring her narrative. She realized, I believe, what many groups have realized; that recording their own stories can serve as a form of empowerment. Contemporary women, not always Westerners, may do life histories of those in their own or other societies to empower themselves, to further cross-cultural understanding, and/or to preserve in written form the history of those whose memories have previously taken only oral form. These narratives have profound implications for

---

    10. Judith Stacey, "Can There Be a Feminist Ethnography?" in *Women's Words: The Feminist Practice of Oral History,* edited by Sherna Berger Gluck and Daphne Patai (New York: Routledge), p. 117.

building a sense of identity—for both individuals and groups. One of the best reasons for doing life histories is the potential empowerment of those whose stories are communicated. As Buss has stated, "[since] memory itself is a political event, . . . creating space for re-memory may be a profoundly liberating and energizing experience."[11]

Berida Ndambuki

I first encountered Berida Ndambuki in December of 1987 at Gikomba Market, the largest outdoor market in Nairobi, Kenya. I was surveying sellers at Gikomba as part of the research for a book, *Trouble Showed the Way: Women, Men, and Trade in the Nairobi Area, 1890 to 1990* (Bloomington: Indiana University Press, 1997). She was a leader of the dried staples sellers, some 400 women who occupied a prominent hillside at one entrance to the market. I found Berida's personality—her intelligence, openness, enthusiasm, liveliness, and talent for dramatization—very appealing, and we developed a relationship that extended to some limited socializing outside of work hours. It was not a close relationship but definitely a friendly one. In 1996, with the completion of the *Trouble* book, I came up with the idea of doing a longer life history with Berida that would show the world the complexities of her life in eastern Nairobi and at her home in Kathonzweni, an Ukambani village east of Nairobi. Berida's unique qualities and the prospect of doing the kind of life history I had envisioned made such a project attractive, as did the possibilities for helping the women's groups in which Berida plays a strong role with any resultant profits. Further plans included doing an accompanying videotape to demonstrate more vividly Berida and her life's contexts. The results you see here.

My choice of Berida Ndambuki as a subject for a life history was not random, although she first came to my attention as one among a randomized sample. In any crowd Berida will stand out. She is physically handsome and has an imposing presence, with articulateness, humor, and ability—qualities that have made her cohorts select her to lead women's groups at Gikomba and Kathonzweni. She has been relatively successful as a businesswoman/staples seller for almost thirty years in Nairobi and elsewhere. She has also coped with the manifold responsibilities imposed by her very large family (she bore sixteen children, ten of whom survived to adulthood, the largest number of children borne by anyone in my survey of some 1,000 traders) and a husband whose irresponsibility and disabilities increased her burdens (I did not understand the extent and full implications of her husband's problems until I did the interviewing for this book). Thus, her particular attributes led me to think that her experiences would be of interest to a world audience, that she would do the work involved in this project adeptly and persuasively, and that it would interest her to do it. In fact, when Jane Ngima Turunga, my research assistant extraordinaire, broached the project to her she readily agreed and became enthusiastic, without any particular prospect of material gain from it.

---

11. Buss, *Forged under the Sun*, p. 31.

As our work progressed she came to understand the advantages of speaking to an international audience. Without her strong abilities, patience, and enthusiasm this project would never have been completed.

Berida also was attractive as a subject because of the more usual aspects of her life. Her double life at Kathonzweni and in Nairobi typified a certain sector of the Nairobi women traders, many of whom began with strong rural roots but who are becoming urban in orientation. This applied particularly to those from Ukambani, the Akamba women, whose entry into Nairobi trade came later than, for instance, the involvement of the Kikuyu, which went back to Nairobi's beginnings in the last decade of the nineteenth century. But Ukambani, the Akamba homeland, is further away than Kikuyuland from Nairobi, and only the press of severe drought and famine seems to have encouraged Akamba women to come to Nairobi to trade in large numbers after Kenya's independence in 1963. Berida is a representative of the first substantial wave of Akamba women to settle in Nairobi on a long-term basis. However, this move is not permanent; she intends to go back to Kathonzweni eventually and in 1999 began that transition.

Berida's values regarding marriage are common among those of her age group who came to Nairobi to trade; in the *Trouble* book (see Chapter 6) I called them a transitional generation in this regard. By that I meant that they accepted the goals and values concerning marriage of those older than themselves, who were born in the 1920s, but also presaged changes that involved those younger than themselves, born in the 1940s, whose marriages often fell apart or became dysfunctional for various reasons. Berida's marriage began with patrilocal residence as in the old system and she arranged her own marriage with her parents' consent, a typical pattern for her generation. Despite her husband's impositions on the family and herself, she has not divorced Ndambuki, but rather has evolved the present separate residential pattern, a clear compromise followed neither by many younger women, who left their husbands when faced with such dire circumstances, nor by older women, who stayed home and farmed. Berida has threatened to leave permanently but also has a strong belief in marital endurance.

Ndambuki's addiction to alcohol reflects a problem common among elderly men in rural areas; it is almost an expected behavior tolerated by most people. His particular addiction, however, is more extreme than most in that it has continued over a long period of time (by her account from at least the early 1960s until the present) and has resulted in unacceptable antisocial behavior that has embarrassed and impoverished his family and annoyed the neighbors. Readers will also find in this account examples of good husbands in Berida's view, men who have built comfortable homes with their wives, and of good fathers like Ndambuki's father, who tried to make up for his son's deficiencies in providing support.

Berida was born in 1936 and married in 1950 at a younger age than most of her cohorts, who married at age eighteen or so. The 1950s insurgency called Mau Mau by the British, Kenya's militant independence movement, disrupted Berida's life as it did the lives of most central Kenyans, although the Akamba were not subjected as much as the Kikuyu were to systemic villagization and internment of the rural population by the British colonialists.[12] There was a lot of movement by Akamba into new areas of settlement to escape colonial exactions, which is what happened with Berida's conjugal family; sometimes these areas were dryer and not as well suited to cultivation.[13] After independence she moved again, this time to Kathonzweni, to land which falls into this category. Conditions there worsened with further cultivation and the periodic droughts and floods that forced many to seek a living elsewhere. When women in such circumstances moved it was often because the husband was not an adequate provider, as in Berida's case. His failure to provide goes beyond mere irresponsibility into parasitism because of his addiction. He was atypical of the husbands of women traders in my sample; of the women who were still married 80 percent had husbands who were helping to provide for the family. But slightly more than half of the 667 women in the sample of over 1,000 traders were either widowed or divorced. Also, because women often disguised the fact that husbands were not helping (a husband's failure to provide was a source of shame for women) this statistic may be overly optimistic. Failure to provide was the most common reason women cited when they sought divorce.

If there is a dominant motif in Berida's account of her life, it is poverty and all of the tremendous exigencies it imposes. Mohandas Gandhi said that poverty is the worst atrocity and Berida is a poverty survivor, just as others are survivors of abuse. Her self-esteem and her triumphant stories most often concern her ability to overcome poverty to enable her family to survive. In constructing a narrative out of these stories I realized that Berida had provided a meta-narrative, a story of this triumph that she returned to again and again at various stages, not necessarily in chronological order. That meta-narrative is presented at the end of Chapter 2 and again in Chapter 3, rearranged in chronological order to reduce confusion on the part of the reader. Other stories are given in other chapters to honor the priorities Berida established for her life history. However, on the whole chronological order is not observed in this history except occasionally within themes. Elsa Barkley Brown has said,

> If we analyze those people and actions by linear models we will create dichotomies, ambiguities, cognitive dissonance, disorientation, and confusion in places where none exists. If, however . . . we can allow the way in which they saw and constructed

---

12. Pre-1950s Kikuyuland and Ukambani were characterized by dispersed village settlements, many of which were consolidated and fenced with barbed wire and trenches during the Mau Mau Emergency. British counterinsurgency measures further included forbidding people to go to their farms except under restricted conditions. There were also concentration camps for captured guerrilla fighters and for those suspected of sympathizing with or aiding the Land and Freedom Army (LFA), as they called themselves. Many atrocities were committed, but more by the British than the LFA; the casualties included fewer than 100 whites and thousands of Africans. Jean Davison and the Women of Mutira, *Voices from Mutira: Change in the Lives of Rural Gikuyu Women, 1910–1995* (Boulder, Colo.: Lynn Rienner, 1996), pp. 45–46.

13. D. J. Penwill noted that there was already little arable land available for new settlement in the 1940s. *Kamba Customary Law* (Nairobi: Kenya Literature Bureau, 1951), p. 35. Penwill was a district officer in Ukambani and developed expertise in the administration of customary law as a consequence.

their own lives to provide the analytical framework by which we attempt to under-stand their experiences and their world, it will provide a structural framework.[14]

I have attempted to accomplish this here. This structure also reflects the par-tial nature of this history, which has no claims to be a totalizing representation of her experiences. It is what she chose to share with us—her "truth," as it were—which inevitably includes societal conventional wisdom, self-censor-ship, political views, religious beliefs, foundational myths, etc. I have tried to be as faithful as possible to Berida's words and priorities.

This account is, however, strongly mediated by my organizational inter-ventions and various interactions and translations among project partici-pants. I have tried to be deeply mindful of the cautions many have lodged regarding the necessity of paying attention to my own biases and interven-tions in this story. I have followed Daphne Patai's dictum that "[t]hose of us who have the opportunity to be heard must not conceal our own role in creating meaning, in defining reality."[15] Nonetheless, as Judith Stacey has stated, "There . . . can and should be feminist research that is rigorously self-aware and therefore humble about the partiality of the ethnographic vision and its capacity to represent self and other."[16] Thus, this life history is a nar-rative written down not by its primary author, who is non-literate, but by a researcher of middle-class midwestern U.S. background, mediated by input and translation by Mbithe Anzaya and Jane Turunga. Mbithe is well educated with bachelor's and master's degrees from Kenyatta University, a husband and children, a model suburban home, and experience in education, home economics, and health care. She is familiar with the locale of the Nairobi por-tion of this study, having taught for a time at St. John's Church and Com-munity Center in Pumwani, where we did most of the interviewing. She is a first-language Kikamba speaker and upper middle class by Kenyan standards. Nevertheless, she shared many dominant values with Berida, such as the ten-dency to blame women for rape or other violence against them. Her work for me was characteristically careful and thorough.

Jane is a first-language Kikuyu speaker, an incisive thinker, and a capable organizer. She completed middle school at Othaya in Nyeri north of Nairobi, has one son whom she supports, and worked as a nursery school teacher before joining my project in 1987–1988. She is the mainstay of the project. After I left she switched careers and began selling used clothing at Gikomba Market while keeping up a correspondence with me and occasionally conduct-ing further inquiries at my request. Their shared experiences in the market and similar class status bridged the ethnic differences between Jane and Beri-

---

14. Elsa Barkley Brown, "African-American Women's Quilting: A Framework for Conceptualizing and Teaching African-American Women's History," *Signs* 14, no. 4 (1989): 921–29. Chronology is not the only linearity imposed in life histories. In *Brazilian Women Speak*, Patai has a brilliant discussion of oral nar-ratives as poetry and the effects of converting non-linear oral narratives, which scan more like poetry, to linear prose (pp. 19–28).

15. Patai, *Brazilian Women Speak*, p. 34.

16. Stacey, "Feminist Ethnography," p. 117.

da to a large extent, reducing these differences to the subject of jokes on occasion (see Postscript). Both Jane and Mbithe are in their late thirties and thus are over twenty years younger than Berida.

I have a Ph.D. in African history with some twenty-five years of teaching and research experience about Africa (four of which were spent in Ghana and Kenya), and a joint academic appointment between the Departments of History and Women's Studies at The Ohio State University. My provenance is problematized by the tendency in the U.S. Midwest to construct African-Americans as the primary "other." My outrage at racial discrimination in the United States and South Africa was rooted in the experiences of coming of age in the 1960s, in the study of slavery, in my experiences as a woman in a strongly patriarchal society, as well as in my contemplation of the incarceration of Native Americans on reservations, which resonated with the policy used by the British in Kenya to place many Africans in "reserves" so that many lost their land. All of these experiences led to my life choice to be an Africanist. My own family history turned out to have more in common with that of Berida than I understood when I began the project. My father, like Ndambuki, was an alcoholic and was deeply patriarchal. My mother was a businesswoman for most of her life, which was unusual for her generation and class. Like Berida, she had her own business and traveled to pursue it. She also subscribed strongly to male-dominated societal values and tried, not always successfully, to inculcate them in her three daughters. Unlike Berida, however, I am a feminist—I believe that women are more often than not (but not universally) oppressed and need to overcome that oppression to create a more equitable world. My feminist convictions were deeply offended by some of the material here that portrays the extent to which many central Kenyan women participate in the construction of the profoundly male-dominant socio-economic system that is facilitated by patrilinearity and patrilocality in rural areas.

But Berida's story rescues itself from being a recounting of yet another sad patriarchal epic, just as it is not merely a saga of a woman subjected to puberty rites that included excision of the clitoris. It can also be read as a triumph of sorts over male dominance, a reclaiming of Berida's rights to her labor, her body, and her spirit. However, like most things in life, its complexity does not lend itself to simple interpretation along any of these lines. Berida does not fit easily into essentialized notions that would make her an uncontested victim, an unblemished survivor, or a triumphantly empowered victor. Although Berida is not a feminist (she even blames feminists for bringing AIDS to Nairobi), the triumphs over adversity, the seizing of control over their own livelihoods and bodies, and the awareness of continuing problems of women of Berida's generation have helped to pave the way for the efforts of younger women to assert themselves.[17]

[handwritten marginal note: reasons for studying this area]

---

17. Claire C. Robertson, _Trouble Showed the Way: Women, Men, and Trade in the Nairobi Area, 1890 to 1990_ (Bloomington: Indiana University Press, 1997).

Nairobi, 1997–1998: The Research Team

Jane Turunga at her former
residence in Biafra, 1998

Nor can one separate Berida's beliefs into "traditional" (whenever that was) and "modern" (whatever that is).[18] Berida is not particularly interested in old customs and self-consciously considers herself a good Christian who has rejected the old ways; she is a purveyor of urban chic and contemporary wisdom to her village cohorts. She has little interest in folklore, can recognize pictures of contemporary political leaders in newspapers, and keeps up with the latest trends (she has heard of face-peeling as a method of rejuvenating women's looks, for instance). At the same time she has trouble grappling with the concept of keeping an animal as a pet rather than for food and with making a clear choice of favorite color or food; all seemed good to one who has suffered extremes of deprivation. She was raised when the old ways that preceded her mother's conversion to Christianity still had meaning, particularly for her grandmother. But these "old ways" are located in time—the late nineteenth and early twentieth centuries—and not in a timeless unchanging past in which everything was done for ritual purposes, as the use of the term "traditional" implies.

Although Berida was not very interested in telling the kind of folkloric stories that were used to instill lessons in children, she is an accomplished raconteur and observer of the contemporary scene; her wicked sense of humor keeps her audience enthralled in laughter (see the tape excerpt 11-98-16-17 in the Postscript, where she decided to tease me). In general, Berida's stories evoke a prismatic portrait of twentieth-century central Kenyan life: of the impact of colonialism, of hunger and the contrast between rich and poor, of hard work and survival, of marriage and socioeconomic change, of addiction and AIDS, of violence against women, of the experience of being the primary supporter of a large family and a leader among women, of rural and urban contrasts, of religious conversion and fundamentalist bigotry, of contemporary politics and ethnocentrism, and of death. In this story there is humor—from Berida's serving as a ringer in local school sports to the men traders who cross-dress to seek advantage—and bathos—from the deserted granddaughter for whom Berida cannot pay the school fees to her favorite brother's death from AIDS. Because it happened after the completion of the interviewing and the vetting of the manuscript by Berida, the death of her eldest son and family stalwart Dominic in late 1998 is not reflected in this account.

In fact, the story of Berida's life provides an excellent way to learn about the complexities of socioeconomic change, especially when we explore the contradictions in what she has to say to us. Some of her actions that contrast with her values are manifested in decisions about her children's education, her selective participation in puberty rites, and her decisions about her own marriage and career. Why does she tell three different stories about the fate of her shop built at Kathonzweni? Why were there three different stories regarding

---

18. Ngugi wa Thiong'o, Kenya's foremost novelist and playwright, offers a cogent critique of the false polarity of traditional versus modern in his Foreword to Osonye Onwueme, *Tell It to Women* (Detroit: Wayne State University Press, 1997), p. 7.

her daughters' puberty rites? Rather than eliminating contradictory material of this sort, I have included it to provide readers with a means of exploring tension points in the narrative. Only by appreciating the paradoxical aspects of Berida's life can we have an inkling about both current trends and the direction of future socioeconomic change and grasp not just a duality but the multi-layered hybridity of her experiences.

Process: The Recording and Construction of a Narrative

The narrative was constructed from fieldnotes and tapes of interviews conducted in 1987–1988 and 1997–1998, at Gikomba Market to begin with, and ten years later at St. John's Church and Community Center in Pumwani, near Berida's home and workplace in eastern Nairobi. Conditions at Gikomba Market prohibited intensive interviewing there; we could not record in Berida's single-room Nairobi home because it was too small to accommodate more than two people and had no electricity. As a deeply religious person, Berida was comfortable with the church setting suggested and facilitated by Mbithe Anzaya, who did much of the necessary on-the-spot interpreting. My Kikamba extends only to rudimentary greetings; the choice was between spending years to learn another language sufficiently to use it with facility and possibly losing the project altogether or doing it immediately without the language.

I would usually begin the morning by saying something like, "Let's talk about what it was like when you were growing up, the place, children's games, particular incidents that impressed you, whatever." Mbithe would translate this and then Berida would select from her memory, which is prodigious, episodes of significance to her. Any of us might have then asked a question but we did not often interrupt the flow. The goal was to get her to speak comfortably and fluently with few interventions so that her priorities would be clear. On several occasions we had to stop in the middle of a long story and continue it the next day. Berida was not shy about ignoring a question if she had not finished a story to her satisfaction, or about interrupting subsequent translation or questions with additional comments to clarify matters. In this text I have eliminated or had Berida restate (which she did on occasion) most questions to improve the flow of the narrative. Many questions were mere affirmations or requests for clarification. She modified the pronunciation of my name to Kilaya, which she used throughout to address or refer to me, and wanted us to call her Berida.

The pace of the telling varied radically. There were times when there were rather evenly balanced exchanges among the four of us, Jane, Mbithe, Berida, and myself, contrasted with hours in which no one except Berida said much. In the Postscript there are examples of both kinds of situations. In 1997 it took several interviews before Berida loosened up and seemed comfortable; from there on things flowed rather smoothly but sometimes discontinuously—that is, skipping around in time, space, and topic; my main intervention has been to put everything pertaining mainly to one topic in one place. Normally we would work from about 10 A.M. to 1 P.M., sharing tea and sometimes lunch afterward; we amended the schedule to account for probable riots associated with pre-election maneuvering and people's commitments. To cross-check my notes and get more of the rhythm of the telling, other research assistants who were first-language Kikamba speakers—Beatrice Mulala, Truphosa Mwololo, Josephine Mutiso, Jayne Mutiga, Mwikali Kioko, and Anita Kiamba—did word-for-word translations/transcriptions of the tapes and I also consulted on knotty points with Truphosa Mwololo. Here I have tried to preserve the expression and tone of what Berida was saying as well as the content as much as can be done in the imperfect medium of English. Very little has been edited out, although I did delete some material that we inquired about but which did not interest Berida greatly and a few repetitions, but even most of those are included because they were intended as emphasis or indicate the importance of certain occurrences for Berida.

To comment on the text in various ways I have included as sidebars actual excerpts from the tape transcriptions at crucial points and other material: accounts by myself, Berida's family members, Mbithe, and Jane of experiences surrounding the taping; newspaper accounts of related material; relevant stories from neighbors, the cameraman, one of the tape transcribers, etc. The transcript excerpts allow the reader to examine the process of changing the sessions into a first-person narrative. There is also a Postscript with more complete transcript excerpts that include Berida's questions to us about the United States or family matters and other interactions that explicate further our relationship and her reactions to my representations of U.S. culture. With the narrative I have included occasional explanatory footnotes in which I attempted to be faithful to historical context; for example, if Berida was discussing her marriage as it was in the 1970s, I might have included a footnote from a sociologist discussing Akamba marriage in the 1970s.

In May 1998 I returned to Nairobi to go over the manuscript word for word with Berida (with Mbithe translating from English to Kikamba), and to clear up things that seemed problematic. This second, briefer period of interviewing had a more relaxed atmosphere and included some extensive discussions among the research team (by then all of us were definitely a team who socialized together and discussed everything) about the meaning of certain language, about the significance of certain actions, and even freewheeling discussions and arguments over topics that ranged from what to do about addiction or violence against women to the best way to terrace a field. Berida interrupted the reading of the manuscript at a number of points, as she was encouraged to do, to make corrections and additions, but did not delete anything. She insisted repeatedly that the real names of herself and her friends and family members be used in this account, although I offered on several occasions to blind it in such a way as to make them anonymous. Berida's judgments of people are therefore here but should be taken as a point of view and not as essentialist statements regarding their worth. They are heavily influenced by her strong valuing of appearances, wealth, and respect for the elders. Rather than intervene in the narrative to edit out matter that might hurt the feelings of those involved, I included it, contravening the principle I have heretofore followed of doing no harm as an imperative of fieldwork. This issue mostly concerns family relationships. I hope that the frankness here might eventually improve those relationships; that was Berida's hope (she wants her husband to stop drinking, one of her daughters to stop insulting her and apologize, and bridewealth to be paid for all of her daughters so that they have respectable marriages), but that might not be the initial impact.

The final form of this account is therefore a negotiated one that also reflects the changing realities over the years in which it was done. In 1987–1988 Berida was in her early fifties and doing well in her business. She was self-confident and physically strong, while in 1997–1998 she had aged visibly and relied more on her daughter Martha to help her with the business and domestic chores. She said that the business was in bad shape due partly to increased political ructions in Nairobi (the Saba-Saba and Nane-Nane riots that took place at the time of the interviewing in July and August before the elections of December 1997) and to a theft. The torrential floods in Ukambani of 1997–1998 had a great impact on her Kathonzweni home and changed conditions there. The dam built by one of the village groups was washed away. Berida's life continues to develop even more complexities. I completed this narrative in mid-1998; it reflects subsequent events only in a brief 1999 update and a few minor changes.

Although this narrative is, as any life history is, a partial representation problematized by all of the participants in its construction, the qualifications that inform this work have improved it. The situation required a mediated voice in this work. The input of those critics of the life history genre who have led the way in promoting caution and fidelity to sources has informed my methodological decisions at every point. This exercise was tremendously illuminating for its participants in posing dilemmas and successes in cross-racial, cross-cultural, and cross-class communication. This project has been my most rewarding at a personal level because of the relationships that evolved out of it. I have tried to present Berida's history as faithfully to her intentions and words as possible, but her stories had an audience who played a role in their unfolding. They are interactive. In this representation of Berida's life history I have tried to be faithful to the trust of both the readers and of all of those intimately involved with this project. To all who participated I am extremely grateful, but especially to Berida Ndambuki and her generous family.

The Videotape: A Viewer's Guide to *Second Face: Berida's Lives*

While the interviewing was taking place, I made arrangements to videotape impressions from Berida's complicated life. To make the videotape, the research team traveled to Kathonzweni, but conditions at Gikomba precluded the distraction of our presence while filming (see cameraman's sidebar in Chapter 3). This videotape is intended to give a vivid representation of Berida's life in Kathonzweni and in Nairobi. Most of the material on the videotape is not in the book (an exception is Ndambuki's speech, which is given verbatim in a sidebar in Chapter 2), but the book provides essential background for the video and helps viewers to understand its context and content. The book and the videotape comment on and complement each other. Visual Productions (Nairobi) and Indiana University ISS Media Services (Bloomington) were responsible for the technical aspects of its production. Dennis Kavinghua, a talented young cameraman, did most of the filming, sometimes under extremely trying circumstances.

In the videotape the cast of characters includes Berida and her husband, Ndambuki; her eldest daughter and workmate, Martha; her sister Domitila (who talks about their father and adventures in Nairobi); her son Muthama (who helped her take a bag of produce to market); her youngest son, Martin Wambua, recipient of her lecture on responsibility and the work ethic; and his wife, Emma, who performs many household chores and is the daughter of Berida's friend and neighbor Elena and her husband John, also present in the film. Women's self-help groups figure prominently: at Kathonzweni, Ndethya Ngutethya; and in Nairobi, the Kasilili dance group and Kyeni kya Gikomba (Mbemba na Mbosa), whose leader, Mbulwa, is Berida's friend.

Second Face follows Berida to work at Gikomba, to her rural home at Kathonzweni in Ukambani, and back to her home in Nairobi. The focus on a relatively successful market woman, mother of ten, and wife of forty-eight years provides a lens that widens to encompass many aspects of contemporary Kenyan life. We see Berida's involvement in women's groups in both places, her friendships and family, the heavy burden of women's rural labor, and the tribulations of life and death in Nairobi. Issues addressed in the video include social and economic changes, environmental degradation and reconstruction, class differences within families and villages, the gender division of labor and women's work, urban and rural contrasts, addiction, care for the aged, and marital and family relationships.

The scenes in the film represent random ordinary occurrences in Berida's life, with the exception of the celebrations and presentations by the women's groups on behalf of me, my family, and the viewing audience. I asked Dennis Kavinghua to follow Berida and her family's daily activities, which he did, usually by himself to minimize the disturbance of our presence. Moreover, while selecting which scenes to include from some eleven hours of film, I chose what seemed most common and/or significant. Although random chance did play a role in what was filmed, there were, I believe, meaningful absences from the footage that say something about the nature of the lives and habits of those in the film. For instance, there was no footage of Ndambuki or Martin Wambua caring for children in a nurturing manner; nor was there a water tank at the Ndambukis' farm, only a pile of stones to make a foundation for one. Viewers can therefore deduce from the film a certain relationship to actual circumstances in the multiple locations of its filming.

Some questions that viewers might want to consider in relation to the issues mentioned above include the following:

1. How has involvement in trade changed Berida's life? What other changes are evident?

2. When Ndambuki says, "I see to it that my animals get enough food and

water," to whose labor is he referring? Is there other evidence of the gender division of labor?

3. How does age affect the division of labor? (What work does Berida do at Kathonzweni?) Who does most of the ordinary household labor (and the farming, although not seen here) at Kathonzweni?

4. Are any differences in wealth evident between neighbors or within families? (Clothing and the presence or absence of water tanks and granaries are good indicators here.)

5. What evidence is there in the film of environmental degradation and attempts at preservation? What climatic differences are evident between Nairobi (elevation c. 5000 feet) and Kathonzweni? What role does water play in the film?

6. Is there any evidence in the film of how addiction has affected family relationships?

7. What impressions are given about childcare at Kathonzweni? What about care for the elderly in Nairobi?

8. How do women support men at Kathonzweni and vice versa?

9. Is there any evidence of the impact of U.S. material/popular culture in the film? How might the knowledge that the film's future audience would be largely American have affected its subjects, especially the women's groups?

10. What kinds of connections are evident between rural and urban areas? How does Berida's life differ in the two areas?

11. Certain symbols crop up repeatedly in the film. For instance, what is the symbolic role of the matatus, the ubiquitous mini-vans that transport people and goods all over Kenya? (Reading matatus may, in fact, be the best introduction to Kenyan popular culture.)

12. Who apparently inherited rights to Berida's father's land at Masii? Ndambuki has threatened to sell the Kathonzweni land, which he might be able to do under Kenyan law without Berida's permission, so then what would happen to the house that Berida built so painstakingly?

Such issues are the stuff of everyday life that have particularly large implications for Kenyan women and children, since most share the situation of effective lack of property rights, whatever the law may say. Few women can afford to hire lawyers to attempt a way through the complicated biases of customary and written law, both of which embody considerable male privilege. The complex legal situation is only one symptom of Kenya's colonial past, during which British law was imposed on a variety of local customary laws. To understand the videotape and the narrative, some appreciation of the historical context is also useful.

The Historical Context: Akamba Trade, the Politics of Religion, and Nairobi

Berida's life began in the 1930s; she came of age and married just before the 1950s Emergency, during which central Kenya was torn by guerrilla warfare in the Kikuyu forests and urban tumults; many urban conflicts centered on African markets. But unrest, riots, and political and economic persecution of

Map of Kenya
John Hollingsworth, Indiana University Cartographer

traders did not end when the country gained independence in 1963, although the later 1960s and the 1970s were relatively peaceful compared to both the 1950s and the 1980s and 1990s. Berida began trading in Nairobi in about 1976. Since then the market she helped to found, Gikomba, has exploded to its present approximate size of over 2,000 sellers and has become a volatile political space that contains many ethnicities and a center of power for Nairobi's growing underclass. Nairobi itself has now attained a population of over two million. The setting for much of this story, then, is imbued with Kenyan history and is increasingly dominant in making that history. Berida's particular story presents a close view of many events that are more often described only generally and adds to our knowledge of women's trading activities in particular.

A relatively dry area southeast of present-day Nairobi, Ukambani is the home or area of origin for most of the Akamba, Kenya's third largest ethnic group, so identified by a common language and culture. Before the imposition of British colonialism in the late nineteenth century, the Akamba had no centralized government but rather had various mechanisms of relatively peaceful dispute settlement conducted by clan elders. There was also a tradition of prophet leaders. Participation in long-distance trade was another part of Akamba history going back to at least the late eighteenth century. Traders first sought dried staples to supplement food supplies in an area subject to drought and famine every five to eight years or so. *Kuthuua* (searching for food) is the Kikamba term used to refer to early trade. Male traders were heavily involved in the ivory trade of the late eighteenth and nineteenth centuries and were active as far away as southern present-day Tanzania.[19]

The cattle trade, one of Berida's more successful ventures, was an important factor in precolonial Ukambani. Although more dependent on horticulture for subsistence, the Akamba had a mixed economy in which herding provided a substantial source of prestige, wealth, and dietary supplements. Cattle and goats were widely used as a form of currency, especially in the most important transactions having symbolic value, such as bridewealth.[20] Ndambuki's story, presented in a sidebar in Chapter 2, stresses the importance of the herding economy, particularly to Akamba men. Precolonial warfare consisted largely of raids conducted for the purpose of seizing cattle and women. Active trade links with the pastoralist Maasai resulted in a constant importation of cattle. Destocking, a colonialist campaign begun in the 1930s aimed at reducing the numbers of cattle owned by the Akamba, was a source of much

---

19. Kennell A. Jackson, "An Ethnohistorical Study of the Oral Traditions of the Akamba of Kenya," Ph.D. diss., University of California–Los Angeles, 1972, pp. 233–34, 342–43; John Lamphear, "The Kamba and the Northern Mrima Coast," in *Precolonial African Trade,* edited by R. Gray and D. Birmingham (London: Oxford University Press, 1970), pp. 75–86.

20. In *Kamba Customary Law,* Penwill made a list of ten Kikamba terms used to describe and distinguish cows used in symbolic, ritualized transactions such as at marriage, for blood money, etc. (p. 119). There were, of course, more common currencies used in everyday transactions in precolonial East Africa, such as pieces of iron or other metals. Much small-scale trade in Ukambani, especially that participated in by women, was done by barter.

bitter resentment that led to a nascent alliance with the Kikuyu who were in rebellion and that resurfaced in the 1950s Emergency.[21] After the establishment of the Athi River meatpacking plant a constant market for cattle ensured the continuation, although not always the profitability, of the cattle trade and allowed some women like Berida to enter a previously male domain.

Akamba women, like their Kikuyu counterparts, stayed mainly in the local staples trade, carrying maize and beans to sell in Nairobi after independence in 1963. Woven sisal baskets (which were previously made of baobab or wild fig fibers) of the type that became popular in the West from the 1980s on proved to be women's most important export. Large versions of these baskets are used locally to haul produce.[22] In Nairobi and Ukambani women formed basketmaking cooperatives and some women became wholesale export agents. Cooperation of mothers and daughters in trade is hindered by a patrilocal residential system that is, however, being modified by urban circumstances, as we see in Berida's case. In this account Martha, Berida's eldest daughter (see genealogical chart), has joined Berida in business in Nairobi and taken over most of the routine chores, an arrangement that did not exist in 1987 when I first met Berida. Akamba woodcarving, an industry that began in the 1920s, has become famous worldwide.[23] Many of these products are produced at Gikomba Market and sold through Akamba Arts, a location that is featured in Berida's account and in the videotape.

Another location that dominates Berida's stories is Kathonzweni, her rural home and the site of a periodic open-air market (rural markets in central Kenya generally meet twice a week or once a week, depending on the density of the population and availability of products). Kathonzweni Market meets every Tuesday in the central open area of the village, a dispersed settlement of low density. Kathonzweni has a Catholic church, several schools, and a row of stores surrounding the market square. The church owns the sole tractor/ earth mover that we observed there, but it was not working at that time. Berida's home is approximately two kilometers from the center of Kathonzweni. Makueni District in general is a relatively new area of settlement; Ndambuki's people were originally from Mbooni and Berida's from Masii. Older residents can remember the presence of wild animals in large numbers in their frontier area. Thus, the settlers in Berida's area are all immigrants, most of whom arrived in the 1950s or later, partly because they were fleeing Emergency re-

---

21. Munro, *Colonial Rule*, pp. 230–31. There were also protests over compulsory cattle inoculations, the forced planting of sisal, and further seizure of land for cattle ranching by colonial settlers, documented in *Muigwithania* 1, no. 2 (1938), File DC/MKS 10B/15/1, Kenya National Archives, Nairobi, Kenya. Also in this file see District Commissioner Machakos to Chief Native Commissioner Nairobi, 25 August 1938; Telegram: "Wakamba" to Secretary of State for the Colonies, 1 February 1939; Intelligence Report from DC (District Commissioner) Machakos to Provincial Commissioner, 21 May 1940; Memorandum of Elijah Kabula to Secretary of State for the Colonies, May 1939.

22. C. W. Hobley gives a historical description of these baskets, called *kyondo*, and their manufacture in *Ethnology of A-Kamba and Other East African Tribes* (1910; reprint, London: Frank Cass and Co., 1971), p. 29. See also Figure 1.3 and Sidebar 1.1.

23. J. Forbes Munro, *Colonial Rule and the Kamba: Social Change in the Kenya Highlands 1889–1939* (Oxford: Clarendon Press, 1975), p. 183.

strictions. Kathonzweni lies on an unpaved road in a dry area, from which *matatus* go at all hours to Nairobi. The trip is arduous; it used to take about four hours to cover the first 100 kilometers in normal times, but takes longer now because of the flood damage of 1997–1998, which cut off communications completely at times. Thus, Kathonzweni is a small trade center of less remoteness than many places in rural Kenya, but with substantial infrastructural disabilities.

If trade is a dominating aspect of Berida's life, religion is a critical sub-motif. A precolonial domain in which some women exercised particular influence in Akamba society was prophetism, or divining. The most famous nineteenth-century prophet was Syokimau, mentioned in Berida's account as a well-known member of Ndambuki's clan, who predicted the arrival of the colonialists: "Behold, some people are coming! With fire in their pockets they travel in the middle of the sea and they will spoil Ukamba." Syokimau is also said to have predicted the introduction of private landownership and the seizure of Akamba land by the British.[24] The prophetic tradition continued under colonialism and helped organize rebellions.[25] With colonialism also came immediate incursions of missionaries. The African Inland Mission was most prominent among those in Ukambani. It was an offshoot of the American Baptist Church, which provided the funds for its establishment. It was also Berida's first religious affiliation, in which she followed her mother, who gave up her functions and status as a diviner. Conversion to Christianity represented a loss of status for some women since they were no longer allowed to hold positions of authority in the new religion.[26] After her marriage Berida followed her mother-in-law into the Catholic Church, where she seems to have experienced a religious awakening. Her hyperfertility can partly be attributed to the Christian abandonment of the prohibition on sexual intercourse during lactation that had been common locally[27] and to the biblical exhortation to go forth and multiply that is stressed by priests and cited by Berida.

The holistic interweaving of Berida's experiences that occur in many locations and partake of many contexts merits particular attention. She occasionally watches and enjoys TV, but she has no electricity or toilet at her Nairobi lodgings. Although she herself had only two days of formal education (as an

---

24. Joseph Muthiani, *Akamba from Within: Egalitarianism in Social Relations* (New York: Exposition Press, 1973), pp. 5, 77.

25. Munro, *Colonial Rule,* p. 114.

26. African Inland Mission ministers and members immediately adapted to the integration of the religious and the political in Akamba society and meddled in local politics, set up their own chiefs, and contested the institution of polygyny. In the early days they had trouble convincing children and their parents that such schooling was important, so in 1904–1905 they adopted the expedient of paying the children to attend. But that stopped when the children went on strike for more pay. Many of their converts were orphans taken in as children and girls fleeing parental control and/or undesirable marriages. Munro, *Colonial Rule,* pp. 101–108.

27. The ethnographic literature is contradictory on this subject, contradictions that may be explained by local variations in the practice and/or change over time. In the 1920s Gerhard Lindblom stated that such a prohibition existed (as it did with the closely related Kikuyu), but Penwill said in 1951 that it did not, so people may have stopped observing the custom in the interim. Lindblom, *The Akamba in British East Africa* (Uppsala: Archive d'Etudes Orientales, Vol. 17, 1920), pp. 29, 79; Penwill, *Kamba Customary Law,* p. 9.

immiseration? replete?

adult), she paid for two of her daughters to attend computer courses. Neither of them has so far put those skills to use in a job, one because she does not have the influential connections necessary to secure one in a neo-colonial economy beset by corruption, and the other because she is doing something else. Berida is capable of spectacular acts of generosity but also not above begging or ordering others to get what she wants; however, these needs are more often than not for her children rather than for herself.

The many problems besetting the lives of ordinary people in contemporary Kenya are obvious in Berida's narrative. Kenya has a capitalist neo-colonial economy, meaning that it depends largely on tourism and exports of cash crops like tea and coffee to earn foreign exchange; most profits are also exported by multinational corporations and government corruption. Those who do primary production—farmers—and petty traders like Berida have increasing difficulties with the erosion of their incomes caused by this situation, while their children cannot find jobs. Class distinctions are rampant and increasing, exaggerated by pervasive governmental corruption and enabled further by President Moi's efforts to keep himself in power. Crime in Nairobi is also increasing as a result, while most people are getting poorer. Those who are armed prey on those who are not; extortion by the police is more and more common, especially when they themselves are not paid. That the "peacekeepers" have turned violent is only one of the contradictions so characteristic of contemporary Kenya, like Nairobi's increasingly opulent skyline that contrasts so starkly with the immiseration of the population of the surrounding shantytowns. Such vast differences mirror those between the booming U.S. economy, which profits from the organization of the world economy by multinational corporations to concentrate capital in New York and other Western centers, and the falling per capita income in many countries, even those referred to as the "Asian miracles." Virtually every aspect of Berida's life is replete with such paradoxes that not only heighten its interest but also place Berida firmly in the late-twentieth-century world and its economy. In these contradictions Berida expresses her humanity and the complexities of life in the contemporary world.

Claire Robertson
May 1999

"We Only Come Here to Struggle"

Berida, 1988, at Gikomba Market

1

"I Am Berida Ndambuki"

Childhood, Family, and Initiation

My name is Berida Ndambuki[1] but it was not always so. My birth name was Mathei wa Moli (my father's name) wa Kivinda (my grandfather's name). That's how we do it. My mother's name was Maria Mbatha. But now I am Berida Ndambuki. Ndambuki is my husband. He married me when I was young. But in 1957 after attending catechism class for four years I was given the name Berida, and everyone calls me that except Ndambuki when he is being bad. He then uses Mathei but he is the only one that does that. After I took more classes I was given the name Lucia to show that I am a complete Christian and accept Jesus. It is fine for you to use my real name here and those of my family; maybe if my husband sees how he looks here he will change his ways.

About myself, when I was married by Ndambuki I became a dutiful wife. We stayed together as husband and wife and got children but we were very poor and we had no employment, so it became necessary for me to come to Nairobi so that we could educate our children. I educated two children, Magdalena and Angelina. But first maybe I should tell you about my childhood so you can see how things have changed.

I was born in 1936 at Masii in the district of Machakos.[2] Masii is very beautiful; we lived at a place called Iiani. I loved it because we were all there, my father, my mother, my brothers, and my sisters. I grew to be a big girl there and danced the Akamba dances there. I eventually married in 1950. My mother had ten children; I had an elder brother and an elder sister, two younger brothers, and five younger sisters. The eldest is Beatrice, then James Mutune, who died last year of diabetes, then me. After me came Bernard Musau, who is several years younger, Esther, Antony, who died in 1993, Naomi, Lucia, Mutinda, who died young, at about age twelve, and the last-born is Domitila,

---

1. Her first name is sometimes spelled Bellita or Bellitor; I have chosen to use the phonetic spelling here for both our names.
2. Hereafter called Masaku, as it is in Kikamba.

Berida Ndambuki - Genealogical Chart, 1999,
with locations of residence

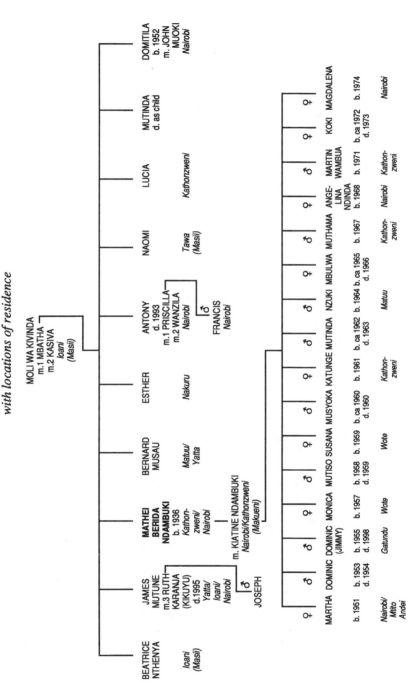

Genealogical Chart: The Family of Berida Ndambuki
John Hollingsworth, Indiana University Cartographer

who was born in 1952 and went to school. I also have half-brothers and sisters since my father had three wives.

My father's clan, to which I belong, is called Mwanzio, Wa Muthike, or Muthike (my children belong to Ndambuki's clan). We were told that Muthike was buried so that rain would come. Daughters of our clan are supposed to be very valuable because we are the ones who brought rain. For the same reason we are supposed to be the first ones to plant after the rains come. We are good farmers. You should see my farm when we have rain; I plant maize, cowpeas, and pigeon peas. There is a tree at Kilala in Makueni that is sacred and the subject of the story we were told about our past. It grows, matures, dries out, and then another shoot comes up. It never dies. This story is about Muthike, a girl.[3] There was a drought. The diviners consulted with other diviners and were told to bury the girl and the rain would come. They gathered together cows to take to the girl's father for her, everyone in the neighborhood contributing, but they didn't tell the girl. She had taken her father's cattle to the bush to graze and the father told them to go look for her there. They found her and she said, "Get someone to stay with my father's herd." They got someone. Then she said, "Cut a stick for me from the *mumo* tree." The stick was cut for her and a cow was killed. A grave was dug. She told them to smear its hide with oil and put it on top of the grave so she could see it. She told them she was going to go and that they should run fast to their homes because it was going to rain. She went singing, holding the stick, which had also been smeared with oil. She fell into the hole still holding that stick and remaining upright. When she fell it rained a lot and the grave was filled with water. She drowned. The stick she was holding grew and sprouted breasts. The whole place was covered with water and sweet potatoes grew there. People began to call the place Kwa Muthike. So that's why our clan is called Muthike's.[4]

Back then we dressed differently from nowadays and even ate different food. We used to cover ourselves with a piece of black cloth the way the Maasai tie themselves over the shoulder. It was tied with sisal string. The rest of the body was left uncovered. It was that black nylon cloth like umbrellas are made of and we bought it from the *wahindi* [Kiswahili; Asians/Indians]. It used to cost fifteen cents. My mother used to tie her cloth on both sides so that all of her parts were covered; she did not wear anything underneath. But my grandmother sometimes used to wear a goatskin when a goat had been slaughtered. It was kneaded and then joined together at one place so that she could just slip it on. The kneading made the hide soft. It was fastened on one shoulder with a piece of skin or a piece of bark fiber from a tree called *kiamba* [baobab] that was also used to make baskets. She used goatskin also as bed-

---

3. Both the Akamba and the Kikuyu trace clan descent to initial female founding ancestors but both are patrilineal, an anomaly that may derive from a transition from matrilineal to patrilineal descent in the far past, an honoring of the female contribution to the clan, or other aspects of their symbolic religious systems.

4. There is a similar Kikuyu story in which a girl is sacrificed in order to save the community. Instead of going willingly, however, she appeals in turn to all of her relatives, friends, and neighbors to save her from drowning but none helps her.

ding. My mother did wear a goatskin sometimes, but only on her back when she went to scoop water from the wells in the sand or when she carried bundles of thorny kindling. People wore hides so they could get through the thorns without being pricked, but I never wore one. My mother and grand-mother used to wear their hair short and rub it into thick little balls; they looked like buttons and stood out from their heads. When they got tired of rubbing it they would shave it off like the Maasai. My grandmother would shave the crown of her head and then leave a little hair around the outside where she would put beads.

Another thing people used to do was to remove certain teeth because, if they hadn't been removed, you could not share a dish with those who had had them removed. Those people would say that they could not share a plate with someone who had to "force food over a bridge [the teeth]." It was considered to be beautiful or fashionable to remove two bottom front teeth.[5] We also pierced our ears and put ornaments in them to make ourselves beautiful. The ornaments were made of wood, carved and shaped by men, smoothed with stone, shiny, and fitted into the girls' ears. My mother did that and my ears were pierced too. I still have the ornaments at home. But I am not wearing them now, why should I? I'll do it when you are taking a photo of me to take to your country. When I was about eighteen I had some scars made. There were men who were skilled at such things and we did it to beautify ourselves.

Back then babies used to sleep on goatskins. Because of being constantly peed on the skins would have many folds which often got bedbugs in them. By morning the baby would be covered in bites. The mother would take the skin outside and beat it with a stick to get rid of the bugs then put it back on the bed. The beds then were different too. They used to make their own with sticks and baobab fiber string [demonstrates]. They got four sturdy pieces of wood for the legs and fixed them in holes in the ground. Then they laid other poles lengthwise and placed a mat made with sticks and string on the poles. That was the bed. Then they made a mattress woven with string from grass. This was done by young men. Even when we moved to Makueni in 1964 we made new beds there like that with grass mattresses.

When I was a child we ate pumpkins, sweet potatoes, and sorghum millet ground fine then cooked in milk to make a dish called *kinaa*.[6] It could be eaten raw too if you were really hungry. The grinding was done by hand using two stones, the lower one flat and big and an upper smaller one. The millet was ground until it was very soft. We didn't eat a lot of greens, but what could hap-pen was that during the dry season or a famine when there was only flour to eat it would be cooked together with some greens to make a dish called *ngunza kutu*. Sometimes the greens were *nthoko* [cowpea] leaves, or they might be *kikowe*, long thin leaves, or *ua* [amaranthus leaves]. We cultivated the *nthoko*

---

5. C. W. Hobley discusses tooth removal as a form of cosmetic alteration in *Ethnology of A-Kamba*, p. 105.

6. Unless otherwise specified, all terms in italics are from Kikamba. This dish appears to have been made with *mwee*, bulrush millet.

leaves but the *kikowe* were wild.[7] Then everyone would be given their share. We didn't eat maize like we do now; where would that have come from during a drought? There were many problems. Even cows were felled and bled so that we could cook the blood to eat. When there was food we cooked *isyo* [food—maize and beans]. We could also pound maize and get flour, then cook it. Normally we ate that one day, and the next we might have *ngima* [a dish made from maize flour], and the day after that *kiteke* [millet flour and milk]. We also might alternate eating pumpkins and sweet potatoes.[8]

We worked a lot, hauling water and watching cows, but we also played games. I was good at games. We would collect wild fruits and pretend they were cows; we sometimes modeled cows and sheds out of mud and pretended we owned them. I played with the neighbors' children and relatives; we competed to see who could make the best and most cows. We played with something called *kima* made using sticks, and another thing called *bila* which looked like this [demonstration]. That was mainly used by boys; they would hit it with a string tied to a stick so that it went round and round. *Kima* was made from a pigeon pea plant stalk which is pointed and one threw it. If it hooked onto the specified object then you were the winner. It was also a boys' game. Girls played with stones. We would take about five stones, throw one up and try to move the rest before the stone came down. That game was called *kola.*[9] We didn't have *bilikoli* [marbles] but we would take stones and smooth them using a bigger stone until they were rounded. We all played with the same set of stones. You threw a stone up and tried to catch it. If you failed then you gave the stones to the next competitor.

We also had jumping games and dances. We would run and try to snatch something from each other like *ngondu* [a wild fruit][10] or we would have races to see who was the fastest. We might also fight to see who was the strongest. If you won, your prize was only that you would be feared and nobody would pick on you! [Laughter.] I was never beaten by anyone. As I grew older I saw people participating in school athletics. They would call on me to run; I was very fast and won many prizes even as an adult. I would win things like blankets, lanterns, plates, soap, spoons, and washbasins. I ran for the school from my home area, Kabaa school, even though I wasn't in school. The teacher really liked me, especially the one they called captain. He would come looking for me calling out my name [she laughed]. If we won locally we would

---

7. Because of desiccation in some places and the increase in cultivated areas, far fewer, if any, uncultivated greens are now in the diet.

8. The original manuscript had a series of footnotes like the following that indicated the location of specific narrative materials in my data. Information in the preceding paragraphs was taken from fieldnotes for 25 and 29 July 1997 and tape transcripts 97-3-8 (year, tape number, page numbers), 97-1-1; 97-3-12; 97-4-1; 98-1-16-17; 98-1-17-19; 98-9-10–11; 98-2-8; 97-12-13-14; fieldnotes 88-19 and 98-1 (year, page number). Except for the postscript and places where locations of tape transcripts are cited, this information has now been deleted as not of general interest. It is available on request from the secondary author.

9. Joseph Muthiani has a fuller description of marble games in *Akamba from Within,* pp. 57–58.

10. Ngondu [or *ndongu* in Kikuyu] (solanum) fruit is mentioned by Lindblom as being used as pretend cattle (*Akamba in British East Africa,* p. 57) and by Hobley as being used in many medicines (*Ethnology of A-Kamba,* p. 67). However, the term *ngondu* also means a medicinal potion in Kikamba.

then travel to Masaku to compete. There was a dance called *mbeni* and another called *kilui* [crow] in which you stretched your neck and hands and strutted like a crow. But old women danced without a lot of jumping, something called *kilumi,* bum, bum, bum, bum, bum, bum [demonstrates]. We still do it.[11]

I even did things that were supposed to be for boys, like the high jump, called *ndui.* We would put poles at two ends and then lay one between them and jump. We would also go where there was a slope and slide down on our bottoms. Boys and girls did that separately at their own places. There was nothing that a boy could do that I could not do. Even if they wanted to fight, I would fight with them and no boy could beat me. I was arrogant even as a small girl; if a kid came and asked me, boy or girl, what I was saying, I would just hit them. You know, my father liked me very much and he was arrogant. Yes, I often acted more like a boy than a girl, and my father would ask, why was I born a girl instead of a boy? Sometimes the other kids would laugh at me and say that I was like a boy. They would even spit on me. And if a boy behaved like a girl the other kids would also laugh at him and call him a girl. We were told that a boy should not behave like a girl but be brave since they would be called on to fight when there were raids or cows had been taken. Boys who lacked courage were never taken to fight; they were cowards like women. Women were timid. But I am not timid. It depends on how you are created. There are people who are timid and scared and look like they are sleeping all the time. Do you want to tell me that that is a person? [Laughter.] Why, if they saw Kilaya, who is white, they would move backwards and start talking in low tones, [whispering] "Who is that?" Such people will never progress at all. But if I had gone to school, by now I would be in Parliament!

I did not go to school because my father was a drunkard and did not send me.[12] So for languages I know mostly Kikamba, but also some bad Kiswahili, and Kikuyu, no English. And I can read my name but I can only write a few letters of it; I have to use a cross to sign things. I learned Kiswahili from selling at Gikomba. An African can never accept the price that you give so they bargain. They will ask, [Kiswahili] "How much is it? What is it? What is it?" That's how I came to learn it. Once I went for some adult education, but only for two days. The problem was that while I was listening I kept being distracted by thinking about my children, whether or not they had enough to eat and so on. I quit so I could deal with all those problems. I really wish I had gone to school so I could read and speak English, be as smart as those who have. White people have become so clever, but it's not that they are white, just that they have education. I feel foolish because I don't read.

Neither of my parents went to school. My father hasn't worked for a long time now. He is still alive and living at Masii but my mother died some years

---

11. *Kilumi* is/was a dance connected to veneration of the ancestral spirits called *aimu* according to Lindblom, for which a big drum was used (*Akamba in British East Africa,* pp. 231, 35). In *Elements of Akamba Life* (Nairobi: East African Publishing House, 1972), K. Ndeti called the initiation dance *kiloe* (p. 91), which he contrasted with *kilumi* (p. 165). See also Hobley, *Ethnology of A-Kamba,* p. 53.

12. Access to Western-type education was closely related to wealth; in the 1930s it became necessary to pay school fees, which many could not afford. Munro, *Colonial Rule,* p. 159.

ago. He just herded cattle. I really liked my father when I was a child. If you see us together, you will see that I am more like him. My father also liked me because I was sharp. If he sent me on an errand I went running off and came back quickly. If he slaughtered a goat he would give me some extra meat, not the others. My father preferred me to them. Even today he always asks first if I have come when we go home. Although father drank he never bothered us except to order us to go work on the *shamba* [farm] during the rainy season. He taught us about cultivating. Even today he still works in the *shamba*. That taught us responsibility and I taught my children to work in the *shamba* the same way. In the morning we would wake up and go cultivate and not come back until 9 A.M. Then we milked the cows. My children worked on the *shamba* on days when they didn't go to school or had been expelled for nonpayment of fees. That was Martha and Dominic in the days before I began working at Gikomba.

My mother was my father's favorite wife, his first wife. There were two others including Kasiva, who is still there. Another wife died after having only one child because she had been beaten badly by a man who wanted to marry her when she refused him. Later when she and my father loved each other and she gave birth, the old injuries killed her. Kasiva had six children. However, Mother had sixteen children like I did (of all those twenty-two children, sixteen survived and my [full] brothers all became successful, not the other ones). Even though Mother died in 1982 he still lives in the house that they used to live in together. Actually, when I was a small child he used to beat her sometimes and she would go home to her family. She was afraid of him. That even happened once when I got older and she asked me to go with her but I refused. He would yell at her and she wouldn't answer him back. She didn't know how; she used to tell me that I am like my father because I talk a lot. Then after awhile they would forgive each other. When the children grew up and the sons prospered my father realized how valuable she was to him and quit beating her. After her death he didn't go to live with any of the other wives. Even though he has land at Matuu and my brother Mutune invited him to come stay at Yatta in a house he built for him, he still stays at Masii in the house where he lived with my mother and he carries her identity card with him. He says, "I can't leave Mbatha alone." They were friends right up until her death. He loved her the most. If you ask him, he says that Mbatha is still a young girl. Even her things are still intact; he does not allow anyone to touch them. He says, "Leave those things alone; they belong to Mbatha." Of course, we will get them when he dies himself.

It is God who created me and put me in my mother's womb and I was born. My mother was very hardworking. We were friends because she gave birth to me. We had a normal relationship; if she sent me on an errand I just went like that. We went to fetch firewood and water together and cultivated together. I helped her. She taught me to weave baskets by first showing me how to make the sisal string and starting a basket for me. It used to be that people would compete to see who could make the best basket for the bride-to-be. The strands of a good basket should all be of the same thickness and woven evenly, tightly.

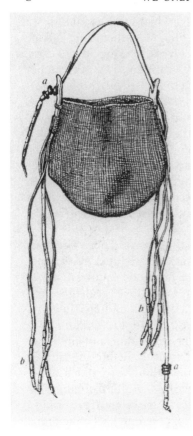

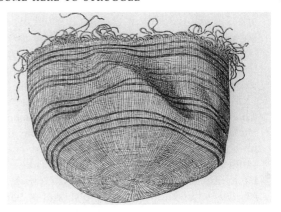

Unfinished basket

Akamba *kyondo* (baskets)
Gerhard Lindblom, The Akamba in British East
Africa, *vol. 17 (Uppsala: Archive d'Etudes
Orientales, 1920), p. 542*

Gerhard Lindblom Describes Kyondo and Their Importance in the 1920s

During the pauses between their different tasks one can see the women sitting in groups outside the village, talking and working at their bags at the same time. One may say that a kyondo is an inevitable appendage to a Kamba woman during her work. When a wife is mentioned in the people's numerous tales, it is almost always added in passing that she was plaiting a bag (*kutuma kyondo*). The bags are plaited with the fingers from two balls. The Kikuyu women make them in the same way. So as to have one hand free they often put one end between the teeth. The bottom is made first and the bag is held with this upwards during the work. The size varies from 50 cms. in diameter down to quite small wallet-like bags for small girls. The largest take a month or more to make. On most bags there are leather straps to carry them, which are placed over the forehead. The Akamba, both men and women, carry loads in this way, and the length of the strap is so arranged that the load comes on the upper part of the back. Carrying is made easier by bending the arms up and catching hold of the straps.[13]

---

13. Lindblom, *Akamba in British East Africa*, pp. 541–42. The chief location of the contemporary *kyondo* industry in Nairobi is at Kariokor Market, where several basketmaking cooperatives are headquartered.

I am like my mother; the only way I don't resemble her is in my height. My character is like hers, even the way I had children is like hers. My mother also had eight sons and eight daughters. I also look after my family, but Mother had three sons who got wealthy. Now only one of them is still alive. My mother had a good relationship with her daughters-in-law. They respected each other. She didn't do anything to displease them. I too, if my daughter-in-law doesn't think I should do something then I don't do it. For example, if I say I am going to the market to buy such-and-such, she might say, "No, don't go, I'll send somebody for you."

Mother was not initially a Christian. She used to go dance *kilumi*. She could tell when rain would come. This talent was bequeathed to her by her husband's mother, my grandmother. People would gather at her home and then somebody would play a drum for her and she would dance until the spirits seized her. Then she would announce: "This year there will be no rain." Those spirits were demons [*masatani*], also called *aimu*. Christians would not have seen such things. You know, there was even a famous prophet named Syokimau from the same clan as my husband. She predicted that the whites would come over water on something like a snake carrying fire in their pockets. She is even written about in schoolbooks. She's dead now. The interesting thing about her was that when her old teeth fell out she grew new ones even until she died. She could see when the Maasai were coming to raid cattle and warned people. Her angels would tell her when they were coming and which route they would take so the Akamba could go, ambush them, and kill them. She could also tell people about their problems. For instance, if people were dying in a home she would do her divination using her tools (gourds and seeds) and tell them why it was happening. I never saw her myself but my parents used to talk about her. The sacred grove [*ithembo*] at Ithaini in Masii where she used to tell people to bring food to sacrifice is still there.[14]

One time when Antony was at school my mother went to the store and saw a black cloth with red and green stripes on it (called *peke*) that was worn at the time. She really liked it but she had no money to buy it. So she asked to have the cloth and said she would bring the money later. Then she went back to the *shamba* [farm] where her daughters-in-law were and they asked her what she was carrying. She said it was her clothing and they said that if Antony saw it he would burn it. She said, "Why would he do that? I would rather take it back." So she did. It was around Christmastime and Antony was going to a celebration for the young men. Antony asked her, "Mom, Ndeve told me you

---

This activity is still ubiquitous; women weave baskets as they sell, walk, listen, or perform any other activity that allows it. Women have adapted their skills and styles to new materials, using wool or even plastic on occasion. The color combinations have also increased in range with the use of artificial rather than natural dyes for the sisal string. The leatherwork has gotten more elaborate with the addition of zippers, tooled decoration, pockets, tassels, and other improvisations, many of which are aimed toward the export market. The leatherwork is usually subcontracted to men. Unfortunately, the Chinese invention of a machine for weaving sisal baskets to make passable imitations has undercut this hitherto stable industry and threatens the livelihood of many women who derive their cash income from the sale of the beautiful baskets.

14. For an illuminating historical discussion of Akamba prophets see Kennell A. Jackson, "An Ethnohistorical Study."

had a cloth with you, what was it for?" You see, that cloth was associated by Christians with demons. He asked her, "Couldn't you find something else to wear?" Mother told Antony that she had already returned it.

Antony went to another home, Somba's, for a Christmas celebration. I was already married at that time but had been invited to go to Masii for Christmas. I woke up in the morning and went to mass. When I came back I went to the house of one of my stepmothers to make porridge for the baby, since my mother's kitchen was being used for the big meal. Then my mother came over and asked, "Do you have any medicine with you? I hear that Antony has been taken sick at Somba's." I said I didn't have any. She said, "Let me go to Karanja [Mutune's wife, a doctor] (Karanja is known by her father's name)." She asked Karanja to go to Somba's. I finished making the porridge and then I heard my mother scream in the distance. I ran out. She screamed and then ran with Ruth Karanja toward Somba's, where she was told that Antony was dead. Normally she wouldn't call my father by his name but rather Mwendwa [beloved], but this time she called him Moli and, after she had gotten him from the drinking spot, told him she had killed Antony. They then carried Antony home. He was already stiff. People gathered and the nearby shops were closed. My mother said, "Tell Antony to get up and burn my cloth. If he has any strength he should get up and burn the cloth." My father said, "That cloth will be bought. If Antony can, he should get up and burn it." Then all the people gathered there said that if that cloth was the cause of Antony's death, then it should be bought and let him rise up so they can see him. They contributed a lot of money to go buy it. After an hour Antony, who was dressed in a suit, got up and hid behind people because he was ashamed of having dirtied himself by defecating in his suit. He called his older brother's [Bernard Musau's] wife and ran into her house away from Mother's house. He asked Bernard's wife for water to bathe, which she brought, and he bathed and dressed in clean clothes. Antony went back to the celebration.

Father took cow's milk and poured it on the ground according to Akamba custom and said, "If it is true, then let Antony be healed. I will buy that cloth." Then my mother went back to the shop and found that the cloth was not there any more. They even went to Nairobi but still couldn't find any. Then Antony died again at school in Mbooni. He was taken to Masaku and checked out. They said he was not sick. They even had to go to Mombasa to get that cloth. Then Antony was all right, he recovered. Mother took all of her divination paraphernalia she used to use to the church and the cloth and they were burned. There were gourds and other things. She was then baptized after she had attended catechism classes to be taught the word of God. That was when she was given the name Maria. Then she stopped seeing all those things, became a good person and died a Christian.

Sometimes people inherit abilities like that. Just this year on 9 March I was waked up at night by my late brother Mutune. He called, "Berida!" and I answered. He asked why I hadn't taken a walking stick to Musau. In the morning I went to one of my sisters and told her about it. She asked me, "What should we do?" We decided to go see the son of our older brother at Gikomba and tell him what I saw. When I told him he said, "Get that walking stick and take it to Musau. Mutune was given that stick by my grandfather, who wants you to give it to his brother." Mutune had been given that stick and told to use it to rule over the home so that there would never be any problems. So I went and bought a walking stick for Ksh.700. Where was I going to find that old one, with me here in Nairobi? I sent for all my sisters and sent a message to Bernard Musau saying that we would go to his house on 30 June. He waited for us, not knowing the reason for our visit. He slaughtered a bull, bought a lot of *lesos* [also called *kangas*][15] for the girls, and his wife made Akamba baskets [*kyondo*]. My sisters contributed money toward the price of the stick, so we all bought it. We presented the stick to him together and I told him that his brother had told me to give him the stick so that he could have it whenever he is called to settle disputes at the various homes. After that I didn't have any more dreams.

> **Berida Refuses to Be Diverted**
> EXCERPT FROM TAPE TRANSCRIPT 97-8-19
>
> *Berida:* Antony got better and went back to the celebration.
>
> *Mbithe:* Antony recovered and went back to the celebration.
>
> *Claire:* He probably had epilepsy or something. Did he ever have any more spells?
>
> *Mbithe:* She is asking, did he ever die again?
>
> *Berida:* I haven't finished the story.
>
> *Mbithe:* She is still going on.
>
> *Berida:* So he went back to the celebration. Then my mother went to the shop and found the cloth was not there any more.

When I grew up and had things I took care of my mother. I wouldn't let her wear dirty clothes. I even told my brothers' wives that if they neglected her I would take her to my house, so she was taken care of to the end and given proper respect when she died. She died the day of the attempted coup in 1982. They wanted to wrap her in sheets but I refused to let them and said they had to pay Mother her last respects. I went to a tailor and had him make a dress like a wedding dress, with a petticoat and a headscarf. I didn't even ask a single person at Gikomba for a donation to help. I told them that Mother said she didn't need donations because she had children. We got everything ready. There were many people at the funeral because her children are well known and friendly with people. Her sons' cars, six of them, followed each other, plus those of her friends. There were more than 100 cars. People came all the way from Kisii and Gikomba. I was saying to myself, "I wish I was the one who had died." It was so nice; there were many people singing in the choirs. I wondered if there would be people to do the same for me. When you looked at her through the glass on the coffin you didn't think she was dead. Hooo, it's getting late. We should stop. Remind me tomorrow where we stopped so we can begin again in the same place. I have trouble remembering.

You are asking about rewards and punishments when I was little? If we were good and worked hard in the *shamba* Mother would grind millet on the grindstone and prepare *kinaa* for us. This was a big treat! It's the best-tasting

---

15. Large cotton cloths with bright colors and sayings on them, used to wrap around women's hips. They are often used for gifts.

food! Or, she would buy us the piece of cloth that was worn in those days, it cost twenty cents. My father would slaughter a goat for us if we had done some particularly arduous work, like digging a waterhole for our animals to drink from, or if we had hauled water for the cattle to drink during a drought. If I had done something naughty I would hide at the back of the house in order to avoid being beaten. I stayed there until I got sleepy and everyone had gone to bed. Then I quietly removed the plank that was used to close the door and went in. I would then wake up very early and leave the house again. One time my mother caught me and beat me for letting the cattle go into somebody else's *shamba*. They had destroyed the *nzuu* [pigeon peas] and *binzi* [beans] in the *shamba*. And we had insulted the owner. He had accused us of letting the cattle in there deliberately, which was not true. We had too many animals to be able to herd them properly.[16]

So my mother really beat us and my cousin and age-mate Nyiva was beaten to death by her father, my grandfather. She was beaten so hard I ran to get his sister. By the time I came back with my grandfather's sister, Nyiva was already unconscious from the beating. She had stopped crying. So my grandfather's sister yelled at him and said, "That's it, go ahead and kill her as I watch!!" in outrage at him. After that he walked back to his home. Nyiva was picked up and taken into the house and Nyiva's mother returned to her home that night and never came back. They came and got Nyiva the next day and took her home too. But she got very sick there so she was brought back to us and treated until she recovered.[17] She seemed fine; even when we were dancing you couldn't know she had been hurt. But Nyiva was pregnant.[18] When the time came for her to deliver, her injuries from the beating flared up due to the strain of pushing. So she got sick and died, leaving the baby. On her deathbed she called her brother and told him, "You see, I am dying. Our father is responsible for my death. He is the one who beat me." Since the man who had impregnated her had not paid bridewealth, the baby was returned to our grandmother's home. We called him Mutiso. She took care of him. She used to feed him by taking some raw milk into her mouth and then spitting it into his. The day he died I was visiting my grandmother's house. I woke up that morning and went to pick up the child from the bed. I used to pretend I was nursing him. But my grandmother said, "Leave him be, he's dead." He was only three months old.

After my mother died in 1982 my father bought land in Matuu. His children were grown and too many for that piece of land. At Iiani it was flat. There was an earthen dam built by the colonialists and even fish in the pond. In fact, it is like my father's land was taken by the earthen dam. We were forced to dig the channels by the chief and the dam was built with tractors. They also sur-

---

16. In the 1940s and 1950s damage done by stray livestock was regarded as a serious matter; the owner of the animals was required to pay compensation to the farmer. Penwill, *Kamba Customary Law*, p. 103.

17. Medical treatment was/is regarded as the husband or father's responsibility, an issue that is raised later in Berida's account with regard to the conduct of Ndambuki and his family.

18. Although the ostensible reason for the beating was the incident of allowing the cows to damage the neighbor's field, the real reason may have been her behavior in getting pregnant by a man who refused to bring bridewealth and marry her. For an extensive discussion of the meaning of bridewealth see Chapter 2.

veyed our land and then gave us the work of planting grass. Then the chief, the assistant chief and the Homeguards[19] would force the other people to come and work there. They would not give us food. We would spend days doing that work. Both men and women did it. Oh, oh it was hard! We were like slaves. It made us very angry. It was even worse if you had cattle. You were forced to lock them into sheds and then you had to go out and cut grass for them and take it to them. The chief who was there then was called Mutinda wa Nzioka. If the cows were seen outside their sheds, they would be confiscated and taken to the chief's place until you were forced to sell one cow in order to go rescue the others. The result was that people reduced the number of stock that they had. Also people moved to Makueni to save their cows. People moved at night because we were afraid.

The happiest time when I was a child was when I had eaten enough to be satisfied, since sometimes there was not enough. I was especially happy when my father would give me some of the food prepared for him. A particular incident that made me happy was the outcome of my father's arrest by the Homeguards. He was forced to join them and then ordered to beat one of his uncles, a relative from his mother's side. He refused and turned in the badge that they used to wear on the hand. He was lucky he was not arrested for that but rather set free. When he was released he came home and slaughtered a goat for us and the gods of the homestead to celebrate. Ever since then my father has never been employed [worked for wages]. He is happy and satisfied; he has three sons who got wealthy and who can support him. There is even a reserved seat for him in one of his sons' *matatus*. If someone else sits there he is told abruptly to move! When we went to see him on our way back from Kathonzweni, he blessed me for giving him Ksh.500; Ndambuki sent only Ksh.100 because he didn't have more than that.

Before I married and left home I used to help my mother look after the younger children. How could I fail to help her? During the times when there was no food, my mother would send me out to do casual labor on other people's farms; whatever I got I would bring back for the whole family. We were not paid in money. If you worked on a cassava *shamba* you were given some cassava, if on sweet potatoes, you were given sweet potatoes. We would go up to the Iveti hills to work for people there. Anyone who had a lot of work needing doing we did it; we asked around here and there from Akamba farmers. When the sun began going down about 4 or 5 P.M. we would be given our due and then we took the food home for the others.

All of my brothers and sisters were friends. My favorite siblings are Domitila, my youngest sister, and two men, Antony and Bernard. I like them a lot;

---

19. Loyalists who were appointed at the time of the Emergency, 1952–1960, when Kikuyu, Akamba, and others fought the British colonial government in the Kenya highlands and in Nairobi for land and freedom. There is an extensive bibliography on the subject including many firsthand accounts of participants in Bruce Berman and John Lonsdale, *Unhappy Valley: Conflict in Kenya and Africa* (London: James Currey, 1992). For women's role in the conflict see Muthoni Likimani, *Passbook Number F.47927: Women and Mau Mau in Kenya* (London: MacMillan, 1985) and Tabitha Kanogo, *Squatters and the Roots of Mau Mau* (London: James Currey, 1987).

we shared everything. My brothers have started their own businesses. The youngest, Antony, got educated because my older brothers helped each other; Mutune got a government job and then got a job for Bernard. They then paid for educating Antony, who became head of Posts and Telecommunications before he fell sick and died. Mutune and Bernard started shops and opened a store to buy foodstuffs together. When they got enough money and their sons got older, they divided up the assets equally and each ventured into business on his own. Both did really well. They have buildings, shops in Masii, Masaku, and Matuu. They also own their own pickup trucks and run about six *matatus*, which are called Mwende.[20] They make a lot of money from all of the businesses but the *matatus* bring in the most profit. Since my children are mostly not working, they can't help me much, but my brothers do. If Antony came and found me with other women in a restaurant kiosk, he would buy us all food. If he had been alive when I was robbed he would have said, "My sister, you don't need to suffer," empathized, and repaid the money. As it was, Bernard sent Ksh.800 [about $13.50 in 1997] for my *harambee*[21] to replace the money and Mutune's wife brought Ksh.500 [about $8.50]. When Kilaya gave me money I gave Bernard Ksh.400. Even the members of the market groups, I am better off than most of them. Some of them sell maize they have gotten on credit. They even consider me to be rich! Right now they say I have a white daughter who brings me a lot of money! [Laughter.]

When I was a child my best friend was my age-mate named Nzilani. She and I are cousins related through my paternal grandmother. She was my best friend because we never fought. If she became friends with someone I would also do it and vice versa. I liked her because we never fought; if she got a sweet potato she would share it with me and I would do the same with her. If she found a beautiful necklace she would get one for herself and one for me. She is also talkative like me. Our blood loved each other. We were very close. Even when I was told to marry that man I didn't like she hid me when I ran away. We either went to her home or into the bushes to hide. When the people who had come for the marriage negotiations had left my homestead we came out. That is what it is to be a friend. She was good like me. Her behavior was good even until now; she has never left her husband. She is still alive and farms at Masii; I see her occasionally when she comes to Nairobi. But if you see her now she looks very old; you wouldn't know we are age-mates. But I don't know her children because she got married in Masii and I got married in Mwala, then moved to Kangundo and to Makueni.

When I had my first menstrual period I didn't tell my mother. We girls discussed these things among ourselves; why should I have told my mother? And besides, I was too shy to tell her. There used to be something special done for

---

20. *Matatus* usually have slogans written on them, which have become increasingly elaborate as time has gone on. This one reflects a more conservative era, meaning "Go" in Kiswahili, but now there are many things painted on the minivans, often referring to U.S. popular culture, sports figures, rock singers and songs, religious sayings, etc.

21. A pre-eminent Kenyan custom, a fund-raiser conducted on behalf of a cause or individual by soliciting (sometimes forcefully, as in the case of government *harambees*) and collecting contributions from attendees, who are usually fed.

girls at their first menstruation and the mother was supposed to have sex with her father to avert possible problems, but I was a Christian. I took care of my own menstruation by being a Christian.

Nzilani and I were initiated together and therefore belong to the same age-set called Asingi.[22] I was happy when I was initiated because no man would have wanted me had I not had the clitoris removed. The other girls in the group were Nyiva, Waio [the black one], Nthenya, Nziva, Kithei, Mutheu [the brown one], and many others. The first stage of initiation was called *nzaiko nini.* On that day we first bathed and then went to the hut. At the door we found some women who held your legs straight and wide apart. Then another woman, the *mwaiki,* performed the initiation, the cut, you are just cut. There was nothing we could do. After one girl was cut she was taken into the hut, then another one came and so on until everyone was cut. After you were cut they covered you with a leaf from a *museve* plant. Then some stayed in the hut until they healed, but some were taken to their homes. The boys and the girls were circumcised at the same time and then separated. The boys, of course, had male advisors.

If the initiate went home then the mother of the initiate had to have sex with her husband that night in order to "straighten the initiation" so that the child would heal fast and well and not swell. For those families whose custom it was to leave the girls with the operator, she became like their mother. It was just like a baptism when you have a godparent. The operator also had to sleep with her husband that evening. In our family the initiates stayed at the operator's home for six days.

The practice of excision of the clitoris[23] is now stopping, but I think it

---

22. Initiation established age-sets, which were to command lifelong loyalty from their same-sex members. These age-sets furthered peer solidarity that crossed clan or family ties, but gerontocratic authority was upheld by the training the girls received at the *nzaiko nene.* Age was formerly the strongest determinant of rank among the Akamba, since it brought experience and presumably wisdom. Gender was a secondary determinant; a senior woman could have authority over a junior male in most cases. Colonialism, however, provided Western-type education on a discriminatory basis to some boys and very few girls, along with the accompanying requirement to convert to Christianity. Only after World War II was any systematic attempt made in British colonies to provide government-sponsored secular education independent of the mission schools, although the Kikuyu independent schools movement of the 1920s had some limited success in doing so. As access to Western education became more common those with wealth and those who were male were particularly favored.

23. The commonest term used in Kenyan English to refer to clitoridectomy is circumcision, which many activists feel underestimates the severity of the operation that removes the clitoris, the labia minora, and sometimes the labia majora. In the United States it has been the subject of much negative publicity and sensationalism, the impression often being that all African women have it done. Although statistics are often difficult to obtain and unreliable, it seems that fewer than half of the women in Africa belong to ethnicities who have ever practiced it; many of those groups have now stopped doing it. As shown here, in areas where it is practiced it is often declining rapidly. An extreme form, infibulation, or the sewing together of the vaginal opening, is practiced in the Horn of Africa (Somalia, Sudan, Egypt) and elsewhere, while clitoridectomy only is practiced in a discontinuous belt stretching from Kenya to Senegal. In a few areas infibulation is spreading along with Islam, although it is not prescribed by the Koran. There are now active women's groups in many countries who are working on its eradication, often using a health education approach in particular. Such procedures are illegal in many countries including Kenya, where President Moi banned it in 1982, but enforcement of such laws has often been non-existent. Kenyan reformers have come up with innovative suggestions, such as "circumcision with words," a modified initiation in which girls are given sex education and moral training, but no operation is performed. For further information see Efua Dorkenoo, *Cutting the Rose: Female Genital Mutilation, the Practice and Its Prevention* (London: Minority Rights Group, 1994) and Claire Robertson, "Grassroots in Kenya: Women, Genital Mutilation, and Collective Action, 1920–1990," *Signs* 21, no. 3 (Spring 1996): 615–42.

Harambee!

A friend hands a donation to the Master of Ceremonies as Berida looks on

Clockwise from left: Berida's nephew, the MC; Berida; Domitila; and a niece

Berida and family outside the nursery school/ *harambee* location. *Back row, third from left:* Dominic; third from right, Berida. *Front row, third from right:* Maggie; far right, Martin

Berida's Family and Friends: The Harambee (Claire's Description)

It was Sunday afternoon, 6 July 1997, the day of Berida's *harambee*. The venue was a neighborhood nursery school near Berida's Nairobi home in a neighborhood called Biafra. Karanja, my driver and security guard,[24] carefully parked the rental car in the gated yard, with the help and supervision of the male guests. Jane, Karanja, and I then participated in a round of picture-taking with the car and Berida's friends and relations. The car lent status to the proceedings. We then entered the spotless room and were given seats of honor at a table covered with an immaculate tablecloth at the head of the room. Although the scheduled time to begin was 2 P.M., the formal proceedings did not begin until about 4:30, when one of Berida's nephews attired in a suit, the master of ceremonies, began by calling for a prayer. Everyone was given lavish helpings of mashed peas, potatoes, and rice. The room was sparsely populated and everyone was asked to introduce themselves. He then announced the purpose of the *harambee,* to collect Ksh.30,000 to replace the money stolen from Berida (see Chapter 3). He used Kiswahili, Nairobi's lingua franca.

The attendance showed Berida's support by her family of origin; none of Ndambuki's relatives were there. There were some twenty people including two of Berida's brothers' wives who had come from Matuu, two of her sons and two daughters, her sister's daughter and her children, her nephew's wife, and a number of male and female neighbors. Conspicuously absent at the beginning were her Gikomba work-mates, although they had contributed to buying the food for the *harambee*. Berida had expected them to be the first ones to come. The guest of honor was an elderly Kikuyu businessman from the neighborhood, who arrived at about 5 P.M. He was seated at the table while others were scattered in chairs around the room. At about 5:30 two women from Gikomba finally arrived. The fund-raising began with helpers selling brightly colored plastic flowers. The master of ceremonies said, "I am donating, would people please assist me?" The money was put in a *kyondo*. A slow process began with people donating small cash for the basket as he announced the amount in each case. Applause resulted when the businessman donated Ksh.50, myself Ksh.75 (I was mortified that I only had with me large bills and could not buy the flowers). The Matuu women were notably impassive in aspect. The master of ceremonies played a game with large contributions on occasion; he wouldn't tell the crowd how much Berida's oldest son had sent unless they gave more. Dominic had sent Ksh.1,000.

There was much fanfare for the businessman's contribution of Ksh.800. After consultation with Jane, I gave Ksh.1,500. Big contributors got leis and had their pictures taken. I also took pictures of many contributors and of others by the car. At about 6:10 we left. The net yield, we learned later, was only Ksh.10,000, a big disappointment that was very upsetting to Berida, who said that she was so humiliated and worried about repaying her debts that she could not sleep.[25]

should continue. Failing to remove it leads to immorality; women run around with many men because the clitoris is active [demonstrates movement with hand]. The women now are sexually active. Excision does not guarantee virginity; it only assures that one does not sleep with everybody, maybe only with one friend, not moving from man to man. There were two types of initiation. Although the one involving the cut was called *nzaiko nini* [the small initiation], yet it was the big and painful one. The other one was called *nzaiko nene*

---

24. Cars left unattended in certain parts of Nairobi make good targets for piecemeal dismemberment or complete theft.

25. See also Chapter 3.

[the big initiation], which involved having a mark drawn, a small cut, just on top of where the pubic hair grows. With *nzaiko nene* a lot of advice was given and information passed along to the initiates. After it the whole group would be sleeping outside on the verandah chaperoned by another woman until the day that the lady who did the scratch would be ready to have sex with her husband. That night is when we were allowed to sleep in the hut, but not in the same room with them, of course. During the *nzaiko nene* you had advisors who were referred to as hatchers [*awikii*], as with eggs. Our hatchers told us the bad things we should not do. They were like our mothers and were paid only, say, thirty cents for doing it. It wasn't a career but a status you inherited.

The hatcher would wake up as early as 5 A.M. and start singing to wake us up. If someone was a laggard or greedy she would compose a song about them. If one was not satisfied and had a big stomach, you got more food after the song was sung. If you were hungry she would tell you, "Don't worry, your mother is still remembering you and will give you food." If someone was hard-headed and wouldn't listen, a song was composed about her to advise her, "Mambalelea, you do not understand/hear/listen when you are told." We were instructed by means of these songs. We were taught that there were bad people, girls who used to have sex before excision, so during excision opening up their legs was shameful because men's sperm had already dirtied the person. We were told not to be hard-headed. If you were sent by your mother on an errand you should go and not answer back or sass older women from whatever clan or group.[26] Those women, all older women, are your mothers; they have given birth to you. If you meet another parent who needs your help, you help your parents. This way you will be an obedient and good child. So as parents go about speaking of you, they will say, "That child of so-and-so is a very obedient child."

They also told us about sex. We were told that we should not have sex during our menstrual periods before we married because we might get pregnant.[27] If you got pregnant and gave birth at your parents' home you would never get married. You were to have sex only with your husband after marriage. Even if you had other friends before you should forget them. And you should not refuse to have sex with your husband because you are annoyed or sulking, telling your husband to take it for himself. If you do that your husband will leave you. You should try to please him and give him what he wants. You don't say [high peevish tone], "Go away, you never bring me anything!"

---

26. The translator used the word tribe here, which is commonly used in Kenya without the problematic implications that beset its use in the United States (primitiveness, otherness, vagueness, or the idea that Africans have tribes but Europeans have ethnic groups, peoples, nations, etc.). Because of its negative connotations in the United States it is more advisable to use specific terms like ethnic group, nation, clan, language group, or whatever most accurately describes the group under discussion.

27. Knowledge of Western-type birth control methods was not current in Kenya in the late 1940s. In a situation with high infant mortality and high value placed on children to perpetuate lineages and provide labor such methods would not have been seen as desirable had they been available. Only in the late 1980s with increased impoverishment of the population did Western birth control methods, which had in the meantime become more effective, become popular.

You need to maintain a friendship with your husband. We were told to respect our husbands so that they would remember us no matter where they went. If you shout or retort back when your husband talks to you he will leave you and forget you. Then you will start moving all over. A good child is one who is able to stay on good terms with her husband. Even when you are sick and do not want to have sex with him, you should plead and explain the situation to him, referring to him as "the father of so-and-so." You hold him, laugh with him, touch him, so that you are friends.

On the day we went home the hatcher accompanied us and our parents were waiting for us. My mother had cooked good food. We could not respond to our parents' greetings until we were given gifts by our parents. The gifts could be a goat or cow or chicken from your mother. You wouldn't speak even for days if the gift wasn't given. The hatcher stayed with you at your homestead until the gift was given and you could respond. *Nzaiko nene* was performed about a month after *nzaiko nini*.

Ah well, it is the whites who made the practice die out and it was darkness. And Christianity. I took the eldest girl to have it done, but not the younger ones.[28] It was a group activity. For the boys, I took them to the hospital for circumcision. My mother-in-law was among the earliest Christians and was happy that some of the girls were not excised. My husband also didn't mind because no one was doing it any more. If there is nobody else taking their girls for excision, can you take them alone? Only you? There was only one man who was saying that he was going to have his girls excised so that they did not "erect" [have a large appetite for sex]. [Laughter.] But it was really Christianity that told me not to do it. People were told in church that God did not require the shedding of blood like that. We came to understand that some of the customs we were carrying out were not useful. For instance, if you were sick and it was suggested that they dance *kilumi* for you to heal you, imagine, will that cure you without medicine? Will you really get well? You have to go to a hospital or you will die. So the white priests from Italy explained it to us and we found out that excision was not necessary. The women who were excisors either got old or converted to Christianity.[29]

Between initiation and marriage I did not move around with men. I worked for my mother fetching water, collecting firewood, and watching my younger siblings. We looked after the cows; I did it when it was my turn. As I grew older I helped with the cooking. I ground the millet flour, which could take

---

28. According to her 1988 account, the four eldest were excised. In 1997 she said that none of the girls had been excised and in 1998 that only the eldest, Martha, had been, after Martha had told us that (98-12-26-28, which is the last excerpt included in the Postscript).

29. Some of the beliefs that support the perpetuation of initiation and its related excision of the clitoris that are not cited by Berida are the promotion of women's solidarity and ideas of cleanliness, modesty, and femininity. The debate over excision and initiation has raged since the 1920s in Kenya; one of its primary sites was the missionary schools, where excised girls were initially ostracized. Today the practice has gone underground to some extent due to illegality and social pressure; some village mothers take their daughters surreptitiously for initiation. In the 1990s only about 20 percent of girls had it done in central Kenya, compared to almost 100 percent in the 1930s. See Robertson, "Grassroots."

as long as four hours. I cultivated; if you got married and didn't know how to cultivate, then how would you cultivate your own farm? We started when we were very young learning even using a stick; in time we learned how to weed and more complicated things. Nowadays children are taken to nursery schools but in those days the nursery was the farm.

I actually did not like men; I only slept with my husband when he married me. And I even cried since it was my first time and it was painful. Before that we teenagers used to go to dances and do an Akamba dance called *mbeni,* danced with the neck like this, oh, oh, oh, oh! [Demonstrates.] And that crow dance I told you about. I will bring you a cassette tape of those who used to sing those things. We did not do *kilumi,* were not allowed to since a young person then was not allowed to sleep with a married man. He might have had a wife with a child who died and the man is trying to get rid of that death; the girl would be cursed. Death was regarded as contagious; that was foolishness. When we used to go to the *wathi* [dance] girls would be paired up with men so that they would go and have sex here and there. I did not agree so I was considered to be arrogant. At the *wathi* there was a leader and an assistant and others called *makanga.* It was the leaders who used to do the pairings. If a girl refused to have sex with the designated partner she was beaten. Or, you might be shown something and told that it is an oath so that if you did not have sex with the man you would die. They would stick some things that looked like the horns of *dikdik* [a tiny savanna antelope] into the ground and threaten you that if you passed them without having had sex with the man you were paired with, you would die. What I would do is just to go around and pluck those horns out of the ground and throw them away.[30] Then I passed and went home. [Laughter.] There were usually three people there who would threaten you saying, "Go ahead and see." Then those people I told you about, those [timid ones] who look like they are dozing, would come there and look down and do what they were told. But I just passed arrogantly.

In our time things were different; it didn't matter if a girl got pregnant before she married.[31] In fact, it was good and sometimes more suitors would appear since they knew that the girl was fertile. We wanted children. People were valuable and so she was more valuable if she was pregnant. There were, however, people who did not want children and tried to abort themselves. Some people got quinine tablets from the army. Other methods were to sieve cow manure and mix it with water, then drink it, or to drink a whole bottle of

---

30. Some Kikuyu women responded to this situation by carrying long wooden cooking spoons under their clothing, which they used to beat any man who sexually harassed a girl. Jean Davison, *Voices from Mutira: Change in the Lives of Rural Gikuyu Women, 1910–1995* (Boulder: Lynn Rienner, 1996), p. 33.

31. The mission-imposed disapproval of premarital sex perhaps never had a strong impact but was certainly well advertised and is still much discussed as a Christian tenet. Many "emancipated" young women do not marry at all but have children in any case, so that the formalities that signal marriage are increasingly ignored and the issue of premarital sex is irrelevant. Among those of many classes there is a diminution in the practice of bridewealth, which symbolized and legalized the marriage, while formal Christian marriages are expensive (see Chapter 2 on bridewealth and Martin's marriage).

ghee [Hindi; liquified butter]. People used to look for medicines; the strong ones are the ones they took. I never tried it, even when I was feeling desperate with all those children. Nowadays I have heard that people insert tablets in the vagina or that one can use suction to extract the baby. Also, there are tablets that you take, wait for four days, and then the abortion happens. I don't know much about it since I am not interested. I don't bother asking about it.[32]

32. In 1999 there was tension between Berida's son Martin and his wife Emma over birth control. His unemployment made support of their three children difficult but Emma was not using birth control.

2

"No woman can know what will happen to her in marriage"

Marriage, Children, and Survival

I was very young, only fourteen, when I married Ndambuki on 1 January 1950. I was supposed to marry another man. If you compare how I was married and how you [Mbithe] were married there is a big difference. Long ago there was no courtship; your father was just given bridewealth and you were married off. If you refused to marry the man who had given bridewealth your father would beat you.[1] That is what happened to me. My father had accepted bridewealth for me from a man whose father was wealthy whom I disliked. He started paying when I was small, but as I matured and saw him I disliked him. I didn't like the way he looked, although he was not old. He didn't know how to dress. He used to wear *mikalya* [sandals] made from tires; his had only one strap instead of the usual two. Whenever I saw that I felt like vomiting. I was just disgusted with him. [Laughter.] If I saw him I would go in the opposite direction. When my father insisted that I marry him I refused and was beaten. My mother could not say anything about it; if she had, she would also have been beaten. Mm mmm! Those things of long ago! Nzilani

---

1. The term used by Berida here for bridewealth is *mali* (Kiswahili; goods). In Kikamba a word for bridewealth is *ngashia* according to Ndeti. *Kuashia* is the verb to pay bridewealth. *Elements of Akamba Life* (Nairobi: East African Publishing House, 1972), p. 66. The terms bridewealth, brideprice, and dowry are often used interchangeably. Dowry refers more properly to exchange at marriage in the other direction, from the bride's family to the husband's, as practiced among the propertied classes in Europe and elsewhere. Since dowry is never called husbandprice, bridewealth is not called brideprice here. Both are exchanges that legitimize the marriage; without it the Akamba did not recognize the legality of a marriage. Statistics for Berida's age-cohort regarding choice of spouse showed that more than two-thirds of the women agreed with their future husbands to marry before consulting either set of parents to seek permission, while only two-fifths of those older than Berida did that. The other 60 percent of the older cohort had marriages arranged for them either by the future husband and the parents together or by the parents only. Younger women had more mutual consent marriages without payment of bridewealth. Robertson, *Trouble Showed the Way*, pp. 192, 206.

hid me. I finally ran and threw myself in the pond. Then they realized I might drown and they rescued me.[2] My father quit insisting and nobody forced me again. My grandfather told the suitor to outline what he had paid and they would repay him because they realized that they might lose a child through death. He was the only one I turned down. You know, you can look at a person and the way they dress and assess whether or not they should be called your husband. And you know, I was beautiful.

The other one I chose myself. Ndambuki and I courted and agreed to marry; then I told him to go to my parents.[3] I first met him at Masii market at a tailor's shop where we had gone to have some dresses made. The tailor was from Ndambuki's place and Ndambuki had stopped by to say hello. After Ndambuki greeted the tailor he asked him, "Where are these girls from?" Then he greeted us. Boys are like snakes, they just slither around. When we left the shop he followed us outside and asked me where I came from and how he could get to our home. Then he came there one day and I just saw him. We courted and he told me he wanted a wife on the first day we met there. I told him to go back to his home and give me time to think about it. I told him to come back on a certain date when I would give him an answer. He went and came back on the appointed date, three days later. I then asked him why he wanted a wife. He told me that he wanted a wife who would take care of the property he was seeking. He was working for the government survey department then as a demarcator, holding the string for the surveyors. Makueni District was being subdivided. He was older than I was by a few years, not in my age-grade. I am not even as old as the lastborn in his family. He is the fourth-born in a family of ten (five girls and five boys). I agreed. He looked very smart in his surveyor's uniform. His full name is Kiatine Ndambuki and he has some education; he went to Standard 1 or 2 [first or second grade]. I liked him because he was not married to any other woman and he was earning wages, so I thought I was not going to get poor and suffer. I also asked him if he was going to beat me and he said no. He was not handsome or charming, just ordinary. If I had only known! No woman can know what will happen to her in marriage.

Ndambuki talked to my parents. They talked and talked and agreed. Then he was told to go home and bring his parents, so he went home and brought back his mother and his elder brother, who acted for his father. My parents outlined to them what they wanted for me. They talked with my parents and liked each other. So since we already liked each other, my parents agreed to the marriage.[4] Since we lived in Masii and they lived in Mwala there was no way to find out about his character in the usual way. His parents came again with beer and then they were given a date to come and get me. The third time I was escorted to the gate by Nzilani, my younger sister Nthenya, and some age-

---

2. Lindblom noted that a girl might commit suicide if her father tried to marry her off against her will. *Akamba in British East Africa*, p. 78.

3. For a more detailed ethnographic description of Akamba marriage customs in the 1950s see Penwill, *Kamba Customary Law*, pp. 1–22.

4. There is no distinction in Kikamba between "like" and "love."

Comparing Marriage Payments

EXCERPT FROM TAPE TRANSCRIPT 97-6-5

Berida: Do they pay bride-wealth at your place?
Mbithe: She wants to know if they pay bridewealth at your place.
Claire: No.
Jane: What do you do?
Claire: In the olden days people gave dowry, which is when the woman's family has to give something to the man's family, so it is like husband-price. But we don't do it any more.
Berida: Here it is bridewealth for women; a woman is more valuable because women give birth.

mates; then his family took me back to their home. After I went to his home before a month had elapsed they had slaughtered a bull for a feast to thank my parents for giving them a daughter. They paid a lot of bridewealth.

At one time they took forty goats and Sh.240.[5] After awhile Ndambuki took them a heifer. He bought a blanket each for my mother and father. It was his father who paid for everything before the month was out. The goats and the money were brought together on one day, the cow by itself later, and the bull also by itself for the feast. I was bought by our father very well, for an amount over and above the bridewealth that was taken initially.[6]

Nowadays many people don't pay bridewealth at all. Some women now even complain about it. That's people who have come up with you [Mbithe]. You started saying you can't be bought, you are not land or property.[7] [Laughter.] But you never finish buying a person and women are not slaves. The mistreated wife can go back to her parents and the bridewealth can be returned to the husband. It is not good to abandon the bridewealth custom because your father has put so much effort into bringing you up; what does he get in return? Your parents have taken care of you from when you were a baby to when you got married. Someone then sees you and admires you. Your parents will not be happy not to be given anything; they might even put a curse on the proceedings. If you ever do anything that makes your parents unhappy you will not

5. This amount was cited in 1988; in 1997 Berida changed it to 42 goats, Ksh.300, a cow, and a bull. C. W. Hobley said that forty goats was the usual amount given by a poor man in the first decade of the twentieth century. *Ethnology of A-Kamba*, p. 63. That the sum had not risen in this case shows its symbolic purpose and perhaps the lack of resources in Ndambuki's family.

6. The payment of bridewealth is usually thought to symbolize that a greater value is put on women than in societies where dowry was practiced, as in Europe, China, and India. The economic value of women's labor in Africa was great in most societies. However, in central Kenya there was also in the old system the practice of payment of blood money in cases of murder, for instance. The amount paid by the murderer and/or his clan/family to the clan/family of the victim depended largely on the category of person murdered. Thus, the murder of a man was punished by a fine of twelve cattle, of a woman, eight cattle. Rape was punished by a fine paid to the victim's clan elders or father. Hobley, *Ethnology of A-Kamba*, pp. 78–79. Thus, there were tendencies to treat women as the property of men and transgressions against them as violations of male property rights.

7. Ndeti stated that the monetarization of bridewealth (he firmly rejected the term brideprice), which used to be paid only in livestock and other goods, was responsible for women becoming rebellious. "[T]he women who were once docile and submissive despise it because they refuse to be sold like manufactured wares." *Elements of Akamba Life*, pp. 66–67. The debate over bridewealth is current in Nairobi newspapers; many young women favor its abandonment because they believe it commoditizes them, that it has, in effect, become brideprice. However, the generations between Berida's and that of the young women of the 1990s placed more value on bridewealth in that, in cases where the husband and/or his family could not pay bridewealth, some women paid it themselves to legitimize their children, a complete transformation of older practices.

succeed in life. I have gotten bridewealth for my daughters[8] and paid it for my sons. For the one Muthama married I took twenty-four goats and a cow, plus a big ram to be slaughtered. I also gave Ksh.12,000 in cash and took rice and flour for cooking to that home. But for Angelina, those people from Meru, her man's people, came to my place with three vehicles and food that they alone cooked and ate. They told me that I had to go get the bridewealth myself from Meru. I never went to get it; where I come from we do not like that. So it is not a marriage because the parents are not happy. And if bridewealth is not paid for a woman, then it cannot be demanded for her daughter either.[9]

Bridewealth is negotiated. Both fathers and mothers receive it. It was handed to the man and then the man gave it to me to keep. After the visitors left then we decided what we were going to do. We each said our needs to see which ones we were going to deal with. What was left over we kept for future use. The only bad thing is misuse of what is given. Mothers deserve a reward for all their trouble. Just imagine the pain you undergo to get children! The man doesn't undergo that. The woman really should get more but remember that the woman was created from the man's rib and therefore will always be lower. [Laughter.]

Back then we did not marry in a Christian ceremony. But now men and women know that formal weddings are important, unlike getting married in darkness, at night, where it is the wild animals who are your witnesses. "The nights are for the hyena." [A proverb.] Bad things happen at night; even thieves rob at night. Night weddings are just dark and one will not stay well with one's partner because the wife will be treated like a slave. But Christian weddings are during the day; there is light and everybody is free and open. I wear a wedding ring because we redid the vows in a Christian ceremony not long ago. When our son Martin got married in a formal wedding (I paid a lot for that wedding!), my husband said that he also wanted to convert his marriage to a formal one. So two years ago I wore a white dress that I will put on so you can see it when you come home with me and we went to church on a Sunday where with many old couples we formalized our marriages. We sat in the congregation and the priest called us when it was our turn. I was very happy; we enjoyed a marriage ceremony when we are old together with our children. Even in church now they respect me more and the priest calls me Berida, Berida.

I think we need to stop now, I am tired. And besides, tomorrow I am going with a group of women from Gikomba, who are in charge of social functions, to help one of them to ask for a daughter-in-law. We help each other by

---

8. This contradicts her detailed account, in which she said that her daughters Angelina, Katunge, and Monica did not have bridewealth given for them. Berida's beliefs concerning respectability for women are strongly connected to the importance the legitimation of a marriage and children by payment of bridewealth. She and many older people believe that without bridewealth there is no marriage, no matter what kind of other ceremony has been performed (Christian, Muslim, etc.).

9. Without bridewealth to formalize a marriage there is no necessity for partners' parents to meet and formalities do not accompany a separation unless a Christian or civil ceremony has been performed, which would require legal action to divorce. When bridewealth is paid the children normally go to their father in case of divorce; without bridewealth they stay with their mother.

pooling resources and buying things for each other. In this case the things will be part of the bridewealth for the son of one of us; she already left today. Then we select a few people to go and present the things we have bought. We call this *kuashia,* to take animals and money to buy a bride. I would be happy tomorrow if we could start earlier and stop earlier. We will leave tomorrow (Saturday) and come back Sunday.

Before I married Ndambuki my mother told me to stick to my husband and not run around with other men. I was also told to get along well with my in-laws because my husband might change and his parents might support me. She advised me always to work hard because I would benefit and people would admire my work. That's why I started doing my own work. The rest about marriage I have taught myself.

I cried when I married Ndambuki because I felt a lot of pain. I had never been with a man before. I was afraid and had to be forced. But even though he forced me I eventually loved him. I got used to the sex. I was having my period when we married and after that I conceived immediately. We were there at Mwala with his parents, three of his elder brothers, and a younger one. Those people at Mwala were not as civilized as my people; we had real beds but they had those beds with poles. We even had lanterns. I come from an enlightened family so I also try to follow in the footsteps of my people to take care of my house and make it look nice. But at their place everything was still left to do. We used to live in a house that collapsed when it rained. Ndambuki built it but he never finishes what he begins. I worked to build a home like the one I had left. I had my house but we cooked together. We stayed there for awhile; I bore two children there and then we moved to my eldest brother-in-law's land to farm at Kikambuani in Kangundo when he moved to Makueni. We went to Wote in Makueni in 1958 when he came for us and stayed there until independence in 1963, then we moved from Wote to Kathonzweni. That was when Paul Ngei [a prominent Akamba politician] and Kenyatta [the first president of independent Kenya] announced that people could have their own land. We got forty-eight acres from a white man named Kiko, who showed us where to settle and organized people to clear the land because there were a lot of wild animals. Before, the chief would organize people to clear it through forced labor. The white man gave it to us for free if we cleared it to drive off the wild animals.

Ndambuki is short and sort of medium-col-

A Story from the Frontier

When we visited Berida's home at Kathonzweni, Mukei, an elderly woman at the party in Berida's house, told this story:

When we first went to Kathonzweni it was wild bush country. We were the first settlers. We had to walk a long way for water to the nearest mountain called Nzaui where the sun sets. I carried a gourd for the water and one for the porridge. We might leave at 5 A.M. and return at 4 P.M. We filtered and reused the wash water and cooked cowpeas because they required less water than beans. Sometimes I used to take a whistle with me as I walked to scare away the wild animals like the elephants, or beat on things to get rid of the buffalos. I told my orphaned granddaughter for whom I was caring and the other children to light a fire in my absence to keep off the wild animals. We first encountered Ndambuki when he came and asked the children who they were with. He also was frightened of the wild animals, which we could hear all the time at night, especially the [Cape] buffalos.

Cameraman Dennis Kavinghua films Ndambuki

ored. When we were first married he did not behave like he does now. I like him because he married me, gave me shelter, found land to work, and never beat me; he is the father of my children. He comes from a clan called Mbaa Mulaya Itema Asii, which means "those who do not eat liver." If they eat any kind of liver their eyes will start watering. My mother was also from that clan. They are also called the lion clan, the one who breaks the necks of the other animals. They originally came from Mbooni in Makueni. We first stayed together at Mwala near his parents' house.

After a while we had a famine and Ndambuki went to look for work in Nairobi. He used to send us clothes and money; he would tell me to buy cows and I would. They used to be paid Ksh.90 at that time. He would send about Ksh.60 and I would buy cows at Ksh.40 and goats at Ksh.12. But there were times when he would come home and leave us only Ksh.5 for food. I fed the children with produce from the farm. But we needed to buy food often during droughts. His father would sell a goat and give us the money to buy food. Or he would buy a bag of maize for us which cost Ksh.10.50. Ndambuki even made me cry once. There was a drought and I had three children. He had left only Ksh.5 for us and was leaving for Nairobi. But he went and drank somewhere and used up all the money for his fare, so he came back and got the Ksh.5. Although I made noise at him about it and asked him why he had given it to me in the first place, he took it! He explained that I should let him have the money and that when he got to Nairobi he would get food from a place he knew and send it to us at home. It was all lies! So I went to my paternal grandmother and told her and she gave me food. Had she not moved from

Masii to Mwala in search of pasturage for the cows I would have had nowhere to turn when I had problems. My people helped a lot with food and clothing. I used to go to Nairobi sometimes and look him up to see if he had gotten tempted. . . .

Ndambuki's father also used to help me until he died in 1965. His mother, however, was bad; she didn't help anyone like she was supposed to. She had five daughters-in-law and she never visited them. She never cooked with any of them or visited their parents, not once! Usually a mother-in-law would help the daughters-in-law when they gave birth but she wouldn't bother. Even her own sons know that she had a bad spirit. She used to brew and sell beer, but would she help with money for hospital expenses? No! I was the one who used to help his brothers' wives give birth, not her. My father-in-law too, he would hold their feet for me. My problems increased a lot when Ndambuki's father died so he couldn't help me any more. If it were possible to bring him back, I would do it in a second!

You see, Ndambuki never stuck to one job for long. In one month he would work for three different white employers. With that little money he would buy trousers. And how much was he being paid, anyway? Very little. Some paid him Ksh.50 or 60. In one week he would work for two different employers. And you can't get any benefit if you don't work consistently. My younger brother Bernard even nicknamed him "the one who does not stick." "The one who does not stick has come back home again," my brother would say. Sometimes he would not even collect his pay. He was never fired. It was more like he would just get discouraged or he would refuse to do the work. Maybe it was something in his head, I don't know. He would want to come home, just to sing and dance. The people from Mwala were foolish, not enlightened like those of Kangundo, Masii, or Masaku. When I got married I went there wearing dresses which had been bought at my home. The people at his place called me a prostitute who has been brought from town. Those people were very backward. The men would just sling a blanket over themselves and underneath they had nothing on, just like Maasais. What made me get married to Ndambuki was because he was working at Makueni and had clean clothes, but those were the only ones he had. When they got torn that was it! You will see when you come to my place. Even the house there, I am the one who built it. He cannot build for anyone, not even a granary.[10] When he is smearing mud on the walls of a house you can see that he has no chance of finishing. Even when we go to the *shamba* you can see that he won't finish the work. His work is just grazing the animals.

Once I got very sick so my husband decided to consult an *mganga* [Kiswahili; healer]. The *mganga* asked me what was wrong with me. He told Ndambuki to buy me certain things so that I could get powers, be clairvoyant [*mundu mue*]. But Ndambuki said he had no money to buy such things. So I left my husband's home on foot. I was so thin and weak it took me three days

---

10. Hobley (and others) state firmly that building a house was men's responsibility. *Ethnology of A-Kamba*, p. 30.

to walk from Mwala to Masii. I had Dominic with me on my back; he was a little baby. On the day I arrived, Mutune, who at that time was in charge of Kenya Breweries, had just been there with my father. When my father saw me, he asked, "What's wrong?" I said I was sick. He called Mutune's wife; Mutune had just left for Nairobi. I had gotten there at about 11 A.M.; by 1 P.M. they had put me in a vehicle to go to Nairobi. Mutune's wife was told to take me to Mutune so he could take me to the hospital. But Mutune went to see Patricia, Ndambuki's sister, who used to work at Mathare Hospital.

Patricia got training as a nurse's aide after she ran away from home to escape marriage with a man her parents had chosen for her. She joined the nuns at Mangu and they trained her. Later she married a Ugandan doctor and they had four children but now they are separated; he has married a Kikuyu woman. Ndambuki's older brother Michael Mukolwe was also a doctor, a surgeon who used to do army physicals during the war. He was among those who were taken to Kabaa to be educated by force; they had no choice.

Anyway, Mutune told Patricia, "Mathai is here very sick and if I get her treated, when she recovers she will never return to your people. I will refund your bridewealth."[12] So Ndambuki's sister told him to bring me to her place. Mutune came and told me we were going to Patricia's. But I told him, "I have been sick for many years and these people don't get me treated." So he told me that if she refused to take me to the doctor the next day I should go to the road just there by Mathare Hospital and wait for him. He said he passed by there several times each day and

> **Ndambuki's Story: July 1997**
>
> My cows were given to me as a gift from my father. I used to go to school. My father would say, "Put aside your books and go herd the cows." When my father told me to stop going to school I stopped. From that time until today I have herded and watered the animals. I later found that herding was profitable for me. Like now, these people have come and I have slaughtered a goat for them. I didn't have to ask anyone for a goat. There are times during the dry season when there's no water for the animals; I always try my best to get them water. I do it so that they will be strong and fat and bring a good price at the market. If a cow calves I have milk to drink; if I need money I sell a cow. If I want meat I slaughter a cow to get it. During a drought I can sell a cow and buy food for the family. I don't work but my children and grandchildren are in school. I sell a cow or goat to pay their school fees —they finish school. The cows and goats are my mother and father because they help me. If my clothes are torn or those of a child are ruined, I can take an animal and sell it to buy clothes. I buy dressy clothes, bedding, and schoolbooks. So—I help myself. As my father said, "Rely on the animals."[11]

would see me. I didn't want to go to Patricia's because she is just like Ndambuki and I didn't think that she would have me treated. But I spent the night at her place and in the morning Patricia bathed my baby, then she bathed me (I was in a bad way). She dressed me and took me to the hospital. I was told I needed an X-ray. Patricia paid for it. I asked her how much it was and she said

---

11. This speech was videotaped. Berida's reaction to this part of the tape was to snort and say, "Has he ever bought himself clothes, even once?" Similarly, in a scene where he joined the digging for the dam, Berida remarked, "Can he dig? He never digs."

12. Penwill supports Berida's account by saying that a husband's failure to provide proper medicine and care for a sick wife was grounds for divorce. *Kamba Customary Law*, p. 17.

Ksh.100. I said, "Where is that Ksh.100 going to come from?" She said that I was worth more than Ksh.100. So I was treated and told not to eat *isyo* [maize and beans] or hard food. I was told to come back the following day, but I had left Martha at home and I began to feel that she was suffering, so I decided to go home. Patricia bought rice and wheat flour for me and gave me money for vegetables, telling me to send my other sister-in-law to buy them for me. She put me on a bus and told me that the food was for me, not her mother, since I couldn't eat hard food. With the money I was to buy things like soupbones and tomatoes. The doctor had discovered that I had no blood! That's why I was so weak.[13]

When I got home my catechism instructor came to see me. It was a Saturday. On Sunday he went to church and asked the white priest at the time, Father Wit, to pray for Kiatine's home; he asked everyone to do so. The teacher told the priest he should come and lay hands on me so he and the whole congregation came to my house. He prayed and blessed me. He blessed our home. I never went back to the hospital.

You know, Ndambuki never had girlfriends but he did bring home a second wife once. She came in 1962 and then I got sick. I stepped on a nail and spent nine months in the hospital. After that Ndambuki said that she had bewitched me and he chased her away. He thought she wanted to kill me. When she came she already had three children; I don't know who the father was. She came from Kyanzave in Kangundo. He met her in Nairobi. He was staying there and I was upcountry. So he probably thought she was pretty since she had bathed, but I was cleaner than she was. He brought her home at about the time I gave birth to my daughter Katunge. She did not even help me with the baby after my foot was pierced. She would refuse to bathe her or help in any way. She also did not milk the cows; the neighbors had to help me. She was lazy and jealous. If she saw Ndambuki coming she would run and jump into bed and say she was sick. She was possessive about him. When she behaved like that I just ignored her and kept on working. It's not good for a man to have two wives. If the husband favors one wife, stays with her overnight at her place, she will tell him that the other one did such-and-such to make him find fault with her.[14]

A good wife is obedient to her husband and a hard worker. She does not

---

13. Anemia perhaps?

14. It is also possible, but rare, by Akamba custom for a woman to take a wife, the practice that in the anthropological literature is called woman-marriage. The woman's wife would then be called an *iweto*. The woman would pay the bridewealth and the *iweto* would take a lover who fathered the children. The children would belong to the lineage of the woman-husband's husband, if she had one. In theory, an *iweto* was to produce male heirs for a woman without sons in order to satisfy the patrilineage of the husband. In practice, senior women of rank and/or wealth sometimes took advantage of the arrangement to the point of establishing de facto lineages of their own, especially if they themselves had no husband. In 1988 I encountered a woman-husband at Shauri Moyo Market in Nairobi who fell into the latter category. Supporting the five children of her *iweto*, however, had become burdensome for her and she wanted her to use birth control or stop seeing her lover. When discussing this topic, which did not interest Berida much and so is omitted from her account, Berida added the interesting information that the *iweto*'s lover should not be from the woman-husband's clan lest he claim the children for himself, and should be chosen discreetly by the *iweto* without the knowledge of the woman-husband. Berida was shocked when we asked if there was a sexual relationship between those in a woman-marriage, and said that women don't do those things.

Berida discusses arrangements with helpers in her doorway

move around with other men. She knows only her husband. If she is single like Jane, she has only one man friend and knows only him. She stays with the children and doesn't go out. A bad one goes to a bar and finds a man one day, to a restaurant tomorrow and finds another one. It is not Nairobi that has made women bad but the person herself, the individual who is bad. Those who are bad want to be bad. I myself came to Nairobi to sell staples when I was young but whenever I needed a man I went back to my husband at home. A good husband is one who remembers his wife and always has her in mind. If he goes somewhere and finds that someone has slaughtered a cow he will take her some meat from it. He cares about his family and stays with the first wife and looks after the children. He sticks to his wife; he does not move around with women who have applied make-up and used Snow [a complexion cream]. Those women are the ones who have *ukimwi* [AIDS]. Some husbands go to the extent of moving about with girls who are the age of their daughters. You never know, sometime he might find himself in bed with his own daughter! It's not good! Some husbands object to their wives going to Nairobi to trade, but they are foolish to do so. They imagine that when they let their wives go out they may sleep with other men and become prostitutes.

Just the other day I hurt my foot separating two women who got into a fight. The younger woman sells next to me at Gikomba. The old woman has left her husband at Mwea. They were fighting over a young Kikuyu man named Ndegwa with whom the old one is now living. The young one did not see the older one coming because she came up behind her and hit her until she fell down on a board where boiled maize ears were sitting on a tray ready to be sold. Then Martha, my eldest, called out to me to help separate the two. When I got there I slapped the older one really hard and, as she was getting up, she stepped on my foot. I think a nerve has been affected [see Chapter 5]. That medicine you brought me for it helped a little; I hope it will ease the pain.

Then there was the time that a husband followed his wife to the market and yelled at her for leaving home. He even tore up her shoes so she couldn't go again. Another husband came to Gikomba carrying a baby. The wife had run away from home leaving the baby. He managed to trace her to Gikomba and when he found her she denied that he was her husband. We as the Market Committee were asked to judge the case and we chased her away from the market, handed her over to the chief, who handed her back to her husband.

I was happy enough with my husband until he began drinking a lot. Why, I have never gone back to my parents' home even once other than for friendly visits! Some women who were mistreated returned to their parents. If the parents had negotiated the marriage and bridewealth was involved, they would get intermediaries to talk to the husband when he came with his family to take the wife back. If he accepted the advice given he would get you back, but if he refused to change his behavior the bridewealth would be repaid and your family took you back. However, usually when Ndambuki and I quarreled we forgave each other. I would tell him where he has wronged me and he says in turn how I have wronged him and says he will beat me. Then I just ask for forgiveness. We cooperated when he came and said he had been unable to find employment in Nairobi and didn't know how we were going to survive. He took one of the cows and sold it and gave me the money to start the business, Ksh.60. But you can't count on him. He is inconsistent. Now he is boasting about me coming there with a white or he might say, "There's my lady from the city." He should value me more; sometimes men would ask Ndambuki to swap their wives for me!

By 1988 Ndambuki and I had changed places. He drank more when he was in Nairobi and I was at home in Ukambani. But then I began trading and left him at home with the children and the goats to supervise the farm. I also had a house-help to cook for the children. I paid her Ksh.250 per month. I was sending money to him to build my house and he would oversee the building process. Only the doors were left to do, but then he started to drink the money I sent for the doors, so I sent the money directly to the *fundi* [Kiswahili; workman]. When Ndambuki found the doors installed, that's when he started trouble. "You give money to your friends!" he said. And these are people who are the same age as our children! That's when I got angry and told

A Different View: Magdalena's Story, 6 July 1997

I am twenty-three and the youngest child of my mother and my father. We were sixteen but six of us died. My father is a farmer who farms fifteen acres at Kiuani village near Kathonzweni. He works very hard herding the cattle. There was a drought and many of his cows died. He had twelve cows before the drought but now has only about thirty goats. He has two helpers, my older sister Monica's two children—a son about ten years old, and a daughter who is about fourteen. They live with him.

him I would never give him any money again (except I buy clothes for him so he doesn't look dirty). I do give him Ksh.100 now and again and I don't care what he does with it. You don't lend money to husbands; you give it to them. He's not paying anyone's school fees.

I don't know how long Ndambuki has been drinking but it has been a long time. It was when he was drunk that he began beating me sometimes when I was there. He would chase me and I would hide. This is an ordinary thing for a man and his wife. After the children got a little bigger they sometimes tried to defend me. For instance, one day Muthama got really mad because Ndambuki was threatening me with a poisoned arrow, so Muthama took his bow and arrow and said to him, "If you dare to hurt her I will kill you!" Finally I got fed up with it. He was again chasing me with his walking stick and I took it away from him and dared him to hit me. I told him I would not hesitate to kill him. After that he stopped chasing me.

Sometimes Ndambuki makes me so mad. For example, at the time when I only had one dress I used to wash it every night and put it back on in the morning. It was nylon and you can imagine how cold nylon material can be. If he waked up very early in the morning he would take with him the blanket with which we covered ourselves so we were forced to wake up also because it was the only one we had! That's typical for those people from Mwala. And now, he has nothing; I even buy him clothes. He sent a woman to tell me to bring that white person home with me so he could slaughter a goat for her. He gets drunk and calls me names in public to embarrass me. A man is only loved or wanted by a woman because of money. That's why you see so many dying of that disease we talked about [AIDS]. I only love Ndambuki for the name. My children cannot be referred to as the children of Berida, a woman. They

---

Mbithe's Story: 29 July 1997

While at Kathonzweni Berida told me that she could do nothing with the land since both she and Ndambuki own it. He says that all of the animals are his and the house is hers. Ndambuki sold two bulls for Ksh.40,000 and bought two smaller bulls; he drank up the difference in the money. If she had asked him about that money they would have fought about it. He yelled at her to go fetch firewood and carry it in a *kyondo* when we were walking on a tour of the property and the dam works. Domitila carried the *kyondo* and Ndambuki fetched the firewood. He told Dennis to ask Berida to prepare tea for him. They began quarreling about his drinking again and Berida, Elena, and Domitila left to go to Elena's, where they talked until 1 A.M. Berida leaves to avoid fights with him.

---

have to be known as the children of a man. He has changed. I would not have agreed for him to marry me[15] if he had been like this then. I get so angry. I feel I'm alone because he thinks of nothing but drink. If he didn't drink I would be a very rich businesswoman today.[16]

I could go on and on about the things Ndambuki has done. He sold animals belonging to me and to Martin (they were given to Martin as wedding presents) without consulting us. I own four cows and six goats, but he treats all of ours as if they are his.[17] He took my shop I built here from me and rented it out; he drinks up the rent money. He said there was no space for a woman to run a business like that and so he took it! He insults my friends and neighbors. He comes to Nairobi all dirty and disheveled; it's embarrassing! That's why I refused to bring him to see Kilaya. Just now he has even threatened to sell the land, so I told him that if he tried that I would get him jailed until I said he could get out! I didn't ever tell my parents about how he treated me and all the problems, neither did my brothers. What could they have done about it anyway? I could keep that knowledge from them because we didn't live together. When my father would come visit us Ndambuki would slaughter a goat for him so he thought everything was all right.

I have talked to Ndambuki at length about drink. His father was also concerned about it even long ago. When he realized how much Ndambuki was drinking he thought that if he gave him permission to drink by Akamba custom, that he might moderate his behavior. They did the ceremony but he was already addicted and it made no difference.[18] I am even thinking of getting him treated for drinking; he may be bewitched. I told him the other day, "Dominic's father, we have children who are grown. It is not nice for them

---

15. Berida made an interesting correction here. Claire had written, following Berida's account, "she would not have agreed to marry him," but Berida insisted that he married her, rather, as above. A woman is married by a man; he is the actor, she the passive object in Kikamba and Kiswahili.

16. Lindblom said "Beerdrinking is the favorite occupation of old men . . . ," who got old before their time because of it. *Akamba in British East Africa*, p. 521. Hobley said that a habitual drunkard might be punished by mob action, *Ethnology of A-Kamba*, p. 81.

17. Penwill said that one of the household head's/father's/husband's obligations was to help his sons and their wives to establish themselves by donating a goat or a heifer so they could start their own herds. Ndambuki therefore inverted and subverted his responsibilities in this regard. *Kamba Customary Law*, p. 112.

18. Penwill described the elaborate precautionary ceremonies that permitted a young man to begin drinking beer that still existed in the 1930s. A father was required to give permission in three stages, each marking the progression of the young man to elder status. Neither women nor children were allowed to

to see you like this and hear the language you use when you are drunk." Sometimes he says he will try to change; other times he denies that he uses bad language. When I arrive home, that day he might not go out to drink. He stays home like a good husband. Then he says, "Let me go check the cattle and see how they are doing." He disappears and the next thing I hear is him coming home drunk making a lot of noise, insulting people.[19]

When you live with someone who drinks he spoils everything for you. If you have some education, maybe up to Form 4 [equivalent to ninth grade], you forget everything. Instead of thinking about your work, your head is full of thoughts about that person and all the bad things he said to you when he was drunk. You get old fast because someone is bothering your head and you don't feed your body properly. Anyone who drinks, that's all they think about, and about their drinking buddies. There is a man at Kathonzweni named Nzioki who used to be a rich businessman, but the drink got him and now he is thin and goes about barefoot like

> Claire's Diary, 28–29 July 1997
>
> At Kathonzweni Dennis Kavinghua, the cameraman, developed an instant rapport with Ndambuki, who invited him to go drinking with him that night or even during the day. Ndambuki boasted of his secret route to the drinking place, an arduous journey through gullies and brambles. The first day we were there he disappeared only once. The next day he got up very early before sunrise and stayed away drinking until about 9 A.M., and left again several more times. He was very thin but did not appear to be disabled in any way and showed no visible effects from the constant imbibing of homebrew. [Later, in February of 1998, he got very sick with malaria and Berida went home to nurse him. She got him treatment and he recovered.]

a chicken. When I say to Ndambuki, "Why don't you go by Bernard's and call him to go to church?" he says, "I can't; I don't feel well." He lies down on a sack. As soon as we leave the house he disappears to drink. His friend Bernard has told him not to spoil his [Bernard's] home as he has already spoiled his own. If he doesn't get anything to drink for awhile he says he is sick, has a fever, and lies outside on a mattress shaking and shivering, complaining that his bones ache. As soon as he has a drink he is all right. His blood is used to the alcohol.

But when Ndambuki's not drunk he can be a nice person. I cannot reject him. I have never even been tempted to be unfaithful to him. If someone else had loved me he would have married me. The one who loved me married me. Even in Nairobi I am called Berida Ndambuki. He is the father of all of my

---

drink beer. *Kamba Customary Law,* pp. 97–99. Snufftaking also required permission from male elders. In Kikamba there were also at least eight terms for the beer drunk as parts of different ceremonies to seal negotiations (p. 121). By the 1940s, however, beerdrinking had become general; the Local Native Councils of male elders were trying to preserve control over the young by fining those who drank beer without permission (p. 100). During the videotaping Ndambuki insisted that we film him and another male elder taking snuff.

19. According to Hobley, a habitual drunkard who drove off his wives, beat up his neighbors for no reason, and generally made a public nuisance of himself was often punished by "mob action," the seizure of an ox and a thorough beating (nonfatal). *Ethnology of A-Kamba,* p. 81. This practice, if it ever was prevalent, seems now to have disappeared.

children. All he has done is change. Things just happen. God must have meant Ndambuki for me or else why did I marry him and not any of my other suitors? I believe he was created like that by God, unable to help anybody. God always pairs people like that: if the husband is hardworking then the wife is lazy and vice versa. So God made me industrious and paired me with Ndambuki. "Two axes together in one bag will inevitably rub against each other." [A proverb.] Good or bad, Ndambuki is mine. I accept him as he is and we will die together. Sometimes I regret marrying him but when I grow resentful I ask God to forgive me for such thoughts since he gave me this husband who fathered my children. I only ask Him to give me the ability to support them.

Many husbands and wives live well together; they consult each other. If you love together and work together you will have wealth in the home. If you court first and obey the ten commandments that is good. They come to appreciate each other and the man knows that your body is his and that therefore you have to stay well together. The man has brains and is well educated. People of long ago behaved the way they did because they were uneducated. For instance, my sister Domitila and her husband are good friends, like you and your husband. John cooks if Domitila feels bad, even if she lies about it. The children sit on his lap. They have five children, three boys and two girls. He pays the school fees. He normally works at the Post Office but they have a place near Matuu in Ukambani and he goes home when it is time to plant.

My brother Mutune was a good husband. He had four wives, one of whom is Ruth Karanja, who you saw at Wote at my father's place. What happened was that during the Emergency Ruth was working at the Mathare clinic where Patricia also worked. Kikuyus were being targeted, arrested, and often tortured by the police. Ruth managed to escape and fled to her friend Mutune, who was working at Kenya Breweries. He then took her to his home where he even put up a dispensary for her. He already had two wives by then. Even though their marriage came about because of the Emergency troubles, he paid bridewealth eventually, a lot of cows that were taken to her place in a truck. That was in 1963. So she became his third wife and then he also married another one later. Altogether he had twenty-five sons and eight daughters. He cared for them all well because he got a lot of property and was very successful.

Even now that he has died they are fine. Each wife has her own land in different places: Ruth is in Masii; there is one at Katangi, and the other ones are at Yatta but in different places. They get along well but that is because they don't live together; if they did they would hate each other. In fact, Mutune's wives did not consider that their marriages were polygynous; each one would say that she was his only wife, even though they each knew about the others! He has built modern homes for all of them with gates. When he died he made provision for all of them and divided up his property so that Ruth's eldest son, Joseph, got the *matatus* and manages all of the businesses. He started by doing accounts for his father. His father told him how to distribute the earnings. Ruth was to get the least because she didn't used to feed Mutune well. Joseph's wife is also very clever; she's an education officer in Matuu, an Mkamba woman. Yes, Mutune also was a good man; if it were possible to raise people from the dead I would go get him. Even his wives wish the same for James!

But there are also those who are worse than Ndambuki. There are more women than men, and women like you [Mbithe] cannot agree to be a second or third wife.[20] There are very many who will help you to give birth but very few who want to take care of you—they are not there—and the children . . . ? It is a problem that is there *kingi, kingi* [plenty, plenty]. I heard about a man shooting and killing his wife. At Kathonzweni at a place across the valley a man cut his wife's throat. They don't know why; he was drunk. He spent five years in prison and then they let him out because the children were alone. That was in about 1975. The family there was destroyed. One of the daughters married a white man and went abroad. That man put up a house there for the other children to live in but he died. That house is in the valley just before Elena's.

At Kathonzweni there was also a man named Edwards who actually beat his wife in the market and stripped her. He beat her so much that her skin, which was light, turned black. The police came while he was beating her but he was so fierce they couldn't stop him. He told her to take a hoe and dig her own grave. She ran away to Somalia. He tracked her down there and brought her back. Her brothers came and got her with the three children but she died from the beatings. Now he has married a young wife who is a prostitute. She is the KANU (Kenya African National Union) chairlady for Makueni and travels a lot.

Elena is my best friend at Kathonzweni. We became friends because we are neighbors and decided to remain friends always. They came from Kilungu looking for a place to settle. My husband Ndambuki showed them a piece of land. They didn't have to buy it because it hadn't been claimed. So we became friends. That was in 1964. One day she said we should have our daughters marry our sons. So her daughter Emma married my son Martin. Actually,

---

20. Polygyny is the correct term for the practice of a man having more than one wife; polygamy refers to any form of multiple spousal marriage. Before central Kenya's phenomenal population growth in the twentieth century polygyny was primarily a means for a man to control more labor and expand lineages in patrilineal societies in which the amount of land worked depended on the labor supply. Polygyny was not universal by any means but was rather reserved for those who could afford to pay more bridewealth. It is now rapidly declining. Ndeti, *Elements of Akamba Life,* p. 66; Robertson, *Trouble Showed the Way,* Chapter 6. Frequently given explanations which naturalize the practice include the necessity for men to have more than one sex partner (in case of one wife's pregnancy or to satisfy instincts) and many children, and the "fact" that there are more women in the world than men who need spouses. The latter phenomenon occurred not because more girls than boys were born—a deviance from the world pattern because of differential age at marriage, as with Berida and Ndambuki. Women married men older than themselves, often by many years. Because there were fewer men aged 25 to 35 than women aged 15 to 19, the usual age at marriage, there was always a surplus of marriageable women.

Elena, Berida's in-law and friend, and Berida catch up on the news

Elena leads a Kathonzweni dance group

Mbithe's Reflections on Kathonzweni, 1998

The experience for me at Kathonzweni was very enlightening. Those people face a
lot of problems but they seem cheerful and even contented. It's like they bend but don't
break with the stress. Instead of sitting and waiting they work hard to improve things.
Their biggest challenge is water. That deep well is so dangerous but they seem unaware
of the dangers. If that wall collapsed with those children there! Why not make a proper
well with reinforced sides and then pump out the water with a manual pump, or even
use a crank and a bucket? Is it economical to hand-water plants if you don't even have
enough water for yourselves? You use so much labor to draw the water and then water
the plants; even then it's not enough and many don't survive. They recycle the water
and expose themselves to diseases. They could have sold that land but Berida enjoys
being there. And Ndambuki!!! Do you think he is aware of what he is doing to his
body? He could get cirrhosis of the liver. Berida thought he wouldn't drink when we
were there and he wasn't drunk when we arrived, but the next morning even at 5 A.M.
he sneaked out! Why does he do it? Does he feel stressed as a man when he's not able
to provide for the family as he should? Berida goes to Nairobi to escape when she
would rather be home. She is trying to protect her family as she sorts out the situation.
The hard work she does!!! But she won't be able to keep it up forever and what will
happen when she can't do it any more? Is her home secure enough for her to go home
and stay there? Maybe she has resigned herself to the situation with Ndambuki. She
tried to improve her situation by working and educating the kids, but that relationship!!! I think she is hopeful that he can change. He needs someone in the neighborhood who will sit down with him and tell him that what he is doing is not right.
Someone who is too close to you won't do that because it risks the relationship. Maybe
there is someone who cares enough to do that and stand by him as he tries to change.
Even their own children have made the choice not to drink, probably because they saw
him drunk and using bad language; it had an impact.

Martin and Emma decided they wanted to get married and we had nothing
against it so we told them to go ahead and get married. I paid some bridewealth but we are friends and we share things. For example, when we get to
Kathonzweni you will see; she will be the first to come and welcome you. She
is a nursery school teacher and younger than I am. I like Elena because she
gave me a daughter and she takes care of my *shamba* when I am not there. Also,
if she notices something is wrong at my home she tells my people to put it
right. She oversees what Martin and Emma are doing. She is a nice person and
also very talkative. [Laughter.] Her husband's name is John. She even might
get on a bus and come to Nairobi to check on me and see if I am sick if I don't
go home for some time. Sometimes if there is no food she gives my family
food. Also, if someone is sick she will give them money for the hospital. What
I do for her is that I send things home from Nairobi to her and the people
at my house, things like rice, cabbage, potatoes, carrots, that they can't get
there. Her cattle graze on my land because her land is small. Sometimes when
Ndambuki gets drunk he insults Elena and seems jealous of our friendship.
But that is just the booze talking. If he is not drunk he calls her Mom and runs
to her.

The way birth went in the olden days was something like this. The woman
who was helping with the delivery, the midwife, would catch the baby in her

Mwenye, Monica's daughter, gets water from the well with a neighbor

Dambuilding

hands and cut the cord with a knife using a piece of gourd to place under the cord [like using a cutting board].[21] If there were problems there were healers who knew how to insert an arm and use their hands to take the baby out. They would massage the stomach and give the mother herbal drinks to get the afterbirth to come out. The midwife was paid for her services, but that was usually in kind; you bought her a dress or long ago people even just gave them food in a basket that was taken to her. I took the food to her along with the baby for her to see. A new mother got soup made from goat broth and millet porridge to help her strength return. She would be given *nzavi* [lablab beans], or if those were not available, plain maize.[22] Porridge made from millet flour is good and so are cowpeas, which have a lot of vitamins. Sugarcane helps with milk production. A goat was killed and soup prepared to give to the woman who had to breastfeed. Not bananas. She was given *ngondu*. In the olden days some birth customs were really bad. After a baby was born they put a charm around the baby's neck on the second day. On the same day the woman had to have sex with her husband so that others could hold the baby. You would be bleeding and sore, with wounds. People believed that if you had not had sex and somebody held the baby and went and had sex with someone else, the baby would die. There are still some people who believe that and consult with healers.

It was usual for a woman to be taken to a medicine man if she couldn't get pregnant. I myself went to a blind medicine man because my babies were dying, one after the other and all boys. Ndambuki went to him and I stayed by his gate. The medicine man knew I was there and sent for me. He told me that my children had died because of that baby that I used to pretend to nurse when I was a child, the one whose mother had died after being beaten by my grandfather. I used to take that baby and put it to my breast, pretending to nurse it. At that time I was pregnant with Dominic. The medicine man said that if I wasn't treated the child I was carrying, which was a boy, would die too. So a healer (they are the ones who do the cleansing and actual treatments) was brought to treat me. I was given some herbs and other charms for protection after the baby was born. I was told to mix the herbs with a little water and apply them to my breast before nursing the baby to wash away the stigma of the child I used to pretend to nurse, who had died. There were no problems with Dominic's birth; after him I never had problems again with babies. Dominic was named after the one preceding him who had died.

There were two children who died between Martin and Magdalena; I was told it was a recurrence of the stigma from that same baby who died. Then I was taken from Ndambuki's home to my father's home to continue the treatment. At my father's home I had to lie on my bed while they took herbs mixed

---

21. According to Hobley, mothers were usually in a squatting position when they gave birth. After a birth they remained in the house for twenty days. *Ethnology of A-Kamba*, pp. 60–61.

22. *Nzavi* have a special association with women in Akamba and Kikuyu culture. They are given especially to nursing mothers and not classified with other beans. See Robertson, *Trouble Showed the Way*, Chapter 2.

with water and applied them to me. They then took a little cooked maize and beans and added it to the herbs and told me to eat it. They said that even though I was married I kept eating food from my father's home and I shouldn't have done that. A medicine man was brought and he mixed the food with the special herbs. He gave it to my mother and me to eat so we had shared food. Therefore, if my babies were dying because of my eating food from my parents' home there would henceforth be no problem. It was all right to do it. After that there were no more deaths.

I bore sixteen children in all, but six of them died as babies, a few months old.[23] Childbirth is so painful! The reason that you hear that a mother has cursed her child so that the child leads a wretched life is because she remembers that pain. The worst birth was Magdalena's. It was the last one. I felt as if I was coming apart at the seams. I really screamed. I used to deliver alone and normally I would just get on my bed and deliver. I would cut the cord and tie it. I wiped the baby off with water before oiling the skin, and then wrapped the baby in a cloth and nursed. After Martha got older I would ask her to heat the water for me and I would wash. I would just spread a clean cloth on the bed, get on it and deliver. People would only know when they heard a baby cry. Then I would squeeze my stomach until the afterbirth came out. After that I would cut the cord, or Martha would help me to cut it with a razor blade after I showed her how to tie it. But with Magdalena I screamed so hard that people came running; my husband had to hold me.

After I bore a child I used to keep away from my husband for seven or eight months usually. But after my seventh child I conceived again after only six months. I used to breastfeed the children for about twenty months or two years. I would also give them cow's milk with a bottle immediately because I didn't have much breast milk.[24] I gave them porridge after six months and mashed bananas. Nowadays children are dying more because there are more of them. Parents may not want children and some girls even do kill babies. Or people are just too poor to take care of their children properly; sometimes when I go home I see such people and give them clothing. We were poor also; the baby used to sleep in the bed with us, the others on the floor or in a small bed.

I have borne eight boys and eight girls; of these six girls and four boys survive. My first child was born in 1953.[25] That is Martha and she went to school up to Standard 4. I chose her name because I used to hear another

---

23. Family planning became widespread in Kenya only in the 1980s; in the 1950s and 1960s, when most of Berida's children were born, very little was available and a strong pronatal ethic prevailed for most people. In the late 1980s the birth rate began to drop, especially in urban areas, so that women now average about five live births instead of the more than eight that was usual. Davison, *Voices from Mutira*, p. 12.

24. Berida's infants who died mostly had stomach ailments and may have suffered from malnutrition, dysentery, and dehydration. Bottlefeeding under less than sanitary conditions has sometimes been identified as a cause of infant mortality, especially if powdered formula is used and watered down because of lack of money to purchase it.

25. This is a logical date for her first birth, since many women who marry very young do not have successful pregnancies until they get somewhat older. The average age at puberty for these women tends to be around fourteen.

woman calling her daughter Martha and it really sounded good. I always chose names from my heart. As it happens, they are all biblical names, but I didn't know that with Martha then. She sells dried staples with me at Gikomba and has her home at Mtito Andei. When she is in Nairobi she stays with me at Pumwani. She is a nice child; she got married and they get along well together. She has never given me problems. It is only that where they went it never rains. Her husband, an unemployed charcoal dealer, sent her to me so that I could train her to trade so that they could feed themselves and she could help her family. When she is away from home her husband and her eldest daughter, who has a baby of her own, care for her younger children. I like Martha for her perseverance. Even though she knows I do have some property she has never come to ask me to solve her problems for her. When I have some food from the farm I might send her as much as three bags of maize, beans, or cowpeas.

How could you distinguish Martha in a crowd of people, you ask? Just look at me and you have seen Martha; the only thing is that she is short and I am tall. And she doesn't talk a lot like I do; my talking is a gift from God. Also, she bore twin boys and I never had any. It's not good to have twins. I didn't know how she was going to rear twins, they are so poor. One of them died before learning to walk. The survivor is in Standard 4. (One of my sisters also bore twins—girls. They were tiny like mice when they were born; I never thought they would survive, but now they are in Form 2. Both of them are called Mwana and they are very pretty.) I like Martha's children but I like better those ones of mine, the children of Dominic and Muthama. Those of Martha belong to another clan but these are mine. You have heard that there are clans called Asii, Atangwa, and Aombe. [To Jane] Among the Kikuyu you have Angare. So these grandchildren of Muthama are mine and I love them; those of Martha belong to their clan and will be loved by their clanspeople. Nobody marries their own people; are you married where you were born, to your own people, Kilaya? No, I didn't think so, even if you only had clans a long time ago.[26] Well, that's Martha's case also.

The second-born who survived is Dominic, who was born in 1954. He was the biggest of my babies and is now the largest adult. His birth was exhausting. I gave birth at about daybreak but didn't come around until about three hours later. When you deliver a big baby you are not going to feel all right. When Dominic was small he was beaten up by the neighborhood bully on his way home from school. The children were fighting over marbles. He was hit on the nose and fell down. It was serious. People came to get us but we found that he had already been taken to the hospital by one of the teachers. He might have gotten epilepsy from it since from time to time he would fall down. He was treated for a long time until we took him to Kenyatta Hospital where he got cured. When he recovered I asked the father of the child who had hit him

---

26. Penwill stated that by the 1940s the prohibition on intra-clan marriage was weakening. *Kamba Customary Law*, p. 1.

to refund my medical expenses. He refused so I took him to court. The case was heard and he was told to pay me but he still refused. Finally people from the court went to seize his things in order to auction them off to pay the fine. Even cows were auctioned. So the things were sold and I was paid my money. This was a court in Kathonzweni. We were paid Ksh.1,600. The boy was expelled from school for doing it and never went back. He just hangs around the market, has no job. Dominic was in Standard 3 when that happened. He went up to Standard 7.

Dominic is a police driver and stays at Gatundu. He is also a good child because like now, when my money got finished, he is helping me, he and Muthama. He helps me the most. If I see a dress that I like he buys it for me. Dominic used to be called Jimmy Rogers because he is a big man. Kilaya knows him; they have been photographed together. He is tall and broad. He talks slowly. He looks like me. He is good because he helps me, takes care of his family, and doesn't bother me. You have taken care of the child and now the child is taking care of you. He tells me that he will take care of me as much as he can. "Because you did a lot for us, engaging in casual labor, collecting castoff clothes for us, I will help you as much as I can. The way you stitched torn clothes, you will never have to do that again, Mother," he says. He sees himself as the eldest and even takes care of his father. His father has given him the responsibility to oversee the family and guide the younger ones. If he sees them do wrong, he will correct them. He tells the younger children that he never wants to see any of them drinking. They all got fed up with beer because of their father. His first son was born bowlegged and had to be operated on at Kenyatta Hospital; I went there to stay with him for two weeks. The mother was so frightened that she couldn't do it; it was her first child.

The rest following him I don't know when they were born, maybe the next one in 1957. I only know that I was giving birth every year like a chicken. Between Martha and Dominic there was one boy who died. I can't remember well. It's up to you who are educated to try and approximate the dates; every year when I was holding a small baby I would find out that I had another one in the stomach.

The one following Dominic is Monica. She was the only one I delivered in the hospital and was the smallest of my babies. I was staying with Ndambuki at the time and he was in the army. He had enlisted voluntarily but they only kept him for maybe six months. That was in 1956. He was set to work in the stores giving out food. Ndambuki paid the hospital cost for her delivery and named the child Carol because he said she looked like a white woman he knew called Carol. But I call her Monica and that is what it says on her identity card. He never calls his children by the names other people use for them. For example, he calls Magdalena Syombui and Angelina Syongulu. These are names from his people; I don't know who they were, but Syongulu was his grandmother. He calls Martha Katoto, a nickname [from Kiswahili for *mtoto,* child].

I never went to school so my brain can't carry all these things; it is full of other things. Monica went up to Form 3 [the equivalent of about ninth or

tenth grade] but she dropped out due to pregnancy. She died after she had had four children. She was working in a KANU[28] office as a
clerk and lived at Kathonzweni. To me it is like
she is dead because I never see her and she does
not help her children. She disappeared, leaving
them. When that happened I kept three of them
and Dominic and his wife took in the other one,
an infant girl who still needed breastfeeding.
One of her children has done so well in the
Standard 8 examination that the teacher wants
her to continue, but I have no financial strength
so I cannot take her to school. She just helps at
home. Monica now works in a bar. No, I don't
know who fathered her children; she never married. Was I there when it happened? I told her,
your husband either died or is not born yet. The
women nowadays just have men friends who are
married to other women and only help their
girlfriends with something small from time to
time. I feel disturbed in my heart about Monica.
Where will her children go if she doesn't buy
herself a place to settle? I am the one who helps
them.

The one who follows Monica is married; her

> **Time Perceptions**
>
> EXCERPT FROM TAPE TRANSCRIPT
> 97-1-6-7
>
> *Jane:* Can you remember when
> Monica was born?
> *Berida:* Who? Monica? I think
> she was born in 1970
> something around the 28th of
> February, that's how I see it.
> *Jane:* Are you sure it was
> 1970?
> *Berida:* Maybe 1970 or 1960.
> Anyway, I don't know; I don't
> want to cheat you [with the
> wrong information]. I have
> told you, try and put them
> in order because I can't
> remember; at the same time I
> never went to school and my
> brain can't carry all these
> things, it is full of other
> things.
> *Jane:* Did Monica go to
> school?
> *Berida:* She went up to
> Standard 13, Form 3.
> *Jane:* Did she finish secondary
> school?
> *Berida:* No, she dropped out
> due to pregnancy.[27]

name is Susana. She is good; where she got mar-
ried she has stayed with her husband. You will see her when we go to my
home. When you see them all you will just know these are Berida's. She went
up to Standard 3 in school then developed ear problems and dropped out. She
also got pregnant then like Monica. She is a farmer; she harvests a lot of food.
She is very hardworking. She is a settla[29] of food. She has six children. She
hears but not clearly and is not as talkative as I am. I also like her husband
because he is very hardworking and they both use their hands to work. This
time when I lost the money, Susana was asking, "How much did Mother say
she was robbed of?" I sent word to her that my white friend from abroad had
paid the debt for me. Even at Gikomba I tell my friends that among my
daughters the one I like the most is Susana. If it was Susana who was at

---

27. The first two interviews in 1997 had more questions like this one; then we passed a point when
Berida got more comfortable and there was less need to interject questions. Anticipating this phenomenon,
we used the first two interviews to establish basic data about herself and her family, reiterating some already
obtained in 1988.

28. For a long time KANU was the only legal political party. It is still dominant but not in the majority,
according to the latest elections.

29. Settler, as in British colonial, white, rich, and enterprising.

Gikomba selling like Martha she would have made a lot of money by now because she is very hardworking. Very determined. She would go to all those places that you hear people are going to look for cereals/food. You should see what they have built at their home. She has bought oxen for plowing, a cow for milk. She and her husband cooperate in their work. Those things are good.

Katunge is the next-born, a girl who reached Form 2 in school but then had a problem with her eyes. She got married to "something" immediately she left school. She never asked me about marrying that man. I woke up one morning and found she was married. Then her father sent for her and she refused to come. She said she was trying to build her own home like we her parents did. We gave up. We were never even given tea [a minimum obligation to visitors]. They have three children. That one she married I will not tell you much about. Katunge is there but those people there look like this [makes a face]. Even me as old as I am I can't accept that. I can't accept it! Let me tell you frankly, that man who married Katunge, I usually sit and look at him and wonder whether Katunge actually saw him or was she blind? Doesn't she have eyes? That man is a young man who is taking tobacco in his mouth. [Men usually take snuff.] He has no looks; he is not well-dressed. She farms at her husband's at Kathonzweni. Now that Katunge is staying there, who will educate those children of hers? I don't even know where her place is; I only see her at the market in Kathonzweni. On the day they had arranged to formalize their marriage I traveled to Nairobi. I didn't want her to marry that man and besides, they are so poor that they had no wedding feast. They didn't even tell me they were planning the wedding, but just asked me to come. I could see that this was just a problem that would be passed on to me. I never go there because they are poor and her husband owes me money; it's embarrassing. Those children of Katunge will eventually be brought to me to care for. If she has problems she will come to me. She is timid. After she married she got work as a nursery school teacher and because those people are backward, the husband refused to let her take it. He just does casual work around there. These are real problems. I just tell Katunge to continue getting many children but never bring them to me. Sometimes she comes home and I give her clothes. You know, giving birth makes a strong bond, to think that I even give her clothes! Just lately, though, they went to visit me at Kathonzweni and took along a small pot of honey, a *kasuku* tin [500 grams], for reconciliation. That was good.

After her comes Nzuki, who studied at the village polytechnic. I celebrated the birth of all of my children, not like those of old did it with the *ngondu* ritual and a charm, but like a Christian. We had a feast but when Nzuki was born it was special. That day Mother [her mother-in-law] had made beer. Ndambuki had been arrested for fighting in a land dispute; he was in police custody at Makueni. When he was told of the birth he sent word that the beer should be given freely to people to celebrate. He had been complaining about so many girls and this was a boy! The brew was made from honey so we called the baby Nzuki [bee]. He got permission to come home for two days (it was only a one-month term) and slaughtered a goat. So we celebrated.

Nzuki went up to Standard 5 and trained for carpentry doing woodwork, but he did carpentry at school only. He lives at Matuu and is not married. He works for my younger brother at the counter selling beer, but he doesn't earn much. He dresses very very well. If you look at him you will think he is a teacher. He puts a pen and a flower just here and when he is walking he is very upright and even wears a tie! He is tall like Dominic. He even does not allow his shoe to have a patch. He polishes it so well you can see your image in it. He refuses to get married. I tell him to get married but he jokes by telling me he will wait for the rains to come so that they can be married by water.[30] It's not that he doesn't like women. If you go to his house it is full of women. Maybe they are his friends. [Laughter.]

Muthama is next, who you know. He is the one who has had his photo taken with Kilaya. He was born at Wote, then we moved to Kathonzweni in 1964. Muthama in Kikamba means "one who moved." His birth was the easiest. I had invited some people to my house for prayers that day and they left around 10 P.M. I got into bed but then started feeling the pains. My mother-in-law was fast asleep. I woke up Martha to heat some water for me to wash. There were only a few pains and then I felt like pushing. As I was getting ready to bathe the waters broke and Muthama was born. The people who had been at my house were so surprised in the morning. Ayeh! They couldn't believe I had delivered! That's why I love Muthama. He didn't give me much trouble. He never even got sick. He reached Standard 8.

Muthama is a bus conductor on *matatus* that go to Makueni. Among my children he is the one who is most talkative. If he sits here he will make you laugh all the time. He is nicknamed Kawembe [razor blade] because he is sharp. If Muthama sees me he runs to me and cries, "Mother is here; Mother is here!" He has a wife with three children; the wife is a teacher. Her name is Rose. Those grandchildren! They usually come to my side and say [whispering], "Susu" [Grandmother]. They tell me if I get hungry I should tell them so they can go tell their mother. He sleeps at Kathonzweni but travels to Masaku with the *matatus*. He might come to my house and say, whispering to the children, "What mood is your grandmother in?" The children say, "Quiet." He says, "Did she have a quarrel with your grandfather?" The children say, "No." Muthama then goes back a few paces and then comes toward the house again calling loudly, "Mother, Mother, I am hungry!" And I reply, "So am I." Then he sits down and says, "I have actually brought you bread." Then we begin talking.

When he comes to Nairobi by the time I wake up I find he has fried an egg for me and made good tea for me; he does it himself. That one I really like. Even if they refuse to wash my clothes, he will wash them himself. Before when we all went to Kathonzweni I passed via Masaku where he was and he

---

30. This is a pun—the verb for to marry, *kutwawa*, is the same as the one meaning to be flooded, *kutwawa nikewu*.

Choma, Muthama's firstborn, joins the inside action

Muthama, Berida's
sixth-born son

asked me, "When is Mama Kilaya coming?" So I said on the 28th. Then he told me, "Here is my boss; let him know that I will be waiting for Mama." Then his boss laughed and even gave me Ksh.100 to buy a drink. They get by with both of them earning but they don't have a lot of money.

The one following him, Angelina Ndinda, married in Meru. She went up to Form 4 and is in [English] "business." She buys foodstuffs and travels with her truck to collect them, things like maize, beans, all produce. She even goes to Mombasa, Ukambani, wherever there is a need for foodstuffs, Namanga, Kitale, Busia. She has three children and lives here in Pumwani. They have bought land in Sultan Hamud [on the Mombasa Road]. Oh Angelina! Let's change the subject! If you see her she is beautiful; if only beauty were edible. If you are pretty in the face but your heart is dark, are you beautiful? It is more important to be beautiful in your heart. When I see her I cover my eyes so that she can pass and I don't see her. She called me Satan. . . . She hurt me so much but she doesn't even know that she offended me, nor does she care! I leave her alone and don't go there. She had the nerve to say to me, "Mom, you are the devil!" I was so upset tears came to my eyes and I said to her, "Leave me alone; I am going." Did she ever come to see how I was, since we didn't say a proper good-bye when I left? Did she come? If she had come to me and said, "Mom, I have come to check on you," I would at least feel in my heart that she is still my child and she still cares for/remembers me. Before when I was paying for her education she would call me, "Mommy, Mommy!" two or three times. But as soon as she got a husband with money she forgot that I was her mother. I feel very bad. Can Satan educate you up to the point where you meet a Meru man? If you were an anthill or were dirty, would that Meru man want to see you? I am the one who cleaned and dressed you up. Did you see what happened when we went there? She was in that very shop; when Maggie tried suggesting that we go there, I refused. Maggie was telling me, "Mother, can't you take them to Ndinda's place?" I refused. I told her Angelina is not my child. I donated her to the Meru man. The way daughters love their mothers! You work for your mother? [To Jane] But I gave birth for nothing.

But now we are reconciled. Birth is hard work and creates bonds; wouldn't you stand by your children if they were harmed? I have forgiven her. Something very bad happened to her and to Maggie, my youngest who was staying with them. Actually, Ndambuki came to Nairobi because of it. You see, Ndinda's husband was running around with other women and Ndinda found out about it. When she asked him about it he really beat her and Maggie too, so badly that Dominic came and took Ndinda to the hospital. He got someone else to take Maggie because he couldn't deal with two of them at once. Maggie couldn't walk for a week. This is the child that Ndambuki says never even had her ears pinched when she was little! You see, Ndinda's husband thought that Maggie and her friends were gossiping about him. I didn't like to go there to Ndinda's place and I still don't, but even if that man had a gun I would go now if I had to, but I took Francis [Antony's son] with me the last time I went in case the man was on the warpath again. That man only paid a token bride-wealth of four goats; Ndinda can come home if she wants to and bring the children. My Ndinda will suffer if she stays there; that man is messing her up because of his lust for women. There are many diseases now; he could bring one home to his wife.[31]

A man should love his wife just like he loves himself because God created Adam and Eve as our examples. To beat your wife is like beating yourself. It is like tearing up your money and throwing it away. He and his wife should do things together and he shouldn't lust after other women even if he finds them more attractive. Let him make his own wife beautiful. And the wife, if she doesn't talk about his women friends she won't be beaten. He won't beat her for nothing. If he is threatening her she should plead with him to stop; she can't fight him because he is stronger than she is. Besides, you shouldn't beat your husband; what would the neighbors say? Those women who do that are wives of drunken useless men like Ndambuki who are not strong. I could beat him but not if it destroys my home. You don't want to spoil your home where you have to stay. But that thief who robbed me, if he hadn't run away I would have beaten him and screamed for help. Everyone else might have joined in then and thrown things at him and beat him until the police came.

Then there is Martin, or Wambua, the one we have left where we were.[32] He went up to Standard 5 and doesn't have a job except farming. After working on the farm he usually goes to church, where he teaches the catechism class. He had a formal wedding and has two children. Neither he nor Emma has a job nor do they have much education. They are the ones I consider to be my children because Muthama has built on his own. Emma has now had her third child. The pregnancies are very close together; one isn't even walking before she gets the next one. The second-born, Mutinda, is so thin. I have had him treated so often at the clinic. If you see Muthama's child he is a big child but he is younger than Mutinda. Martin and I pay for the medical care; he might sell a chicken to pay for it. He needs a job; Kilaya, can you help him get a job, maybe as a gardener at a white's place? Jane, what about if he began selling secondhand clothes at Gikomba? *Mali kwa mali!* [Kiswahili; Goods for goods, the cry of the sellers]

We haven't had any food from the farm since he became responsible/got his mind together. Before I left Kathonzweni I told him, "Wambua, take care of the farm." He needs to get up early and get going, work hard. You really get poor if you aren't working to improve your situation. I thought of bringing him here to sell at one of my stalls, but when there's no money what can he sell? Even if he worked for five months, say, he could buy some dried staples and get started selling. If a man is hardworking and doesn't let himself be distracted by women he can do well trading. If Martin could get started that way then I would be free to go home and stock my shop and stay there. He can learn about business by watching like I did. I never went to school. And he

31. Angelina and her husband later separated.

32. By Akamba customary law the youngest son often took over the father's landholding in exchange for protecting the mother's interests; older sons were expected to set up on their own. Penwill, *Kamba Customary Law*, p. 42. Such a pattern contributed to constant expansion of Akamba settlement.

did go up to Standard 5. He has helped me a little when he has come here. But you can't force it if you don't have the gift for business. My Martin once told me, "Mom, I am not gifted in school." He was at a school in Kangundo, a technical school. He even left my fees I had paid there and came home from school. He said he wanted to farm and then do business. He didn't like woodworking. I tried everything to get him to stay at school: I beat him; I bought him things; I gave him money. But no sooner did I take him back to school than he came back again. That school still has my Ksh.700. If I start him in business with me I will try it out for two months, say, and if he does not do well I will stop him. Each evening he would have to put the money on the table so that I can see how much profit he has made.

I even paid for a beautiful wedding for Martin and Emma, Elena's daughter. I will show you the pictures of it. Elena and I did the arrangements and paid for it. It was worth it to see them so happy. With such a wedding, not like the ones in the old days, you are actually giving your child to God. You know, that baby of theirs, Mutinda, who is always sick, gets better when he is with me. I often bring him to Nairobi with me and would have done it this time had I not been coming to Kilaya's school. The new baby, Kibonge [something big], is very big, the size of this TV set, and very healthy.

Lastly, there is Magdalena, who reached Form 4 and has gone to a computer course but she is unemployed. She just sits at home, even Kilaya knows her. We found her at Ndinda's place. Maggie's was the most difficult birth because I had gone so long without having a baby. I had forgotten how to give birth. I didn't even know where that pregnancy came from. It had been six or seven years. That's why it was so painful.

One time when Magdalena was very sick she was treated by a priest named Fra Enzio from Italy. She was very sick due to poverty. He helped me very much with clothing and food. When he died I felt like my father had died. Magdalena never used to go to church because she had some problems with her feet; the priest even brought the Sunday school nearer so that she could be able to attend. We let him use our land for it; remember the place under the tree where we have a bell for calling the children and everything? (See photo, page 92.)

Back in 1987 when you were here before I had to bring a case about Maggie. She was in Standard 5 and one day was coming back from Sunday school. We had a neighbor who had no proper feet, only stumps. The son of that man grabbed her and tried to rape her. She screamed and the neighbors rescued her. Ndambuki wanted to beat both of them but the neighbors stopped him. The boy was arrested and they were fined court expenses. He had epilepsy and was a bit older than Maggie. To avoid paying the fine they sneaked away to Kambu. I heard later that both of them had died.

Maggie takes after me. She doesn't like men. Her age-mates already have two children. She wants to get an education; she wishes she had passed to go to the university. She's not a complicated person; she tells me that the day she gets a job she will take care of me and I can relax. She earns something in that hair salon where she works. She buys her own clothes. I don't see her as being beautiful; I see her as my daughter. It's Angelina who is so beautiful. Maggie has the complaint form to fill out about Ndinda's husband, but she hasn't done it yet.

It makes me sad to think about all those babies who died; I don't like to remember them at all. You know, before they are born they could be anything. You could even be carrying a snake! But afterward they are people and you love them, so that when they sicken it makes you sick and worried. They would suffer with diarrhea and vomiting. After Nzuki there was a girl who died and another one after Monica. One of those was already walking when she died while I was in Kenyatta Hospital after being pierced by a nail. The worst was Koki, a beautiful girl born before Maggie. She had even learned to walk by then. That death was really painful. I had so many problems. I didn't even have clothes to put on them. I would go where people had moved out and collect the pieces of cloth they had left behind, stitch them together and then put them on myself and the children. That was in 1965. I stitched them with a thorn. It was because of lack of money that Dominic and Martha didn't go far with school.

When my children were babies I just played with them; this made me happy. I would praise them a lot and say, "You have done well." As they got older when I was happy with my children I would reward them by bringing them a suit and a watch from Nairobi. I used to buy the boys and girls the same thing; they looked like they were in uniform. I bought dresses for the girls, though. One of the best things any of them did was that when Muthama was small we would leave him at home to go work in the *shamba*. But he would follow us there and make us all laugh by trying to sing the song we sang while digging. At that time he couldn't even talk properly, but he would tell everyone to stop singing because he wanted to sing the song for us. "Ena hey, ena hey, ena hey!!" We really laughed!

The worst thing anyone ever did was Nzuki's behavior one day. I had gone to the market leaving Susana in charge. Monica came running to tell me that Nzuki had cut Susana's fingers with a *panga* [machete]. He had cut these two fingers; they were dangling like this [demonstrates]. I rushed her to the hospital and they fixed them. Now you can't tell it happened. The children had gone to the *shamba* to work and Susana told each of them to dig up one section. She told them that anyone who didn't finish the section would not get food. When they returned home she told Nzuki he wouldn't get food because he hadn't finished his section. That's when they started fighting.

When I was growing up we were so poor; I decided my children would never wear rags like I did. The biggest problem for a parent, especially the mother because she feels the most for her children, is to see her children not having food to eat, clothes to wear, or fees to go to school. My children weren't going to school and they had nothing to wear. I not only scrounged clothing from homes abandoned by their owners due to the famine, but I also had the problem of where the children would sleep. The little house where they used to sleep collapsed on them one night from the rain. I heard them screaming. I didn't even have a lamp to see. It was a square hut made with poles and mud and a thatched roof. The children had hidden under the table so they weren't hurt, but three goats that were asleep on the verandah died. At that time I realized nobody would get to the Father without going through the Son, Jesus. So I prayed and God gave me the idea to start trading so my children would not suffer poverty any more.

Then there was an incident that was the last straw, that really woke me up. This was during the Atta [whole wheat flour] famine, so called because that was all that we had to eat. I used to have oxen for plowing. One day we went to plow a field for a man named Mutua. We plowed and he gave my husband money. My husband told us, "You stay here and I'll go and buy food." He went and bought one packet of *atta* for Ksh.2.50 and oil for 10 cents. That's what we were supposed to use for making chapatis.[33] Then we picked greens that grew wild during the rains as a vegetable to accompany the chapatis. So I made the chapatis and gave my husband two of them and one to each child. I had eight children by then. I saved a little flour to make porridge for the baby the next morning. Nzuki was the baby then; he was about a year old, just beginning to walk. But my husband said he wanted to show us how Indians make their chapatis. He took that flour, mixed it into a dough, patted it into a flat shape, and threw it in the fire on the hot coals. We didn't do anything because we were scared of him. We just watched as he ate that dough. The next day we were in the *shamba* at around 11 in the morning when I was told that Nzuki had collapsed from hunger. I ran and picked him up. I had a little sugar and a little cocoa in the house. I heated water and made the cocoa for him.

My father-in-law had just taken the animals to graze. I followed him to where he was grazing the animals and told him, "If any of the children die, I will take you to court." Saying that to Ndambuki would have been useless. By saying it to his father I thought that he would get us food. After I told him that he called Jimmy [Dominic] and told him, "You and your father will take this goat to sell at the market. And tell me if your father takes even one shilling from that money." Ndambuki was in the habit of selling a goat and then taking some of the money, lying about how much he had gotten for it. All of this one was to go to me for food. But he did it again; he sold it for Ksh.16 and took Ksh.6 of it for himself. With the rest of the money I bought food. I was on the verge of going back to my parents with all of the children.

Ndambuki ran off to his mother's to avoid being beaten by his father. His mother was still at Wote. He always did that if he was in trouble with his father. His father would come and stay with us to see to it that Ndambuki behaved. His mother didn't know what Ndambuki had done; she thought he was just coming to visit. His father only told her later that Ndambuki was not providing food for his family. When she finally heard she was very angry with him. She really felt badly. She would send food to us when she had it. But she couldn't punish him; he was not a child to be beaten. She just talked to him and showed him all the bad things he was doing. She asked him, "If you knew

---

33. Pan-cooked unleavened bread of East Indian origin.

you couldn't care for a family, why did you get married at all?" So then Ndam-buki went to Nairobi. There was a family there where earlier he had tried to buy a wife and had given them Ksh.90. He went back to ask for the return of that money and he was given it. He was going to give it to us for food, but he drank up Ksh.30 of it and only brought home Ksh.60. He told me to pay school and activity fees for Dominic and Martha. Tuition and activity fees were each Ksh.20 per child. So I went to the teacher and told him that I was going to pay only the tuition but I would pay the activity fees at the end of the month. I started buying food to sell with the Ksh.40.

The important thing is that I gave my children an education, those who wanted it. Those who didn't want it, what could I do, beat them? Those who didn't think like me, their children don't even know how to say [English] "one." Those children went to school only when Nyayo [President Moi] an-nounced that there would be free education but the parents couldn't even pay the activity fee. So they got expelled. Nyayo has given free education but he doesn't pay activity fees so those children are just sent home. They get hired by people to look after their cattle. But me, I have paid a lot to educate my children.

Has it helped them to get better jobs, you ask? Like who now? I don't think education has helped any of my children. I feel like I threw my money away.[34] Take Angelina, for example, she and Maggie got the most education. I edu-cated her thinking that she would be the one to help me when I started getting old. But then she went to study computer and met a Meru man at computer school and got married. That's it. Her only thanks is to call me Satan. If I had to do it over again I wouldn't pay for their education; why should I pay for something that is not going to help me? If I had saved that money in the Post Office or the Bank, it would be there to help me when I get too old to work. But everyone now knows that education is wealth. Nobody who has the means will refuse to educate their children. Even Kilaya left her country to come here because of education. If she had never gotten an education, where would she get the money she is giving me for this work? Education only helps those with a good mind. It doesn't matter how much education you get, even if you are saturated with education as the professor [Claire] said, if you have no will to help your parents, that education is useless. Helping parents is a very im-portant thing; a person is blessed by their parent. Any time you see a parent who is pleased with his/her child, that child is doing well.

You know, it wasn't only my own children I had to worry about. I had a sister who lived at Masii with her husband, who was an alcoholic and a wom-anizer. My sister died there, leaving three children, two girls and a boy. I went there and found that the children were really suffering. I took them and brought them to Kathonzweni. Then I also had two of my brother's children with me in 1988 when you were here before, a girl and a boy. As more came

---

34. Berida's disillusionment with the value of Western-type education is widely shared; it requires more and more education and good connections to get a job that pays enough to support a wage worker.

I just divided what we had into smaller portions. I have asked the girls not to bring me more babies to support. Mothers should teach them not to run around with men. That is very important. When I was earning a lot I was also putting away savings for my old age, but now, I don't know. How much help will my children give me? But girls usually help more than boys. They are kind and remember their mothers, while boys take on girlfriends and stay in town. Or, he might get a harsh wife who will keep him from helping the parents. Even if a girl only has ten shillings she will use it to buy her mother tea.

Now I am supporting them all, even those who have wives. I am the one who pays the bridewealth. I support Martin and his wife and children. Even Ndambuki, I buy clothes for him and built a house for him to sleep in. There is nobody I don't support. I buy all my own things. There are Monica's children; the one who did so well in Standard 8 had to repeat because I had no money to send her on to the next level. I tried to take her to the National Youth Service recruitment but she is very young. She is only fifteen years old and they only take them at age eighteen. Angelina did help Magdalena, however, by paying for her course.

When I was having children we did not know how to stop giving birth. Once I asked, "Where are those people who bewitch people and kill them, why don't they bewitch me so that I can die and stop giving birth?" I used to wish and wonder if there was a place where I could go, across the ridge, where people never gave birth. If you had given birth to children and had no clothes for them, what would you think? People used to think in the olden days that if someone had many children they were rich. Yes, if you two were my daughters, or you had six or eight daughters, you would get a lot of wealth. Even men wanted to have daughters because girls brought in [bride]wealth. But I didn't think about that. My giving birth came from God. In church the priest used to say, "God said you should multiply and fill the earth."

"Family planning" [English] was there but people didn't use it. There's a limit to the number of babies you can bear; can you deliver your intestines? We hear about "family planning" on the radio and all over now. It is good; I have seen children going naked and starving at home. Without it people would be conceiving while they still have children on their backs. And all of those children with nobody, nowhere to take them! Even now I tell my daughters-in-law, if you give birth to many you will just "pinch your own ears" [pay for it, Kikamba proverb] just the way I pinched mine. I am telling them it is not good to have many children, three or four and that's it. Today things are very expensive. The food, school, clothes. I too would only have four if it were today, two boys and two girls. Even my daughters I tell them the same thing. Because the suffering I underwent was due to having so many children. Otherwise, I had enough energy. I tried brewing liquor; I fetched firewood and sold things. If I had had fewer children I would not have suffered the way I did. I even could have done better in business with fewer children to feed. But God gave me all the children that I have for free. I didn't have to pay anything. And also, despite the problems that have encumbered me, He has ensured that I have the means to care for them.

3

"Now I was in business"
Work: From Kathonzweni to Nairobi

When Ndambuki and I first married we worked together at home and on the farm. We worked together in union. Even if it was just eating, after I had cooked I would bring the food and we would eat together. If it was going to the farm he would lead the cows and I would hold the plow. When it was time to eat he would take the cows to water while I would go home to look for what to eat. I was not selling then. We had four oxen for plowing. If we wanted to build a granary he would go and cut the poles and I would cut the grass for thatching. Men were in charge of cutting the poles for building and doing the walls and women did the thatching. I would hand him the poles as he worked and he would throw the grass up to me as I thatched. We tried to find help with the planting. One person would lead the oxen while the other held the plow. You drop the seed into a furrow and cutting the next furrow covers the seed in that furrow. Ndambuki would put the seeds in his pockets and drop them into the furrow just before the next furrow was cut. We also used the oxen to weed, cutting furrows between the rows. We put a kind of net over the oxen's mouths so that they would not eat the crops as we plowed. We weeded by hand between the plants. Both men and women did that and even children. On Saturdays when they were not in school you gave them hoes and they went to weed. People who don't have oxen use *jembes* [short-handled hoes] to make holes for putting the seeds in. Now things are much the same but people might weed millet using a plow by leaving a furrow free between each row.

When we first moved to Kathonzweni there weren't rivers like there are now. The land was flatter and the moisture would soak into the soil instead of running off. It is the cowpaths that have caused the erosion. Those without cattle have better land. We try to dig trenches, terracing to prevent erosion. It is difficult, however. Terracing is hard work but we have to do it or we don't get a crop at all; all the water runs off. We have to clear first because the *jembes* get caught in the trees if you leave them there. Sometimes we plant trees but they get eaten by ants. I planted a lot of trees, fruit trees like oranges, mangoes, but those ants attacked them and they died.

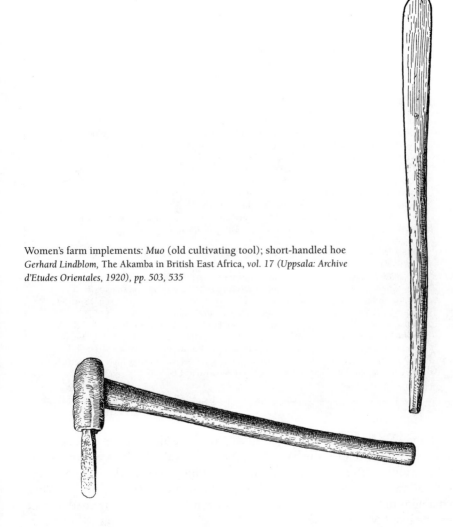

Women's farm implements: *Muo* (old cultivating tool); short-handled hoe
*Gerhard Lindblom, The Akamba in British East Africa, vol. 17 (Uppsala: Archive
d'Etudes Orientales, 1920), pp. 503, 535*

You ask about changes in the division of labor. A long time ago[1] women
used a *muo* [a small sword-like implement with a short handle] to cultivate. It
was made by sticking a sharpened flat piece of metal into a slot cut into the haft
in which it was mounted and burned to hold the blade in place. When you
bend a lot using it your back will hurt. At that time it was only women who
cultivated; the men were busy drinking. Women were like slaves; they had to
fetch water, look for firewood, look for and cook the food, go to the farm, and

---

1. She is probably referring here to the early twentieth century since she does not mention that men's
hunting, trade, and warfare (mainly raiding) were hindered by colonial rule, which began in Ukambani in
the late nineteenth century.

Translation to a Narrative[2]

Mbithe: Has the division of labor changed?

Berida: A long time ago women used a *muo* to cultivate. At that time it was only women who cultivated; the men were busy drinking. When you bend a lot your back will hurt.

Mbithe: What do you mean by a long time ago? Was that before the colonialists or after?

Berida: Even after the colonialists came and before the colonialists men did not do any work. Women were like slaves; they had to fetch water, look for firewood, look for/cook the food, go to the farm, open the cowsheds for the cows.

Mbithe: When did the men start doing the work?

Berida: Men became wise and found out that because they loved their wives they did not want them to get very tired doing all the work by themselves. Because a long time ago women were not important; they were only slaves and for having sex with.

Mbithe: Did Christianity teach men to help their wives?

Berida: When Christianity came people started being enlightened and men considered how they could take care of their wives . . . [long disquisition on marriage here included in Chapter 2].

Mbithe: Does that mean that those marriages that took place a long time ago made women slaves?

Berida: Yes, because men did nothing because they had donkeys to do all the work for them. The women of long ago would be given this cupboard and told to carry it; it was put on their back and they were told to carry it. She would carry it even if she did not have the strength to carry it because she was afraid of her husband.

Mbithe: Women haven't stopped carrying those burdens; I have seen them.

Berida: Women carry that which they have the strength to carry. Even me, if I have the strength to carry this chair, I can lift it and carry it. But if I don't have the strength I won't carry it. But a long time ago you would be forced to do things which you don't have the strength for; someone is standing there with a stick.

---

open the cowsheds for the cows. They would be walking with a child on the front, carrying a load at the back, while the man walked with a walking stick, striding along. [Demonstration.] Men did nothing because they had donkeys to do all the work for them. They thought women were their donkeys. When a man got married he saw that woman as his property and he trained her the way he liked. Women of long ago would be given [objects as big as] this cupboard and told to carry them. A woman would carry it even if she did not have the strength because she was afraid of her husband. You would be forced to do things you didn't have the strength for; someone was standing there with a stick. Because for men a long time ago women were not important; they were only slaves and for having sex. It was men's stupidity that made them do that.

Today women also pocket money. Men have become wise and found out that because they love their wives they don't want them to get very tired doing all the work by themselves. It was Christianity that taught people to be en-

---

2. This excerpt illustrate how sessions characterized by many questions and answers became a narrative.

lightened and men to consider taking care of their wives. Also, there was a famine around 1975 and no food. When it rained men took hoes and off they went to the farms. At my place today it is Martin and Emma and Muthama and Rose who are doing the farming, helped by the children of my late daughter when they are not in school. We should do terracing, but it costs 50 shillings per stride [two or three feet] to pay someone to terrace. The cowpaths cause erosion and the ants take the trees. Ndambuki only looks after the cows because he is old and cannot cultivate. Now if a man's wife is sick then the man will go to the kitchen and prepare food so they can eat, but otherwise it is the wife who cooks and brings the food. That day when I was so hungry, it was because I hadn't had anything to eat the night before. Ndambuki was here but of course he didn't cook for me. That old man, who would he cook for?!

Even before and now women haul the water and the firewood. But when Emma was pregnant she didn't do it; Mwenye [Baby], Monica's daughter, and Muthama's housegirl, the daughter of neighbors, do it. Sometimes Martin helps using a wheelbarrow or a bicycle. There is an old bicycle at Kathonzweni that I bought for Dominic so he could fetch water with it. That was in 1962 and it cost Ksh.240. That is the one we use to take my bags of produce to Kathonzweni. Now Muthama has bought one for himself. Emma also chops the firewood. I need to buy a new ax for that; the one that is there is the wrong kind for splitting wood. It is not even sharp. It was bought by Ndambuki a long time ago, before we had children.

My childhood training was for cultivating only. None of my relatives traded. I did learn how to make change when I was a child because my mother used to send me to the store. I was very good at it. My mother would tell me how much change to bring back; if the shopkeeper didn't give me the change she had told me to get, then I would leave the things I had been sent to buy. When I grew up and became a woman I was engaged in giving birth, collecting firewood, fetching water. I would dig, dig, dig and then harvest. I was very very poor then and when the rains failed I had nothing to give my children. I taught myself to trade because of poverty. When you are like me God opens your eyes wide and you learn. I learned how to calculate more when I began in business myself. I started by counting each grain and putting them into tins. If each tin was Ksh.100 then ten tins cost Ksh.1,000. I used to figure out stuff at night before I fell asleep in my head, almost like I was educated. For example, if I sell forty tins, how much do I get? But even before that, after dinner, I would start my figuring, taking one commodity like *ndengu* [mung beans] and calculating how much I would get if I sold two or five tins; then I would start on beans, then maize, and so on. After Angelina got educated I would ask her to write down how much I had made. She would ask me, "Mom, do you understand arithmetic?" I would challenge her to add amounts together. While she was busy with a pencil I would add the sums in my head and tell her the answer! Sometimes the person sitting next to me would write things down for me. But I haven't gotten so much money that I need help; there wasn't that much left over after I paid the school fees. I haven't been cheated in trade because of not knowing how to read, but I have been by people not repaying debts. I count my profit by doing calculations after I sell a bag. I measure the bag in 2-kilo tins. Say I bought it at Ksh.450. There are about forty tins to a bag. If you count you will see that after selling each tin at Ksh.15 I will have Ksh.600. My profit is Ksh.120 after costs. If the bag falls short a tin, that's my loss.

I began in business by brewing beer to sell when we were at Mwala. If I had bought sugar at Ksh.2 I could brew and then sell a 1-kilo tin at Ksh.4. I would put water and sugar in it and stir, also *miatine*.[3] You brewed secretly so no one saw. It might be stopped for some time when people were drinking too much. The chief or assistant chief might stop it. But the efforts to stop it did not always succeed. You could brew secretly and then sell to people in cups, hiding it. Then they went home quietly instead of singing drunkenly so that they were not caught. They are usually noisy because they are arrogant and it's a habit; you can be quiet like I am if I drink something.

At the time of independence there was a terrible famine in Ukambani, so that food even had to be airdropped to us by the Americans. You know, I showed you the place they dropped it; it is called Nunzu-Nunzu, a marsh at Wote. We even composed songs calling upon America. One of them went "*Na Kaloki ndukinyange mbola, ndukese kunginya uiendanja andu, mwolyo naw'o ni wa America, na Kaloki ukiwikia mbuka.*" [Laughter and applause] [Translation: "Well, Kaloki step slowly so that you don't step on me as you push people. The food aid is from America and Kaloki you are acting in haste."] There were people who were selfish and greedy who would get a whole bag for themselves while some women got nothing. So they were being cautioned to tread slowly because the food aid is from America. Men would jump the queue to get it. They would hide it and take it to their wives at home. So one woman composed that song. We were being given maize, peas. It was rumored that the yellow maize that was given was fed to cows in America, but people ate it anyway. Since the yellow maize grain was so long we could put it into our

---

3. A long gourd-like plant used for making homebrew which helps with fermentation.

mortars for pounding into *muthokoi* [cracked maize, a staple and favorite food] to remove the skin. That softened it for boiling.

I reached a point of extreme poverty until I met a relative of mine who told me that I could buy foodstuffs and go sell them at Athi River town [near Nairobi] and get some money. I got maize from my granary and ground it into flour and took it to Athi River. It was my aunt Munee who introduced me to the business, my father's sister. She saw my poverty; I had no clothes to change and no shoes, was walking barefoot. When we began my aunt's husband gave us a ride up to Athi River in a police car; he used to be a police driver. I took my own produce from my granary to sell. I went twice and got enough money after the second trip to buy myself some rubber shoes for Ksh.12, which was the cost of a bag of flour. I had to buy those shoes because my feet were getting frozen there at Athi River and I couldn't walk. I had pierced my foot with a nail I had stepped on and was in the hospital for nine months. When I was admitted Katunge was a small baby. Since I could not breastfeed her she had to be put on a drip. I was admitted to Machakos Hospital for six months. The heel was completely eroded by the supports that were placed to support the leg. Then I was admitted to Kenyatta Hospital for another three months [demonstrates foot]. It was very serious because even my hair fell out; my nails fell off too and I shed my old skin, just like a snake does. A person can really suffer in this world! I left the hospital wearing a "plasta" [plaster cast], with crutches and my baby. I went to Wote and got fed up with the cast because of the itching. So I called someone and gave them a saw and we removed the cast. Then I applied a medicine called MB to the wound and it healed. You scratched an MB tablet to make a powder and then applied it. It was illegal to sell it.

When I went home from the hospital I was informed that there was better business at Burma Market in Nairobi. A bag that at Athi River cost Ksh.12 would sell for Ksh.24 there. At the time I was carrying Muthama on my back. We moved from Wote when Ngei and Kenyatta declared that those without land should go and search for their own land. (When I have money I even hire a tractor to plow for me because the land is so big.) Anyway, I came to Burma Market once when I brought my flour there to sell. I did not know how to sell it. I displayed it at the market for two days. Nobody even asked me how much I was selling it for. After three days I went to see my younger sister Esther, who was working at the Norfolk Hotel. I explained to her that I had brought flour yet nobody was interested in buying it and so I was stranded. Her husband came with me to Burma and we were advised that I should take a sample of the flour from shop to shop and ask if anyone wanted to buy it. If they did, then I would bring it to them. I took the samples to Kaloleni and a shopkeeper requested the flour. I went and brought it; he measured it and gave me the money. I had about three bags. He bought all of it and I went back home and decided to bring more flour. At that time at home the 2-kilogram tin of flour was costing 20 cents. Then I prepared six bags of flour and took them to the shopkeeper. He bought them and gave me my money. When I got the money I went back home and spent all of it.

After that I had no money. There was famine and I had nothing to give to my

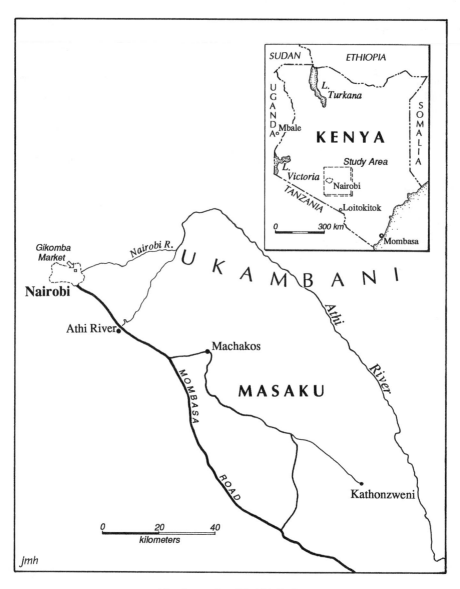

The Geography of Berida's Trade
John Hollingsworth, Indiana University Cartographer

children, so I had to work with my hands to feed them. I went to do casual labor at Loitokitok working for Maasais and Kikuyus. When I was paid in kind with food I would send it to Emali, where it would be sent to my children on one of the vehicles which goes to Kathonzweni. Usually they gave me maize in a *kyondo*. I stayed there for a month, after which I had accumulated five bags of maize and one of beans. I went to Emali and sold two bags, one of maize and one of beans. I sent the other three bags to my children at home. So then I had money, Ksh.300.

Some women at Emali told me we could go to Tanzania and start buying clothes and come sell them in Kenya. We went and at the border, Loitokitok again, we changed the money to Tanzanian currency and therefore I had Tsh.800. We went to Telekea in Tanzania. We bought materials, tablecloths, blankets and *kangas* [women's cloths]. I was with six Kikuyu women. I was the only Mkamba woman. Coming back we heard that the Tanzanian customs officers were arresting people so those women decided to use a shortcut to avoid them. When we had bought our wares I felt suspicious of the other women. I thought that since they were all Kikuyu they might gang up on me and maybe rob me, so I dropped behind. I decided I would rather be robbed by the government and to go straight through customs. I took four of the *kangas* and tied them around my waist, with one to cover the rest. Then I put on a sweater. I looked very fat and waddled along [demonstrates]. It was hot. I took one blanket together with the tablecloths and put them in a paper-covered bundle that I carried in my hand. Then I put the other blanket on my head and marched forward through customs. When I reached the barrier the officer lifted it and I passed through it. Then I ran as fast as I could without looking back until I reached a place called Ndalala, where I downed two bottles of soda. I waited for a vehicle to take me to Loitokitok. I went to the police station on the Kenyan side. I arrived around 5 P.M. and told the police that I had only two blankets and nothing else. I was told to pay Ksh.12, which I did and then went to look for somewhere to sleep, still at customs. I woke up the following morning and tied on my *kangas* and went to find a vehicle. When we passed the customs post, people were ordered to alight from the vehicle. I showed the officer the note saying that I had paid the Ksh.12. He told me to go back to the vehicle. I reached Emali, sold my wares, and got money. Those Kikuyu women got arrested; I didn't!

After getting the money I was advised by another man, who is now Dominic's father-in-law, to go into selling cows because it was profitable. That was in 1975 during the drought of Kilangazi [from the Kiswahili word for drought; *kiangazi*]. They were buying cows and taking them to the Kenya Meat Commission at Athi River. So I bought a cow at Ksh.100. This man told me he had an order to deliver one cow for himself and offered to take one cow for me to Mombasa, while at the same time he would give me his National Identity Card so that I could deliver one cow for him and one for myself at Athi River. I saw this was a good idea. I took my cow to Athi River and sold it at Ksh.800. But the cow that was taken to Mombasa was condemned, or rejected. They only paid Ksh.4 for it but it had been bought at Ksh.170 on credit from the Maasais. Even today I have never asked for the Ksh.4. I repaid the Maasais anyway. With the Ksh.800 I bought three more cows at Ksh.200 each and kept Ksh.200. When I took those cows for sale they were bought at Ksh.3,000.55. After that I went to a place called Simba and bought ten cows for Ksh.900. The cows were going cheap because there was no pasture and they were dying. I would buy them for Ksh.110 or 70. One of those cows died. I took the nine cows to Mombasa and sold them at Ksh.15,000. We could even get Ksh.3,000 per cow. And so it went, until I got more money than I have ever made since, Ksh.70,000.[4]

Then the drought ended and there was rain so the Maasais stopped selling their cows. Since my house at home had collapsed due to the rains I went home to build a house. I arranged for the bricks to be made. After I built the house the money I had was almost finished. I couldn't afford to buy any more cows—they had become more expensive. So I started farming and with the little money left I started trading in dried staples. From my produce I got one bag of cowpeas [nthoko], which I took to Gikomba. At that time a 2-kilogram tin of cowpeas was costing Ksh.2.50. When I had sold the bag I got Ksh.250. Then I went back home with that money. I sold three bags of cowpeas for Ksh.700. I started all over again in business from [English] one, trading at home with that Ksh.60 Ndambuki had gotten from those people in Mwala. I began with contacts from the school. I had gone and explained that I was go-ing to postpone paying the activity fees so that I had some capital to start trading. I started buying foodstuffs just there at Kathonzweni market and selling them to those who came from Nairobi. The people from Nairobi were buying the staples at a good price of Ksh.160. That was ndengu and I had bought it at Ksh.40. So I had money and went to the tailor and had uniforms made for Dominic and Martha. The next market day I went and bought food from the local people and sold it again to those people who came from Nairo-bi; this time I got Ksh.200 and went to the tailor and had trousers made for Ndambuki for Ksh.25. He had been going around with his buttocks show-ing. Now I was in business.

At the end of the month I went and cleared the fee of Ksh.40. The same teacher I paid said that they had heard I was buying foodstuffs, cereals, was that true? I said yes it was true. The teacher sold me a bag of beans at Ksh.160. Then I asked how the beans would be transported to the market. The teacher said that the ox-drawn cart called ikasya would bring the beans. So the beans were brought to market. As I left the market there were signs that it might rain. Then another man from another town called Ikasu near my place came and also wanted to sell beans to me. By that time I had only Ksh.100 in my pocket. I asked how many bags of beans the man had and promised to go and have a look at them. When I went the man said he was selling the beans at Ksh.210 per bag.

I told the man that I was going to come back, left, and went to the market. I went straight to the richest man in the market; he was called Kieti wa Kamba and he gave me Ksh.110. It was a Monday. Then I went back to Ikasu and bought the beans. I told the man to have the beans transported to Kathonzweni by bicycle up to where the other bag was. They took them to the grain store of the man who is now married to Martha. My people started quarreling with me saying, "Berida, you are a fool for buying at that price!" They told me

---

4. Equivalent to over $1,000 at the present exchange rate, but probably worth more in 1975.

that that amount already included any profit I might make so how was I going to sell them at a profit? I told them I did not know; he had just said his price and I bought the beans. I told the man to weigh the beans for me. The bag that I bought for Ksh.210 was weighed and it was 90 kg. [the usual bag weight] plus another three *debes* [one *debe* is approximately 16 to 18 kg.]. The following day was a market day. I sewed up the two 90-kilogram bags and took the five *debes* to the market and sold them. I gave Kieti wa Kamba his Ksh.110. Then I went home that day and it rained. As I was preparing the oxen to go to the farm, people were coming and asking me to sell them beans to use for seeds. There were two varieties of beans, *mwee umwe* [one month, for its short growing time] and *kikala* [also called *kakunzu*].[5]

From then on I was in business. After it rained I went to market and sold a bag at Ksh.700, then went and picked the second one at Ksh.700. By 3 P.M. I went home with a lot of money in my pockets. I called my husband and we sat down and I told him that I had a lot of money. We counted it and it was Ksh.1,400. My husband was happy and asked me where was I going to buy more staples? I said I was going to Kilala Market, so I went and bought seven bags of maize there. I was charged Ksh.5 to transport a bag from Kilala to Kathonzweni. This was very expensive because normally it was only Ksh.2.50. The transporter was very arrogant and said that anyone who wanted to have a bag transported could either pay the Ksh.5 or it would be left there. So I paid it; it looked like it was going to rain and it did. It rained so much that the river called Kaiti flooded for two days. I sold the maize and got a lot of money because I was the only one who had maize. I even hired a vehicle to go to Mwala and bought fifteen bags of maize.

But at that time when I had made a few trips to Nairobi to sell, we realized that that was more profitable. I took the money home and we counted it and it seemed like a better idea to go to Nairobi. Ndambuki said, "Go and trade so that you can help us." So we decided it together. So there I was, now I had money. I bought a cow for milking and continued and continued with the

> **Reaction of Jayne Mutiga, tape transcriber, to Berida's Story, May 1998**
>
> Berida is a very courageous woman. Many women in that situation would just have given up because they don't have the courage that Berida has. There would be pressure on them not to trade because people would think that if they went to Nairobi to sell they were prostitutes. Many women would not leave their homes. Their husbands drink and the rains fail. They know what they need to do; they are intelligent. But they don't have the courage to go. Also, Berida knows about the situation with wife-beating in Akamba culture, that if she fights back his brothers will come and beat her. That may be why she would not say that a wife could defend herself against her husband. She didn't boast about it but she cleverly stopped it. She's a fighter and never learned the etiquette of a wife who sits at home.

---

5. Beans have particular associations with women, who grow, process, and sell them. Knowledge of particular varieties is considered essential to being a woman. See Robertson, *Trouble Showed the Way,* Chapter 2.

business since I had money. When the rains stopped I stopped doing business. I went back home. While I was doing business I had organized for the bricks for the house to be made. I was paying five cents per brick. I would tell the worker that I would pay on Tuesday because that was the market day when I would make money. Then one day Ndambuki asked me why I was having all those bricks made. I told him that it was possible that one day one of our children would grow up and build a house. Then the building began and went up to about four courses [levels of bricks]. Then my husband came and said it was not done right and had it demolished. So I kept quiet and continued to keep quiet. Then he left for a place called Kambu [toward Mombasa]. When he went I went to one of the teachers at the Technical School and got him to measure for the house. The house was built in four days. When he came back he found a finished house. He swore never to enter a house that had been built by a woman. . . . But where was he going to stay? He still stays in that same house. Then we continued living and eventually I built a shop. [Laughter.]

So I began my life in which I sell mostly in Nairobi but I go home on buying trips for produce on occasion and to farm when it rains. I sell here at Gikomba for maybe a month then go home for a month. During the rainy season I might go home for three months to cultivate. I harvest and then I come back to Nairobi.[6] Beginning in 1975 I would go to Nairobi to sell produce that people brought to the market at Kathonzweni: maize, beans, pigeon peas, cowpeas, *ndengu,* millet, sorghum. When I began staying in Nairobi for long periods of time I would sleep at Akamba Arts, a woodcarving shop owned by a man named Mwololo. It was cold and smelly and there were bedbugs but it was nicer then than it is now. There were even beds that you could sleep on if you paid Ksh.2.50. If you didn't have that you could pay one shilling and sleep on the floor. Now Mbulwa sleeps there and it is more crowded; the beds have been removed. It's dirty and unhealthy, damp. It costs Ksh.15 per night to stay there on sacks on the floor. Once in a long while the owner has people remove their mattresses and they sweep the room. People steal from each other; if you hang up your underwear to dry it will be gone in the morning. It's not outsiders doing it. The shop has a metal door and the owner's house is very close. If you want to enter at night you knock and he asks you to identify yourself. If he is satisfied, he will open the door for you. Those women who have been buying their produce stock come back really late and have to do that.

Then that old man [Kiswahili; *mzee*] came to see me, Ndambuki's older brother, and told me to stay with him and his family near Gikomba by the Kaburini cemetery. The house had one room and a kitchen. I was given space in the kitchen; that's where I put my bed. It was very crowded, especially when my children would come and his. They couldn't even all fit on the floor. I stayed there about five years, then I started looking for a house. I found my present room, where I have been since 1980. At the beginning it cost Ksh.150

---

6. Berida probably spends much more than half the year in Nairobi.

Gikomba, 1988

Hero of the resistance:
Ex–freedom fighter/
dried staples seller
occupying privileged
stall

Dried staples sellers
on break among the
stalls

Out in the hot sun:
Dried staples sellers
after destruction
of stalls

Jane Turunga's Story: Life in the Secondhand Clothing Section

I began selling used clothing after you left in 1989. I sell trousers, sweaters, men's jackets, women's and men's coats, dresses, and skirts, which are now very expensive. I buy one bale of clothing at a time. They mostly come from Canada and are imported through Mombasa now that the trade is legal. I have a stall on the road on the other side of the market in the used clothing section, where I have been selling since November, 1997. I used to have two inside stalls in not so desirable a location, for which I paid Ksh.100 rent per day to a cousin. They each cost Ksh.3,000 per month. If I was not there one day I didn't pay for them. Ksh.100 per day is the standard rate for one stall. At the end of each day we had to clear out our goods. In 1998 I began paying by the month so I pay even if I am not there. Now I don't have to clear out the goods daily. So we in used clothing pay more. At our place you can't buy a stall without a lot of money, sometimes even Ksh.90,000. Chagga people from Tanzania have them.[7]

Where I am in the market we don't have all those rules that Berida has, fining people for misconduct like fighting, for instance. I used to employ a boy to sell for me at Ksh.50 per day. Ksh.20 of it went each day for his lunch but I kept Ksh.30 back which was paid to him at the end of the month, so Ksh.900 per month was his take-home pay. There was a high turnover in employees; they stole from me by wearing two pairs of trousers or exchanging my good merchandise for bad things. They thought I wouldn't notice when I counted the merchandise, but I did. So I had to sack them.

---

for rent paid to Wanjiru, my Kikuyu landlady. Now it costs Ksh.1,000, up from Ksh.800 last year [1997].

I am the founder of Gikomba Market. When I came long ago we used to spread out a sack on the ground to sell on. We were given this place by PC Waiganjo [Fred Waiganjo, former Nairobi Provincial Commissioner]. Here at Gikomba there was a lot of garbage and many bushes; people had defecated all over. We got together and went to see the PC. There was a group of women; some have now died and others have gone back home. We each contributed Ksh.1 and went to the PC and talked. He told us to go to the chief at Bondeni, called Ogolla. He is the one who was told to show us where we would be selling our wares. He took us and allocated everyone a plot measured by the length of a sack. We used to sleep here and then start selling very early in the morning, about 6 or 7 A.M. Then we would run away so the [Nairobi City Council] police wouldn't catch us when they started persecuting us.

---

7. Chagga involvement in the used clothing trade came about because of its illegality in Kenya and large-scale smuggling of bales of used clothing across the Tanzanian border. The used clothing is shipped in bales from North America and Europe and sometimes includes new clothing that discount stores did not succeed in selling. Front-page photos of police burning confiscated bales were a regular feature of newspapers in 1987–1988. This trade was made illegal in order to foster Kenya's garment industry. Part of that industry is housed in a myriad of small stalls in the three multi-storied legal buildings called Quarry Road Market, which exists side by side with the illegal sprawl that constitutes the rest of Gikomba Market. As of 1997 the trade had been legalized. It is perhaps the most profitable trade conducted at Gikomba. Certain male partnerships play a dominant role and a host of temporary workers who sell their services on a daily basis—young men who yell "*Mali kwa mali*"—reflect its origins in barter. For more information on this important trade see Karen T. Hansen, "Transnational Biographies and Local Meanings: Used Clothing Practices in Lusaka," *Journal of Southern African Studies* 12, no. 1 (1995): 131–45.

Gikomba, 1988

Used clothing for sale

So the stalls were given to those of us who came long ago by the District Commissioner [DC]. Then we rented the stalls to those who have come recently. We don't pay rent ourselves. We only paid Ksh.2 for the fare to the DC's office. There weren't many people then. I had three stalls. One of them I bought for Ksh.11,000 about eight years ago (Domitila would know exactly when since she went with me to buy it). Since I couldn't be in all three at once I rented out two of them at Ksh.300 each per month, one to a man named Kamau and the other to a woman. Those are ones for dried staples down the hill, not in such a prime location as the one I use myself. The amount of rent is determined by the commodity sold there and the desirability of the location of the stall. For example, the stall where there were dried staples before now has used clothing; the owner is paid Ksh.30,000 for six months' rent. I sold one of my stalls for Ksh.25,000 last year [1997], which I put into an account at KCB [Kenya Commercial Bank] on Jogoo Road. Actually, I only put in Ksh.9,000 and used the rest to pay the hospital bills. Since it is a produce stall I wanted to sell it for Ksh.35,000. You can't sell clothes there. People prefer the stalls on the outer edge because you get more customers where they can see you.

One day I heard that in Uganda the variety of beans called *rose coco* [a type of pinto bean] was being traded at Ksh.2 for the 2-kilogram tin at Malaba. So we went and brought the beans which we could sell at Ksh.28 for the 2-

kilogram tin. Then I was approached by an Asian called Kalani who wanted to know whether I could do business on a large scale. I said if I had money I could do it. So he gave me Ksh.2,000 and I went and bought nineteen bags of beans which included *rose coco, nyayo*,[8] and *kavika* [a yellow bean]. Kalani bought all nineteen bags for Ksh.30,000. Then I went back to Malaba and we were arrested because we did not have a permit to buy foodstuffs. Since there were many of us we decided to send a delegation to President Moi at his Kabarnet home to get him to help us. We were not able to see him so his guards referred us back to Bungoma to see the Senior Superintendent of Police, whose name was Nzau. He referred us to Mulu Mutisya.[9] We went to look for him in Nairobi, found him and told him what our grievances were. Mulu requested his secretary to call the District Officer (DO) of Busia. We waited until 7 P.M. in the evening. I was with Mulu Mutisya in his office when the telephone call came through. I listened as Mulu asked the DO why people had been arrested while they were buying food to take to Ukambani where there is famine and hunger. Mulu instructed the DO to release the confiscated food to the traders. There were many of us from many areas including Maasais, Kikuyus. He agreed to release it the following day at 9 A.M. on condition that we carry our identity cards with us to Malaba. Mulu was kind enough to request a bus to take us to Malaba overnight. A bus from the Akamba Public Road Services took us to Malaba and we got our food back. We sold the food and then we would go back for more. If one of us did not have the identity card we would borrow it from a friend to enable us to go buy the food. I gave the Asian the money and he deducted what I had borrowed from him and gave me the profit.

The demand for food was very high indeed. We could arrive at 6 A.M. from Malaba and by 8 A.M. we had already sold all the food. People were coming from all over Ukambani to buy the food, also from Murang'a, Thika, and Kitui. We were selling here at Gikomba. We sold beans and a kind of Kikuyu pea [Kikuyu; *njugu sika kikuyu*, pigeon peas] that we referred to by its Ugandan name, *nzepa nthika*. We also sold *ndengu*. We might also smuggle in clothes, shoes, and especially the *kitenge* type of cloth. What we would do with the shoes was that one removed one's old shoes and crossed the border barefooted, then bought the shoes and put them on and made several trips across if you needed more than one pair. The Kenyan government was not allowing in goods from Uganda. If you needed to buy *kangas* from Uganda then you could cross the border without any, buy some in Uganda and wrap them around yourself and pretend that they were yours. That's how we smuggled goods in from Uganda. Once you had as much as you needed then you boarded a vehicle to Nairobi. We sold those things at Gikomba also. I also went on buy-

---

8. A kidney bean that is the most popular bean in Nairobi; it was given President Moi's nickname because it came into Kenya at the time of his accession to office in 1978.

9. A veteran Mkamba politician and chair of the Masaku branch of KANU, said to be a close ally of President Moi.

Gikomba, 1988

Akamba women
selling a specialty,
chickens (housed
in withy cages)

A wholesaler arrives

ing trips to Makueni and Yatta, buying at markets and from people's homes. And, after I had sold all the produce from home I would buy more stock from Kalani and sell that. That was back in 1975. But after a while the small sellers like us were pushed out of business by those who have trucks.

In 1988 I was buying from Gikomba wholesalers and also going on buying trips when I couldn't find what I wanted at the market. Those people with trucks would come to the market and tell us that there weren't any cowpeas or *ndengu*. So I heard that they were available at Mtito and off I would go. There was a terrible drought and famine[10] in 1985–1986 at Kathonzweni so nothing came from there; people were eating staples that came from the Kenya Maize and Cereals Board. We also had a lot of trouble selling here because of the Nairobi City Council police [Kiswahili; *askari*]. We had built stalls and I had even covered mine with iron sheets. We hired people to survey the area and lay out straight lines and then build neat stalls, all roofed with corrugated iron. But the *askari* came and tore down everything; they even bent the roofing sheets so they couldn't be used again. They sent bulldozers while I was at home. When I came back and saw what had happened I really cried. Even my twenty bags were buried in the rubble. I was a very healthy and fat lady, but then my head was full of thoughts. I had three children in school then at Masaku and another small boy, Martin, in Standard 8 at Kathonzweni. We only come here to struggle.[11] The only thing that is yours is what you eat; the rest you give to the children.

By the time you were here before [1987–1988] I had made some money and decided to go home with the plan of building a shop and selling there. That was Ndambuki's idea; he sometimes has good ones. I did well because when I came to trade in Nairobi I was able to pay for Angelina, Monica, Katunge, and Magdalena to go to school. When I would go home I would even hire casual laborers to help with the farming, maybe three or four and pay them Ksh.100 per day. I could tell I was doing well because even after paying the school fees I still had a little money left. I knew that one day I would be too old to trade so I went and bought a plot and built the shop. I built it at the same time that I was paying for Maggie's schooling. I had about Ksh.60,000 and built at a place called Mwisa in a small shopping center. I have just locked it up. I used up my money paying school fees. The shop is there, useless because I have no money for stock. Let me tell you, the last time that Kilaya was here, I had money although I used to pay school fees. Now it is finished completely. The money finished with Maggie finishing school. That together with my son's wedding. All that money got finished completely.

Also, I used to lend people money and they didn't all repay it. There is even

---

10. In Ukambani famine can easily come from either drought or floods, which cut the supply routes and wash off the topsoil.

11. In 1998 when Berida heard this sentence she said with emphasis, "That is true!" and added the following sentence. She approved of using it as the title of the book.

Gikomba, 1988

Luo sellers in
the fish section

one person who owes me Ksh.10,000 and another one Ksh.1,000, another
one Ksh.1,300. They were supposed to repay me with interest. Where I was
seated there were many Luos around me. I became so popular among them I
was nicknamed "Mama Jaluo." They took staples on credit from me to sell to
the hotels. They began by repaying me regularly, every fifteenth of the month.
Then one day they just didn't pay. They would plead bereavement in order
not to pay me. But now I have had enough; I am fed up. If it weren't for those
Luos cheating me, I would have my own car today.

If I had money now I would stock my shop at home. Nairobi is not safe
these days with the riots. My trade now is not as good as it used to be. I still

Gikomba, 1988

Men sellers: Tea break for a
veteran notions dealer

Selling sacks in front of the
staples section

travel sometimes; even in March and April I was travelling to Kitui and buying *ndengu* and selling them at that staples market in Ngara in back of the petrol station. Their prices are better than at Gikomba because they sell to the Asians. We would go to Muingi and buy a bag of *ndengu* for Ksh.6,000 but since we had to make a profit we had to sell for Ksh.7,000; people started complaining that we were selling for too much so we went back to our stalls. I went with another woman named Jane from Muingi who is a wholesaler. I used to go with only a little money and buy four or five bags. One time my younger sister Esther gave me some money and I bought six bags. When I came back I gave her two bags and was left with four, which I sold here. She took hers to Nakuru. When we got back we discovered that they were not paying good prices at Ngara so then we came back to Gikomba because here we could sell a 2-kilo tin for Ksh.220, or Ksh.8,000 per bag.

It's very important to have lots of stock so people can find what they want. A shop without much stock won't be visited by many customers. All I have now is the little stock remaining and it isn't moving. You can stay for a week with your stock, nobody buying anything. When there was money, by 8 A.M. I would have sold Ksh.2,000 or 3,000 worth of stock. Now I sell maybe only Ksh.500 per day and some people don't even manage to get Ksh.100. The market is bigger now and there is more competition. If you don't have a lot of stock you won't be able to sell; who will even see one bag? Now I am selling peas, *ndengu, nzuu, nyayo*, cowpeas and *muthokoi*. The beans are often dusty when they reach the market from being threshed on the ground. We have to clean them and remove any bad ones. We polish the beans to attract customers, using the hulls that come from maize kernels after they are

Filming at Gikomba: Dennis's Story

In 1998 I asked Dennis Kavinghua to talk about his experience filming Berida's activities at Gikomba on 9 August 1997. He told the following story in which Gikomba's reputation for roughness is justified.

Gikomba is a really tough place and the filming was difficult. People are very suspicious. When they discovered what I was doing they asked me if I was going to sell this film to the whites and get money for it. They thought I was a tour guide or a journalist. One man who was buying beans from Mbulwa said, "Why have you filmed me? You have violated my privacy." Mostly I didn't answer in case I provoked them further. I did promise money to some of the sellers but I didn't pay them.[12] I covered the camera with a plastic bag so people wouldn't know I was filming them. Most people don't want to be filmed. I was really afraid of being attacked or having money extorted from me. To get the aerial shots I climbed the stairs of that tall building near Akamba Arts. On the top floor someone was breeding German shepherds for guard dogs. They kept the adults in cages in the rooms but the puppies were milling around in the corridor where I was. It was really dirty with sawdust and dog feces everywhere. The pups kept nipping at my trousers. I had a hard time keeping the camera steady! I was very happy to finish that day. Berida and I went to a bar and I had some sodas while she drank beer.[13]

---

12. This went against the policy otherwise followed in this project; we either told people ahead of time that they would not be paid for brief contributions such as a two- to five-minute interview for the market census of all sellers, or promised and followed through with payment for longer involvement. I asked Dennis not to repeat this behavior.

13. Theft is a real problem at Gikomba, as we discovered. In 1988 a still camera used to take pictures at Gikomba was stolen from the car while Jane, Berida, and I were sitting in it interviewing near Akamba Arts. It was hot; the windows were open and two men used a common device of one person distracting the marks so the other can grab the object.

pounded for *muthokoi* or maybe sawdust from the woodcarving industry here. We wet it a little and rub the beans in it. Since the hulls are a little damp, we rub the beans in them until they are clean, like they have just been harvested. Sometimes the beans have pesticides on them so I use something to cover my nose when I am cleaning them in order not to get a cold. People who don't have masks start sneezing as soon as they begin to clean the beans.

Those men who used to pound the maize back there to make the *muthokoi* are gone and it is done by machine. Some of them are now selling maize and beans themselves. Long ago selling staples was women's work, but now men can't get jobs so they also sell them. The women don't mind that since those men are their children and are unemployed.

With the money you gave me last week I will only be able to buy one bag of beans at Ksh.4,500. I will sell that for Ksh.5,000 or so, maybe 4,800. Prices vary all the time by season and conditions. Before the present harvest we were buying a bag of *nyayo* beans at Ksh.7,000 and you sold it at a profit of Ksh.500. It got finished quickly because of the shortages. We were also buying maize and mung beans at Ksh.7,800 per bag with a profit of Ksh.200 on their sale. But now a bag of *nyayo* is Ksh.3,400 and we sell it at Ksh.4,000. Mung beans are now bought at Ksh.4,000 and sold at Ksh.5,000. The thing is that profits are higher during the harvest season because so many people are selling small quantities of their own produce. If I am lucky I will get a customer from somewhere where there is a shortage and they will buy a lot. All kinds of people buy here at Gikomba, but mostly Africans. We don't distinguish between Akamba, Luo, etc. here at Gikomba. Even some whites come. Some even took my picture and I danced for them. They don't buy anything; they are tourists.

If it had been like it was before, I would give Martha a stall to sell on her own. But am I going to give her a stall with almost nothing in it? I have no stock. Martha has been training with me since last August and has only one sack she is selling. She sells her little stock and when it runs out she buys some more. The reason I don't give her her own stall is because she has no money since their place doesn't get much rain. She will look for money for some time and then go home. Our place is a bit better; we have food there. So sometimes I give her money and tell her to buy stock from wherever she can; after she has sold it she can refund me my money. Martha is doing a good job, working hard. Even if I leave anything of mine here, for example, money, Martha will not touch it unless I say she can take it to buy food. If she had money and I left her that stall, she could cope very well. She usually tells me, "Since you spent money educating the others, give me the money you would have spent on my education and I can use it to trade." [Laughter.] So I tell her, "You missed your chance, go and ask your father for the money." But she is joking when she says it.

In 1988 the stalls were well stocked; now there's no money so no stock. At that time I was an important person in the market but now I am nobody because I don't have money. People only consider you to be important if you have money and things. And all those people who still owe me money . . . !

Corruption Nairobi-Style: Assaults on the Poor, Denial among the Privileged

The following story was told to Claire by an informant who wishes to remain anonymous to avoid further persecution by the police. The informant has been robbed by the police three more times since their initial extortion.

Last Friday night two policemen came to my door near Berida's home at Biafra.[14] They were not dressed in their uniforms and did not show their IDs. They had guns which they used to threaten us. With them was a friend who had been arrested in a bar [Swahili; *hoteli*] and accused falsely of illegal dealings in business. The police told me that if my friend and I did not come up with Ksh.200,000 on the spot he would be taken to jail and tried. I asked them, where did they think I could get money like that? Even you, Claire, would you carry Ksh.5,000 in your pocket? Another friend was there at the time and can vouch for the truth of this story. They were threatening to arrest me too if I did not pay up. I was so frightened; it is really difficult to talk about it. I had just been paid but that wasn't nearly enough to cover it; I negotiated the amount down to Ksh.47,000 [about $800 at the prevailing exchange rate in 1998], which meant I still had to find more money. So I went to another friend's house who had also just been paid and asked for that money, which was given to me. I paid the police and they left, leaving my friend. My friend has promised to repay me. Now I am very afraid they will be back since they saw that I have a TV. Maybe I will move.

Note: When Claire told this story to a prominent law professor at the University of Nairobi, his reaction was to say that it was a "fairytale" and completely unrealistic since the police had demanded Ksh.200,000, an egregious amount. He said that even law students would not be asked for that much, much less poor people. Why should Claire believe this story? (The implication was that it was invented to somehow get money from Claire.) Claire responded that law students, attired in suits, would not be victimized in this way and that denial was one way that people like him allowed this system to continue instead of doing something about it. There are many stories of police arresting or threatening to arrest everyone in a bar unless they pay an arbitrary amount. The only difference in this one is that the amount demanded was much larger than usual.

Have you ever seen a poor person who is popular? For example, when I lost that money and asked people to help, Kilaya saw how few people turned up at my *harambee*. Long ago a lot more people would have come to my *harambee*. I felt so sorry for myself that I would cry at night and ask God, "Why?" I couldn't even eat, my stomach felt so nervous. And I never even mentioned the money I had lost; I only talked about my friend's money. That is what worried me the most. If all of that money lost had been mine, I wouldn't have bothered with the *harambee*.

What happened was that I was walking down the street at about 5 P.M. leaving Gikomba on Pumwani Road with two other women. Juliana was in front, I was in the middle, and the other woman at the back walking along. I had all my documents and my working capital in a small purse that was in-

---

14. Biafra is named after the fledgling state in southeastern Nigeria, whose independence was contested and defeated in a Nigerian civil war in the mid-1960s.

Crime in Nairobi

"10 SUSPECTED ROBBERS KILLED,"
DAILY NATION, 5 MARCH 1998, P. 1
BY NJONJO KIHURIA AND KARIUKI
WAIHENYA

Ten suspects were killed yesterday—six by police and four by a mob. The six were shot dead by police at the Kanjeru Village in Kikuyu early in the morning, while the four were lynched by a mob in Dagoretti, Nairobi. . . . This followed a series of violent robberies on Tuesday evening and the shooting of a police reservist at Wangige market. The suspected gangsters had earlier raided a home at Kahuho Village, beaten up the owners and robbed them of more than Ksh.10,000 before fleeing in a car. The police were alerted by telephone and cornered the suspects at Kanjeru at 3 A.M. The six were killed in an exchange of fire, which lasted about an hour. . . . In the Dagoretti incident the four suspects were killed after a failed robbery attempt. Witnesses said the group of five men, armed with stones and crowbars, had stormed into Mr. George Robert Muchene's house at around 2 A.M. But residents, woken up by the noise, came to the rescue and apprehended one of the attackers. Mr. Muchene said the suspect led residents to a house where the others lived, about a kilometre away. The other suspects were dragged from their rooms to a nearby shopping centre where the residents, numbering about 70, beat them to death. Yesterday morning hundreds of residents milled around the half-naked, partially burnt bodies. The residents identified one of the dead as a man called Moses, who they said had been employed as a watchman at a local bar. They said the area had been hit by a crime wave. Langata police boss Daniel Kebenei . . . urged the residents to hand over criminals to the police instead of killing them.

side a big bag, plus money to repay my creditor for staples I had taken to sell, about Ksh.60,000. A man cut the strap and took it, in broad daylight! He also robbed Juliana and then ran away. I didn't tell the police; if I had it would have been useless. Where would they find the thief anyway? The real shame is that I had even seen my creditor across the road and was heading toward her to repay it, but some people with pushcarts intervened and she just waved at me and said, "Bye-bye, I'll see you tomorrow." Then it was all stolen and those women were embarrassing me about repayment. Those wholesalers are younger than I am and they were making fun of me, saying that old mama can't even repay them! They said Juliana and I had just drunk the money together. They sit down there on the road.

The theft is getting so bad here and there are lots of thugs at the market! Even yesterday I saw a man being attacked in the street; they were trying to strangle him with a board. I was so afraid; I didn't want to get involved. So I looked away and just passed by slowly. They would have attacked me too had I interfered. They cut him and removed his shoes. He laid there for an hour before he could get up and he couldn't talk because of the strangulation. My neighbor at Gikomba, who is called Wairimu's mother, was also robbed and they took her documents too, the National Identity Card, her checkbooks. She had squeezed them between some sacks while she went to the toilet; when she came back they weren't there. The thieves watch people; they must have been watching me too when I was counting all that money at the stall before I was attacked.

Crime is one of the issues we talk about in our women's group and on the Market Committee. For us here belonging to these self-help groups is really important. At Kathonzweni I belong to one group called Muomo wa Kathonzweni [Gateway to Kathonzweni] and another called Ndethya Ngutethya [Assist me, I assist you], which is for both men and women. We help each other with expenses and the neigh-

Kyeni kya Gikomba (Mbemba na Mboso): The Committee

Kasilili Dance Group goes into action

Everyone takes a break, with Mbulwa in charge

bors help with the harvest. I always go home then no matter how much stock I have here. In Muomo wa Kathonzweni there are two male members who are dance leaders. At Gikomba I belong to Kyeni kya Gikomba [The Light of Gikomba], which is for dried staples sellers. Mbulwa and I founded it in 1985 as a "merry-go-round" arrangement. My nephew had explained it to me and it seemed like a good idea. We have T-shirts that say Mbemba na Mboso [Maize and Beans] on them. That is our uniform; I'll wear it for you tomorrow. We each make contributions as needed and on a regular basis in the first and last weeks of the month. We help each other with medical bills and school fees. All of these groups do at least some dancing. But we are mere amateurs here; we don't dance seriously. We just dance. The dancing of the Gikomba groups cannot be compared to what you will see at Kathonzweni. Those old women turn around like a marching band! That's the real thing. You know, the Akamba dance more than the Kikuyu, who just put anklets on their legs.

Kasilili is the real Gikomba dance group that escorts President Moi and gets paid for dancing.[15] They make and sell beaded wares. They have elaborate costumes they make themselves with things sewn on their clothes; I have never looked at them properly to see what they are. They wear so many ornaments. They have even gone abroad. But something bad happened after Kilaya left. There is one woman, I call her the chairlady of lies, who claimed to be their chairlady but wasn't. Last Christmas she was spreading it about that Kilaya had sent me money that was supposed to be for them but I had never given it to them. That was not the only thing she had lied about. So they threw her out for that and because she was always meddling in matters that shouldn't have concerned her. That's why I wanted Kilaya to go talk to them this time and explain that that rumor was not true. I am happy she met their chair and secretary so we could clear up this misunderstanding.[16]

At Kathonzweni the members of the groups aren't businesswomen; they mostly stay home. The Muomo women farm some land together where we like to plant cotton or beans. We decide together what to plant and everyone contributes seeds. On our own farms we plant what we want. We contribute Ksh.20 per week but we don't have a bank account. With that money we have bought goats which belong to the group but are kept by different people in the group. When the goats have kids they are given out to members. If the kids are male and grow into big goats they are sold and we buy female ones. But we also do different things with the money, not just goats. For example, if you

---

15. Davison stated that candidates exploit women's dance groups to win elections, and that, particularly in rural areas where there are more adult women than men, women's votes are needed, so the support of the women's groups is crucial. *Voices from Mutira*, p. 9

16. The secretary says he has been secretary for twenty years and doesn't want to do it anymore but they won't let him resign. The chairwoman is an older Swahili woman, indicating the influence of coastal Kenyan culture on Nairobi dance groups. See Margaret Strobel, *Muslim Women in Mombasa, 1890–1975* (New Haven: Yale University Press, 1979) for more information about Swahili women's dance groups.

don't have a good house you can ask for *mabati* [Kiswahili; metal roofing] from your share of the money. Or you could request household things you don't have, like dishes or utensils, and they will be bought with your share of the money. Ksh.5 goes for refreshments for the day of the meeting. We meet weekly. When I am not there I leave my husband Ksh.200 and tell him to pay the Ksh.20 to the group. Yes, he might drink up the money, but then he will have to sell his own goat to pay the Ksh.20; all the same, he will have to pay! [Laughter.] That is the group for the older women.

It's the younger women who are building the dam. That Ndethya group has a man as a chairman. He took those wheelbarrows that Kilaya gave them to his house, but I fetched them back again. Muomo also gave them Ksh.1,000 for the project, but they have been having problems with that dam. It washed away in the floods this year and it washes away every time they get to the point of finally blocking the water flow to create a pond. It just breaks apart in the center. They are wishing that Kilaya would come and hire a tractor for them to pack down the soil so that wouldn't happen again. That tractor costs Ksh.3,000 for one hour's rental. It's at the church. Something else happened too. Elena and a group were going around collecting money for building water tanks, Ksh.300 per person. But the only ones who got tanks were Elena herself and one other! Elena told me that I was next and to bring the money and collect rocks for it. You can still see them there near Martin's house. You know, elections are a very difficult thing. You elect people, then when you give them money they eat it. Then what do they have to buy the tank with or do anything else? I don't like being lied to.

President Moi was having a *harambee* for women's groups in 1997. We made compulsory donations. My friend Mbulwa and I are elected members on the governing committee for the group and we had to decide where a compulsory donation of Ksh.5,000 will come from. Each group had to open a bank account and take a donation to the chief to show the contribution. The Ksh.5,000 was to be given back to us plus double what we have put in the bank. Only those with accounts will get money from him. Whatever you have in the account will be doubled. We were told to open the accounts last May. He says this is his way of promoting small-scale women traders. So the forty-three people in my group are each contributing Ksh.150. The excess over Ksh.5,000 was to go into our account. We got that Ksh.5,000 but no more; we thought it would be more. Mulu Mutisya also contributed to the account. He gave a contribution to 190 groups, Ksh.5,000 each. He told us that after one month we could withdraw it and distribute it among ourselves. But we didn't take it out because my identity card was stolen so I couldn't go to the bank and withdraw money. I am the treasurer. But now I have another ID from the KANU office. Yesterday Mbulwa asked me, "When are we going to withdraw the money?" I told her, "Let's contribute other money and leave that in the bank alone," so that's how we decided to contribute Ksh.150 per person. We didn't really know how groups work but now we are being encouraged to form groups so we can be given money.

We already had groups called Mwethya in which we would contribute money and give it to one person, then to a different person the next time, and so on.[17] For Kyeni kya Gikomba we would meet and contribute on the fifteenth of the month and at the end, another group it was every day. That one had 130 members here at Gikomba, all selling dried staples, and we used to contribute Ksh.100 every day. So if it was your turn on the merry-go-round you got the Ksh.13,000 and you could buy lots of dried staples to use as stock. But you could do what you wanted with the money. We stopped doing that because of the drought. Money became scarce and we couldn't contribute daily. Now there are twenty of us who just contribute Ksh.20 daily. The way we decide who gets the money on what day is by writing numbers on pieces of paper and we each pick one; there are as many pieces of paper as there are people and one number on each piece of paper, 1 or 2 or 3, etc. So we moved from 1 to 130 and then started all over again. And we'd pay Ksh.10 to the person collecting the money. Some people might pick two or three times if they were contributing under three names.

Kyeni kya Gikomba had 130 members but now has only forty-three. There is a Ksh.200 membership fee plus we have asked everyone to contribute Ksh.1,000 toward the account, which all but three have done. It is this group that now has the bank account and is raising money for the *harambee*. At the meetings we do things like talk about defaulters, those who fail to pay. Some people are reluctant to pay because they think they are being cheated out of their money. We have had to remove three of the forty-three in the group because they didn't pay the Ksh.1,000. In fact, that original group of 130 could have had a lot of money in the bank but some people started complaining that those who were illiterate were being swindled by the others, so the number decreased. We have to decide whether or not delinquent payers should be refunded their money and expelled from the group, or if the money should remain with the group. Has she defaulted due to financial problems or just because she is not serious? If we decide that she has a real problem we give her time to come up with the money. If she stays she has to look for money to pay up her arrears. And she will be the last to be given any money. We also settle disputes at the market, for example, theft at night. If theft occurs the *askari* we have employed is brought before the committee. The committee may decide that he has to pay for what was stolen, since he did not do his duty properly. Those watchmen are Maasai. Depending on their grade we pay them Ksh.1,200, 800, or 600 per month.

When we get the money from President Moi we will help each other with

---

17. These groups are called rotating savings groups in much of the literature; in Kenya they are sometimes called roofing societies [*mabati* in Kiswahili], while in parts of West Africa the term for them is *esusu* or *susu* groups [from Yoruba]. They operate on the tontine principle described here by which all members contribute a set sum to a common fund and each receives all of the fund in a scheduled rotation. Sometimes an individual is allowed to contribute double the usual share and thereby receives two turns in the scheduled rotation for receiving the fund. An early study describing the Nigerian practice is William Bascom, "The Esusu: A Credit Institution of the Yoruba," *Journal of the Royal Anthropological Institute of Great Britain* 82, no. 1 (1952): 63–69.

it. For instance, if there is a drought and someone's business is going down, we might contribute the money to them. But we will divide it
among ourselves. We might approach our local
Member of Parliament [MP] who can help us
to acquire property like a plot on which we can
build, which is what the Nyakinyua women
did.[18] We could go to a bank to borrow money
to develop it. Maybe we could build our own
houses on it if it is large enough. If we built even
a small house here in town we could rent it out
and get money. There are plots being given out
near the airport; if we are allocated plots there
that is where we will build. We are just deposit-
ing that money that we started keeping last year;
even when we are struggling so much we cannot
withdraw it. We do distribute the money that the
MPs are giving us, though, after leaving it in the
bank for five days. For instance, Mulu Mutisya
gave us Ksh.10,000 the other day. We took it to
the bank and then withdrew it and subdivided it
among ourselves. He gave it to us to improve our businesses.

> **"Houses Demolished in City,"** *Daily Nation*, 6 July 1999
>
> More than 50 families at Nairobi's Dandora Estate have in the past week slept in the cold following the demolition of their houses by the provincial adminis-tration. About 20 houses belonging to a self-help group . . . were demolished on instructions from a district officer, who said he acted on the provincial commissioner's orders. The group's leaders, Reuben Mwirikia (chairman), John Nduke (secretary) and Shadrack Kitheka (treasurer) said the 15 acre plot was allocated to the society in February last year.

We might also set prices. In most cases we buy the staples at the same price
so we decide on the selling price together. It does not matter if someone
undersells the others because that person will be losing. When we bargain I
may give a discount of 50 cents per 2-kilo tin; if someone buys in large
quantities maybe a Ksh.1 discount. Since I am at the edge of the market
sometimes someone may sell me the staples cheaply. In that case I would also
resell them cheaply. You know, business is a secret. It is like giving birth; no
one can really tell another the exact situation.

I also sit on the elected Committee for the whole market; Mbulwa and
myself do it. My best friend here is Mbulwa. I love her because we were elected
together and we do things together. We are the ones in charge of the market.
Ever since we were elected she has never shown any jealousy or hatred toward
me. When I lost my money she was sad on my behalf and even cried. She felt
very sorry because that money even belonged to other people and how was I
going to repay it? Mbulwa and I eat lunch together often. If one buys lunch
today the other will do it tomorrow. And we decide about things for the market
together, like what happens with the money for the group.

The chairman of the Market Committee is a man named Moses. The Committee takes care of market affairs for this part of the market. The chairman

---

18. This was a group named for the oldest authority-bearing women's age-set among the Kikuyu, which
was founded in Kenyatta's time (he was president from 1963 to his death in 1978).

and those men who sell tomatoes help us when the city council wants to destroy our stalls. You can find the council demolishing the stalls across the street from us and leaving ours alone. When I see the *askaris* from the city council coming I run to call the chairman. He goes to the council offices to plead for the women's stalls to be left alone. There are about eight tomato-sellers on the committee. Aside from Moses, there are also Joseph Mbiti, Karanja, and others. Joseph sells mangoes and other fruit like passion fruit, lemons, and oranges from Mombasa. Karanja sells things like *nduma* [arrowroot]. Then there is Kioko, who has a restaurant stall.[19] Wa Gathoni sells tomatoes and onions together with Moses. Waiganjo is an old man who supervises the watchmen who guard the produce and questions them if something is stolen. I don't know all their names. There are also eight women on the committee who all sell dried staples. Before we used to have only women on the committee. But because "women are light as paper" [proverb] we realized that we couldn't manage on our own and decided to elect a man chairman. He is a good chairman. There is another chairman for the other side of the market; our committee is only for those who sell produce. There is no overall head of Gikomba Market except the city council member for the whole of Kamukunji [which also includes Machakos Country Bus Stop and an area for metalworkers]. I don't know about the organization of those people in the buildings making clothes; it is those with licenses for the shops in there who know.

On the committee we settle a lot of cases. For example, if somebody steals from someone else we have to pass judgment. That usually involves those watchmen. Can a seller come to the market at night to steal from another one? So we tell the watchman to pay; if he doesn't we deduct the money from his pay. We ask him, "This person who came to steal, how did he get by you if you were supposed to be watching?" We fire him. We also talk about how to be more united, to work as a group. We know that "one finger can't kill a louse" [proverb; *Kiaa kenoe kewaa ndaa*].[20] If we had been united when I lost my money, for example, they could have come together and contributed a shilling per person and the money would have been enough.

We settle debt cases. We do not allow stealing from each other. It is bad to take your neighbor's money and not give it to her. For example, while I am here now talking to you, I have displayed my commodities at the market and I know how much there is. If my neighbor sells some maize for me and does not give me the money I will definitely know it. I would first ask her about it; if she denies it or refuses to acknowledge that she has that money, then I would report her to the Market Committee. Recently we settled a debt case. There was a woman who gave another woman dried staples to sell a year ago

---

19. The names here indicate the multi-ethnic nature of this Committee—Kikuyu and Akamba. Similarly, in Berida's family there has been Kikuyu-Akamba intermarriage, as with Mutune and Ruth Karanja. Intermarriage is a tradition rooted in precolonial trade relations. See the beginning of Chapter 4 and Robertson, "Grassroots," 615–42.

20. See Ndeti, *Elements of Akamba Life*, p. 204.

on March 5. That woman took the beans and sold them, and then ran away to her upcountry home. Until today that lady has not repaid the debt. When we discussed the case we decided that she had to pay it. We felt pity for her; she has nothing. She is engaged in selling *sukuma wiki*,[21] tomatoes, and other greens. She explained that she could not get all the money at once and so it was agreed that she would pay it in installments, Ksh.200 per month for five months until the whole Ksh.1,000 is repaid. The Committee will collect the money until it is all paid and give it to the owner. We heard the case in April; she paid in May and June and we are now waiting for her to pay the July installment.[22] If she had refused to pay then the owner of the money would have had to decide what else to do. She would either take her to court or go and *kuiga kithitu* [place a curse on her and her family]. If you take someone's property unjustly, then that person has a right to do whatever they want to you. Usually people are given about three months to clear their debts when they are brought to the office accused of owing money or produce. We first ask the person whether they want to continue selling in the market or not. If they do then that is the time when we decide when the person should clear the debts. If you do not pay you are banned from the market.

We also settle just plain quarrels. We decided that if you insult somebody in the market you will be fined Ksh.600. Anyone who fights in the market without sufficient reason will be fined Ksh.600 the same day. If you do not pay you will be banned from the market for three months even if you have stock to sell. People shouldn't be insulting each other in the market. That even happened to me. You know, generally I like people. God has made me in such a way that I forgive easily; I don't hold grudges. I always remember what I was taught in catechism class, that if somebody does something wrong to me I should be angry for only two hours and forgive by the third hour. But the owner of that stall over there, she once knocked over my sack. We used to place the sacks on stones; we didn't have any boards then. One day I had gone to see someone in hospital. When I came back I found the stones removed. I was told that that woman had done it while saying that I had extended my stall too far. Her name was Kavila. She took the stones and threw them across the road. When I returned I called her over, Kavila, Kavila, twice, and asked her why she had done it. In response she removed more stones and the sack fell over, spilling the contents. I cried, "Kavila, you have attacked my private parts. I will beat you!!!" and I did. I beat her until people had to restrain me. They were asking if I had taken *bhang* [marijuana]. I asked, "How can my food be thrown by a woman who is like a dog?!!" She was bleeding from the mouth and the nose. I was fined Ksh.2,600 by the Committee. It was a lot because I am a committee member and should know better, set an example to others. Kavila left that day and has never returned to Gikomba except to sublet her

---

21. Kale, called *sukuma wiki* in anglicized Kiswahili because it is used to eke out a scanty diet toward the end of the week when people have no money left over from their pay.

22. In 1998 Berida said that the woman had finished paying off the debt.

stall. But it wasn't because of me that she left; it was because she had no money. Since that day I haven't hated anyone else. [Laughter.]

Christians shouldn't get annoyed. Everything I have done has been with a free heart. You shouldn't go to God with sadness in your heart. But I do have my troubles. Like the one who kicked me—what happened is that that older woman I mentioned before passed behind Mutio who sells next to me. Mutio was busy recording something. The old woman grabbed Mutio and began beating her. My Martha called me and I ran to help the lady. She had a carton with her; as she went to pick it up she kicked my foot. But at Kathonzweni I don't have problems. When we go there you will see how popular I am. I entertain them, tell them stories, make them laugh. If they want me to dance, I dance.

When I look back I can see that this work has removed me from a lot of slavery. Even when I am only earning something small, that something small is what enabled Angelina to go to school, even Maggie. No matter how small my earnings were I would go and pay their school fees. I am very grateful for my job. I can help myself and I don't have problems. I could educate my children and pay their medical expenses. I really thank God for my work.

4

"The Akamba are a peaceloving people"

Ethnicity, Religion, and Politics

A long time ago the Kikuyu and Akamba were brothers and sisters, friends. But the Kikuyu did not have cows so they used to get products from cows in exchange for maize and *nzavi*.[1] They would even arrange for meetings where the Kikuyu would bring their foodstuffs and exchange them with the Akamba for livestock products.[2] They intermarried. Even one of my grandmothers was called Mwihaki and she was a Kikuyu. When the Akamba would go in search of food in Kikuyuland the Kikuyus would capture them and take them as hostages. Likewise, if the Kikuyu girls came to Ukambani the Akamba would also capture them. My grandmother was captured and married an Akamba man. She was from Gaichanjiru in Kiambu.[3] She was married before colonialism. My father was friendly with a Kikuyu from Gatundu. One time that Kikuyu brought us three bags of maize and my father slaughtered a goat for him and gave him a cow.

You know, even in the fight to send away the colonialists [the Emergency from 1952 to 1960] there were Akambas and Kikuyus involved. Oh, the British were not always bad. For instance, in about 1947 there was a bad famine. (I remember when because there was an eclipse of the sun and it frightened us badly. We were out gathering firewood far from home. Everything got dark

---

1. Lablab beans had particular religious significance for the Kikuyu, who call them *njahe*; they are a favorite food. They are especially associated with women.

2. See Claire C. Robertson, "Gender and Trade Relations in Central Kenya in the Late Nineteenth Century," *International Journal of African Historical Studies* 30, no. 1 (1997): 23–47.

3. K. Ndeti stated that intermarriage between Akamba and Kikuyu was common, "since anyone can remember," and that they have a myth of common origin. *Elements of Akamba Life*, p. 81.

and we ran all the way home because of our terror. By the time we got there the light was returning.) Anyway, we got famine relief during the Makopo famine. They brought us sorghum, cassava flour, wheat flour, and lima beans. There was a governor we called King George [VI?], whose house was here in Nairobi. They would give a sack of food to share between two people, or a big family would get a whole sack. There was enough to feed us all.

But there were also things like they made us terrace our farms; a white named Lumbai would make us dig. Now we might see that as a good thing, but back then we didn't think it was useful and the labor was really hard. That and the destocking of cattle[4] were very unpopular and so we had the Mau Mau movement, which actually got its name from the fact that when the colonialists came to the homesteads people would be alerted and told, "uma uma," which means "come out." So that they would run to safety. This was around 1952. During that time Kikuyus were being victimized. They were arrested because it was believed that they were the ones who had taken the Mau Mau oath. The way of distinguishing them from the Akamba was through pronunciation; that is, they would be asked to say the word for grass, *useki*, in their mother tongue [Kikuyu; *kaliseki*], then the distinction would be made [between Akamba and Kikuyu]. My elder brother was in Nairobi then and he offered to hide Ruth Karanja, the Kikuyu lady I told you about. She was fleeing the police who had tortured her. Some women were being raped with bottles to get them to confess to having taken a Mau Mau oath. She is from the Mang'u area on the way to Thika. At that time and even before we had to carry passes, which meant that to come to Nairobi you needed to go to the chief and get a letter. Then you took the letter to the DC to be stamped. When all that had happened then maybe you would be allowed to go to Nairobi. And you couldn't graze your cattle on your own land. If they were found grazing you were fined. You had to cut grass and feed them in their pen.

Once I got involved myself in an incident in Kikuyuland during the Emergency. We had taken the cows to Kikuyuland because there was a shortage of grass for grazing the cows at home. The day that it was announced that [the Mau Mau leader] Dedan Kimathi had come, there was fierce fighting and we had to leave Kikuyuland. I had no bus fare; I even offered to take off my dress and give it to the driver for fare because I had nothing else. The fare then was Ksh.5. It was all right; they let me board anyway. My father-in-law took the cows home.

When I was in Murang'a [central Kikuyuland north of Nairobi] I used to apply dust and soot to my skin to make myself dirty so that I would not be taken by the Johnnies, that's what we called the whites. They used to capture people day and night, any time. They were very bad. They really terrorized us. One time I came face to face with them when I was looking for some lost goats. I was so fed up that I dared them to shoot me if they wanted. They did not

---

4. Joseph Muthiani has a useful account of the protests associated with destocking and land alienation that began in the 1930s, which resulted in marches to Nairobi. *Akamba from Within*, pp. 117ff.

shoot me and I ran away dancing until I disappeared. The whites laughed and did not notice my disappearance [demonstrates dancing, running]. I had two children then but I looked very young; one might not even have known that I had children. I was a *mayanga* [fashionable]. When Kenyatta and KANU fought for us to get independence all that stopped.

You can't tell Kikuyu and Akamba apart when they are not talking. We look alike and we understand each other's languages. But we Akamba are peaceloving people; those who steal have been taught by Kikuyu. You can even sleep outside with your money and no Mkamba would bother you. If you steal from an Mkamba, you know you are dead. They will do a *kithitu* [curse] on you. But when an Mkamba comes to Majengo he is taught to steal by a Kikuyu; then he is the one who always gets caught because he is stupid and doesn't know how to escape from a robbery. Kikuyu are bad, the stealing! Even the Maasai have been taught to steal by the Kikuyu. Otherwise, all that the Maasai knew how to steal was cattle from us in Ukambani! [Laughter.] If a Kikuyu has a hotel/kiosk restaurant, he will tell the *askari* to steal food [from the market] and he will buy it from him. God actually gave Kikuyu that talent. When a Kikuyu child is born they put a ten-cent piece in its mouth. They love money. But Jane here, do you think they think of Jane as one of them? Even Jane's brother would kill her to get her money.

But me, I have given up all those things, the *kithitu*. I am a good Christian. Before I married I belonged to the AIC, African Inland Church, be-

---

Ethnic Relations

EXCERPT FROM TAPE TRANSCRIPT 97-10-25-26[5]

Claire: Does she think Kikuyu are different from Akamba or are they pretty much alike?
Berida: No, they look alike. You can't tell them apart when they are not talking. But we understand their language.
Claire: And do Akamba like money as much as Kikuyu like money? [Laughter.]
Berida: These people are too greedy for money; and they are thieves too. [Laughter.] You can even sleep out here with your money and no Mkamba would bother you.
Jane: It's because they are afraid of witchcraft.[6]
Berida: If you steal from an Mkamba you know you are dead. They will do a *kithitu* on you.
Mbithe: If you steal from an Mkamba, just know you are going to die. They are going to consult the witchdoctors. Actually, that thing was taken so seriously that even if you cheat a Kamba, that you don't give them their properties and all that, they consult witchdoctors.
Berida: But when an Mkamba comes to Majengo, he is taught to steal by a Kikuyu; he is always the one who gets caught because he is stupid, doesn't know how to escape from a robbery. Kikuyu are bad, the stealing!

---

5. These remarks were made half in a joking mode, playing on the ethnic stereotypes common in Kenya concerning the Akamba and the Kikuyu. Many Kikuyu jokes told by Kikuyu and others center on Kikuyu love for money, hence the laughter here. Jane is Kikuyu, so that the serious content of what Berida said was somewhat offensive to her; her riposte was to bring up witchcraft in relation to the Akamba, thus playing on another stereotype. Ethnic relations in Kenya have varied historically, but most agree that interethnic hostilities were much exacerbated by colonial and post-independence divide-and-conquer policies. British colonialists defined the "tribes" of central Kenya, South Africa, and southern Rhodesia (British white settler colonies) and confined them to reserves; most of the land was allocated to whites. Thus, "tribal" identity was created to some extent by European modes of thinking and policies, which imposed firm boundaries on the relatively fluid clan systems described at the beginning of this chapter. Africans served as cheap labor for the settlers and could not often be self-supporting on the increasingly crowded reserves. Significant portions of Akamba land were alienated.

6. Penwill noted that the Akamba have a venerable reputation for witchcraft. *Kamba Customary Law*, pp. 93–94. More men than women were thought to practice it.

cause my mother belonged.[7] But when I married my husband's mother was attending the Catholic Church. My mother-in-law was troubled by evil spirits but after she went to church that stopped. She was baptized Monica Kithikwa. So my Monica is named after her grandmother.[8] I followed my mother-in-law into her church because we were at her home. I was given the name Berida when I first converted to Catholicism soon after I married. But when my children were dying I went back to our tradition. Afterwards, I came back to the Church. At Kathonzweni I go to church as often as I can but in February my feet were hurting and I didn't go. I am more faithful about going to fellowship at people's homes, which are nearer. We pray together. Here in Nairobi I go to Saint Teresa's, which is nearby. However, I only go once in awhile, maybe once or twice a year, because business cannot be combined with churchgoing. I ask myself, "Should I go to church and lose business because others are still selling?" My competitors might beat me. When my customers come and don't find me there they will go to buy from my neighbors. We also have prayer groups here, sometimes at my place.

The way I really became a Christian had to do with that time that I was so sick and went to Nairobi and then didn't go back to the hospital. When Ndambuki came back from the healer he just came and told me that if I wanted to die I would die because he couldn't afford to buy the cloth and things he had been told to buy for me. How could I get involved in witchcraft when Ndambuki didn't have anything? What would have happened to me? The idea was to give me the kind of powers my mother had, but instead I ended up at the hospital in Nairobi. So me, I went and accepted Christianity. I had begun before that by going to catechism class to be taught the word of God. We used to sit under a tree, but I would sit apart from everyone else. I didn't pay attention to what was being taught. I wouldn't listen because as I sat there I would see somebody pass in front of me covered in a white sheet.

But when I left the hospital and returned home I continued the classes and started paying attention. I told you already that the priest had come to my house and prayed for me, touched me so that I would get well. The whole congregation had come. He prayed and gave them blessings. Then the priest asked me, "Where do those [in the white sheets] come from?" I showed him just where they passed. Those people who were doing that were not good. Otherwise they wouldn't have tortured my body so. For example, if I was lying in bed she would come and sit at the head of the bed without talking and the

---

7. The African Inland Mission, or Church, a Baptist-influenced American organization, was dominant among Christian churches in Ukambani until World War II. J. Forbes Munro, *Colonial Rule and the Kamba*, pp. 101–108, 154. Catholicism has now become very important in Ukambani. In some areas U.S.-based Pentecostalist Protestants have gained increasing influence and many Africans have converted to such faiths—"born-again" Christianity is now an aspect of the religious scene in Africa, as Angelina's case demonstrates.

8. It is usual to name the first two girls after their grandmothers and the first two boys after their grandfathers. The reproduction of the lineage in such a manner is an interesting bilineal aspect within a strongly patrilineal, patrilocal system. It is also one reason that even those who believe strongly in the use of contraception to avoid having more children than one can support usually say that a woman should bear four children.

other one at the foot of the bed. I would be terrified, leave my room and go lie down outside. They were a vision, not real people. The priest gave me incense to burn at the four corners of my bed and a cross to hang above my bed until it got light. He taught me how to pray with the cross. He blessed the home and sprinkled holy water around the room. I was supposed to go back to the hospital but instead I continued going to catechism classes. Then I began to learn.

There were seventy-four of us in that class. When the priest came to examine us, the Lord directed all of the questions to me. I was eager to answer because I knew all of the answers. The other students were amazed at me. I had been the one who had seemed most reluctant to learn. They were wondering how I had learned. So the teacher was very happy. It was decided that I should be baptized. Only four out of the seventy-four were baptized, and for one of those it was because she was old. She didn't really understand much. Even the bright ones I surpassed. I learned about how God created the world and Adam and Eve and many other things. I was baptized and they weren't. That's when I was given the name Berida. The teacher told me he wanted me to continue to the next stage and receive *kivaimala* [may mean confirmation]. A white priest from Msongari was going to come and give us *kivaimala* to pass to the next level within a week. I asked the teacher if I could be ready within such a short time. He said he would teach me day and night. At that point you receive a second name so that you can be a full Christian. So he came to teach me in the evening at my home. The following day we had to go to Kabaa and he continued teaching me on the way there. So I was given my second name, Lucia, and I stopped seeing the visions. I became a Christian.

When I think about it I believe that if I had stuck to Akamba tradition I would have been like my mother. I would have inherited the way my mother did those things before, for example, making Antony die. Christianity has benefitted me. If I weren't a Christian I wouldn't be talking to Kilaya now. I would be afraid of her. But now through the power of the Lord I am afraid of nothing.

When Angelina married she was a Catholic. But after she had three children she converted; those people came to pray for her at her home. They are Pentecostalists. They call themselves *kuokoka* [saved]. Then she started calling me Satan. I really don't know who those people are; one of them is called Mwangi. She wanted to pray for me but I refused. I am already a Christian and I don't need another religion. That's when she called me Satan. How come Angelina all of a sudden needs a different religion? I have given her education and brought her up to where she is. What makes her think she can call me Satan? Can Satan raise a child? A devil walks around naked, no clothes on. I get so angry. When I think of Ndinda tears come to my eyes. She even used to teach Sunday school at our place where I showed you. The small children who don't listen sat apart from the older ones; we arranged that they all got gifts at Christmas.

Ndambuki is not a true Christian like I am. He can't be because of his behavior. He is a big drinker. If he were a good Christian he would drink in moderation only. If you drink, don't bring problems to your home. He disturbs everybody, chasing them from home and beating them. And the following day

Berida shows off
the Sunday school

he denies doing it at all. When I am home I call a church group to come and pray for him; maybe he can change.[9] I sent a message to him before we went to Kathonzweni telling him not to drink. [She laughed.] Did it make a difference?

You know, in this Kenya there are many problems. It is not just alcoholism. There are all the troubles now that are stopping our trade. You remember that back in 1988 and even before we were struggling over selling where we are on that hillside at Gikomba? I told you that the city council had bulldozed my place and I even lost my stock. That was after the chief told us to go sell down by the river and we had refused. He told us he had the power. Then he went to the city council, conspired with them and they came to destroy our things. So we went to see Nyayo. We sang,

> Nyayo's isn't far, we'll get there on foot;
> open the door so the women of Gikomba can enter.
> A call came from Nyayo;
> we got the call and we went [to Nyayo].
> When we got to his office we asked him,
> "What did you tell us?
> You told us to plant a fruit tree to show cooperation."

9. Convincing a husband to be saved or have a religious awakening was a tactic used by many women to curb their husbands' drinking; in some cases in 1987–1988 it worked and enabled the couple to establish a more prosperous lifestyle in which the spouses pooled their earnings and the husband spent his evenings at home instead of drinking with friends.

The Politics of Anti-Hawking and Slum Demolition Campaigns

EXCERPT FROM *TROUBLE SHOWED THE WAY*, PP. 267–268

The climax of a steadily mounting anti-hawker campaign came in October 1990, when all of the central city illegal markets were destroyed. . . . [O]n 11 October 1990 at Machakos Bus Depot 300 NCC [Nairobi City Council] police took on hawkers with teargas and batons and were met with active resistance including stonethrowing from residents of an adjacent estate, hawker-constructed barricades, a bonfire lit to disrupt traffic (successfully), and fisticuffs. Most business in the central city stopped and the situation was not gotten "under control" until late in the day, when armed groups of NCC police still patrolled, presumably to stop the few shabbily dressed "crafty hawkers" who were trying to sell vegetables and fruit on the streets to homeward-bound workers. On 16 October Gikomba was bulldozed and other illegal markets destroyed. The impact of the destruction was major; traders roamed seeking temporary places to sell. . . .

The ferocity of this attack was clearly linked to political causes. In Nairobi in July 1990 there were demonstrations centering in congested areas near or on the site of some illegal and legal markets. . . . These became riots when the demonstrators were attacked by the police and achieved international notice since they involved supporters of a multiparty political system, whose leaders had been imprisoned. . . . [T]he destruction of predominantly Kikuyu residential areas at Kamukunji (Muoroto) and Kibagare . . . resulted in the displacement of over 40,000 people. Wanjigi protested the demolitions, [likening it to the massive removals of Kikuyu from Nairobi under the Emergency], which cost him his position as MP and his member-ship in KANU. . . . Dissident politician Koigi wa Wamwere was arrested and accused of organizing illegal hawkers and matatu drivers, and promoting a "defiant culture."

It was a song of love—because at Gikomba we loved each other. But we ac-tually never reached Nyayo's office. Our MP, Maina Wanjigi, took up the is-sue with the president that same day and we were told to continue selling here. It was the city council that was in the wrong. Moi had made a telephone call to the DO [District Officer] and said everybody was to be given back their space. We were sent along with the DO back to Gikomba and told we could remain where we were in the stalls. So everybody went back where they were before, even the people who were selling clothes.

But they kept demolishing our place, even when you were here before and I told you that because I am as brown as you are you should build for me. We were just selling under umbrellas to keep off the sun and the rain. They call those men at Kamukunji *jua kali* [Kiswahili; fierce sun] because they had no shelter, but look at what we had![10] Now I have rebuilt my shelter, just about a month ago. We didn't do it before because we were afraid they might be demolished. And the investment, they don't realize the cost! I don't think they will be demolished again. You see, the big man [Moi] passed here when he was

---

10. The Kenyan government, under the influence of the 1972 International Labor Organization report *Employment, Income, and Equality: A Strategy for Increasing Productive Employment in Kenya* (Geneva: ILO, 1974), defined only those workers involved in manufacturing (namely men, since the garment industry was not included) as participants in the informal sector worth helping. Thus, the male metalworkers have had less contested occupation of land across the Nairobi River (which is only a stream at that point) from Gi-komba. Their rhythmic hammering is a hallmark of the neighborhood.

Stories of Saba-Saba (7 July[11]) and "Solidarity"

Domitila, Berida's youngest sister, told us what happened at Gikomba on the first Saba-Saba on 7 July 1990. She was selling dried staples at Gikomba with Berida. A riot developed in the area and the police teargassed the crowd. Berida told Domitila, "I wasn't born with money!" and just left her there to guard the staples and ran away. Domitila stopped selling then and also left. She thought it was a joke but Berida said it was serious and trouble was coming. So Domitila was teargassed and everyone ran to the river and used the dirty water, or their own saliva, to wash their eyes. Everyone stood in the river.

Claire's diary entry for 7 July 1997 noted that it was "trouble day." What began as an Opposition rally downtown progressed throughout the day, from eastern Nairobi in the usual areas to the University of Nairobi, where students were attacked, to Nairobi Cathedral, where the police pursued demonstrators into the sanctuary and beat them.[12] Because of the scheduled demonstrations I planned no interviewing. Instead I left Muguga, where I was staying west of Nairobi, and went to Limuru, which was peaceful, accompanied by Karanja. At one point we got lost, ending up in the dooryard of a house, whose cordial Kenyan owner greeted us by asking where I was from in the United States. When I said I was from Indiana, he informed me that he had gotten his medical degree at the Indiana University Medical School. On our return we found tires burning at Muguga on the motorway, an attempt to get motorists to slow down so that they could be robbed, Karanja said. It seems that every political demonstration turns into a riot in which class warfare becomes salient. Poverty will not be suppressed. At Muguga I learned from participants in a KEFRI (Kenya Forestry Research Institute) workshop that seven people had been killed in the riots today. We watched TV in the dining room. The workshop people laughed[13] when the police were shown beating people who escaped. The police were aiming for the genitals.

On 11 August we had a confrontation with a man at COTU's Solidarity House. Kasilili, a Gikomba dance group and Berida's Kyeni kya Gikomba had agreed at the last minute to be filmed. When we arrived at Gikomba she led us behind Solidarity House to a carpark and grassy space suitable for dancing. Almost immediately an irate older man erupted from the building, a managerial type, and asked us what we were doing. I told him about the filming. He objected that we had not gotten prior permission and began ranting that these women were not workers but just business-women who hang around. I said, angry despite my best intentions, "You mean they don't work? They support their families!" We left, sought and received permission for filming at the DC's compound down the road, and finished.

going to the workers' house [Council of Trade Unions (COTU) building]. Solidarity House, which is their headquarters, is just here near Gikomba. I danced for him holding the container we measure cereals with and he told me [Kiswahili], "*Mama kaa tu, kaa ninakuambia kaa.*" ["Woman stay, woman stay, just stay, stay. I am telling you to stay."] So he gave us permission to stay selling here at Gikomba. Even now, since we were given this place by Nyayo, when the council is chasing people away we are not affected. You see the people across the road on this side selling clothes and those on the verandas of the shops? The council usually chases away all of those and takes their stuff. The

---

11. Saba-Saba means seven-seven in Kiswahili, for the seventh day of the seventh month.
12. The next day both the international and the local media were full of pictures of the beating of the Presbyterian minister Reverend Timothy Njoya in the Cathedral.
13. This example well illustrates the different causes and salience of laughter in different cultures.

Mbulwa, Berida, and Mbithe join the discussion outside Solidarity House—while other group members await the outcome before putting on costumes

Daily Nation editorial, Saturday 14 March 1998

FINDING A SOLUTION TO STREET VENDING

It is so depressingly commonplace that it is becoming a permanent feature of Nairobi and Kenya's other towns. It is the spectre of Kenyans waking up to see council askaris demolishing all manner of structures or engaging hawkers in running battles through urban streets. . . . [L]ocal authorities and the Central Government . . . engage in short-term measures that bring about only a temporary cessation of hostilities and engender construction of structures that are soon declared illegal. After that, it is only a matter of time before the cycle begins tediously anew. The brute force that has been employed by askaris and both Administration and regular police in eviction of kiosk operators and demolition of their premises, and removal of hawkers from city and town pavements and the attendant mayhem are unbecoming of civil society and should belong to a forgotten past.

We would like to suggest that the recently constituted civic authorities look afresh at the twin issues of kiosks and hawking with a view to finding a lasting solution to them. City and town halls need to ask themselves a few questions. One: Should they identify parcels of land and set them aside for kiosks and hawkers? Land can be found in different parts of the city or towns where markets can be set up. These markets can operate on specified days or certain goods can be sold on specific days. Or the civic authorities could decide that different markets could sell different goods. Two: Set part of the city centre aside for hawking activities and close this part of town from vehicular traffic. Again, this can be done on specific days, say, weekends, and hawkers would be invited to set up stalls and adhere to certain specific standards of cleanliness. Three: Let civic authorities get hawkers to organise themselves in societies, arrange for them to obtain credit and set themselves up in small businesses. Four: Let these authorities encourage the idea of boot sales or weekend markets countrywide. These are just four ideas, but there are many more that could be explored by city and town halls.

---

people along this other road that goes down there, they have licenses so their clothes are not taken. But we women, who do not have licenses, we were told to stay there free. We were called *"mama mzazi"* [Kiswahili; one who has given birth], who should be taken care of. The council does arrest the wholesalers across the road at Ziwani, however. That is not Gikomba.

Gikomba is the biggest market in Kenya. Some say it is Karatina, but I know it is Gikomba.[14] Even Moi will be coming here again soon. You ask, how did Gikomba get its name? When I came here it was already called that so I don't know, maybe it was from Maasai. If you ask around many people think that Gikomba is for the Akambas because there are so many here. But that name seems not to have an owner. You know, this market for dried staples was given to the Akamba women. We, the women, when we came we became friends and became one thing. Even when we go to Nyayo you can find us singing Kikuyu songs like that one, "Nyayo's place is not far, knock, knock, knock, open to us; we are coming from Gikomba." We are just one thing. Even when we go to see the big man we go as one.

---

14. She is correct. Karatina in Nyeri north of Nairobi may be the largest *legal* market, however.

Nairobbery: Excerpts from *Daily Nation* Articles

4 MARCH 1998, P. 1
GOLDENBERG CORRUPTION CASE STARTS

The long-delayed Goldenberg [International, Pattni's company] case started yesterday, with the State submitting that businessman Kamlesh Pattni and his co-accused [former Treasury Permanent Secretary Wilfred Karuga Koinange, former Central Bank Deputy Governor Eliphaz Riungu, and colleague Michael Wanjihia Onesmus] were implicated in the theft of Ksh.5.8 billion belonging to the Kenya Government.[15]

31 OCTOBER 1997, P. 1: EDITORIAL
INVESTIGATE SALE OF CITY PROPERTY

Nairobi Mayor Dick Waweru is making serious allegations. . . . [H]e says the City Council stands to lose Ksh.2 billion through the "dubious sale of houses, clinics and plots to private developers." This may sound normal to Nairobi residents familiar with the shameless parcelling out of public utility plots to reward Government functionaries. . . . The Government, as the custodian of the citizens' rights, must in this case explain to Nairobi residents what is going on. It should also assure them, especially the low-income earners and the very poor, that this "privatisation" is not meant to take away even the skeletal medical services they have. . . . It is a pity that . . . political interference, greed and other vices are driving Nairobi to the dump.

A RESOUNDING "YES" TO CHANGE

A near-unanimous yes-vote yesterday saw Parliament endorse a Bill to amend the Constitution to provide for greater freedoms and explicitly recognise Kenya as a multi-party state.

28 FEBRUARY 1998, P. 1
MONETARY FUND DASHES HOPES FOR QUICK AID

The Government has not satisfied conditions set out by the International Monetary Fund for the resumption of funding. . . . The Government was said to have failed to maintain budgetary discipline, with the example given of over Ksh.4 billion spent on the last [December 1997] elections although the Budget allocation was Ksh.2.1 billion. . . . [President Moi was re-elected; the Opposition was severely split.]

20 JANUARY 1998, P. 1
BODY DETAILS ELECTION FLAWS

The Election Observation Centre of the Western Donor Group says there were irregularities in polling and counting of votes in nine constituencies during the last General Election, making it flawed.

Sometimes [whispering] men even wear dresses like women when we go to see Nyayo because men are not allowed to go in there, because the place was given for women to do their businesses so they can help their children. [Laughter.] Men don't help them. The dresses are just a disguise. They don't wear them at the market, only when we are going to see the president. Those

---

15. After the 1997 elections Vice President George Saitoti was implicated in this scandal and removed from office. He was widely thought to be the most corrupt politician in Kenya. His removal from office was due partly to pressure from foreign governments and aid agencies, which response also included setting up an office to get rid of governmental corruption. However, the first attempt made by this office to indict persons in government for corruption resulted in the dismissal of its head in July 1998.

men usually hunch down in the back seats while women are at the front. No man can speak; only the women talk, so that they are not beaten. [Softly] Those who dress like that are those down there who sell tomatoes. They want to go and hear what women will be told by Nyayo. You know, men are the shield; we couldn't stop them from going. They protect us. When there are riots they go in front and say, "These are women, leave them alone!" Why should they feel embarrassed? Since they want to go there, they have to dress like women. There was a time during the last dry season when we from Gikomba gave Nyayo donations to take to the hunger-stricken people. We alone gave seven lorries worth of food. We took it to him so he could distribute it to the areas where people were hungry.

You know, politics is bad. The police come and beat people. It's ruining our business. Now there are all these parties. They have spoiled things. They are just disturbing us ordinary people [Kiswahili; *wananchi*]. We have nothing but they always do all right. When they come and beat us and we run away to our homes, are we going to be able to eat our houses? When I look around I see it is the Kikuyu who are bothering us. It is stealing that is causing all the problems.[16] But I blame the existence of opposition parties for the problems. What were they created for? What use are they when they haven't helped us at all? I thought if there were two parties, if one made things too tough for us, the other would help us. If one party made prices too high, the other would lower them. But when they came, that's when prices went up. They do nothing. I wouldn't say that KANU should be on its own, but having many parties has spoiled things. We are grateful to Kenyatta and KANU because before, when the whites were here, they fought for independence and stopped all those things the whites were doing to us. But now it's not that I like KANU only; I like whoever is looking after us, helping us.

---

16. These observations at once demonstrate the success of President Moi's tactics of divide-and-conquer, through which he has set former allies against each other, and a tradition of what has been termed kleptocracy that was established by President Jomo Kenyatta in Kenya. President Moi is a Kalenjin from western Kenya and President Kenyatta was a Kikuyu.

5

"I ask myself, why did I have my children?"

Life and Death

In Nairobi my day begins when I get up at sunrise at about 6 A.M. I wake up because the neighbors make noise with loud radios, and there is a bell that rings at the Shauri Moyo police station. I can also hear the Muslims praying. Then I know it is time. I heat water on my paraffin stove and bathe. I make tea and put it in a thermos. I have to buy the water by the can at Ksh.1, 1.50 a jerry can [four gallons] or more.[1] It comes from a tap at Kinyago, which is not far from my room [about a half a block]. There is no toilet at my place and no electricity. We go to other people and ask to use theirs, like where Jane stays; she has one. We also don't have a shower so I bathe in a basin in my room. Even without all those things I still pay Ksh.800 for the room. By the time I have finished bathing and made tea it is usually 6:30. I take my tea and then I leave my room to go to Gikomba. Or I might do the laundry before I go. If I am not feeling well I may not get up until 7:00 A.M. and then I wouldn't get to Gikomba until 8:30 or 9:00 A.M. I take a *matatu* or I walk to Gikomba.

When I get to Gikomba I might buy commodities to add to my stock straight off or I wait until I see something. I buy on any day at any time I see something selling at a reasonable price. Yesterday I spent most of the day at the hospital and when I came back I found the people who bring me *ndengu* waiting for me. I told Martha to measure it since I wasn't feeling well. She did

---

1. In 1997 there was a water shortage and the price was Ksh.2 and up for a jerry can. Because Nairobi's water-pumping and storage facilities are inadequate for its population and are poorly maintained, even in times of plenty (as in 1998 with the El Niño rains) they often malfunction, causing shortages and rationing. The poor condition of Nairobi's infrastructure in general is a consequence of political corruption, the pocketing of moneys intended for upkeep and expansion of infrastructure. An extreme case involved the failure to maintain the Mombasa-Nairobi Road, a large portion of which washed away in 1998, thus depriving Kenya, Tanzania, eastern Congo, Uganda, and Rwanda of their major supply line.

it and in the evening came to tell me that she had weighed it and it was worth Ksh.2,800. So in the morning I gave her the money to go and pay them since the sellers had spent the night there. At Gikomba I open my stall, then wait for customers. If they don't come I just sit there. You can spend the time cleaning beans or talking to your friends if customers don't come. It can be boring but morning is usually the best time for customers. Since I left my home to come to Nairobi to trade at Gikomba, I will sit there until 5 P.M. I will sell to any customer who comes, then close at 5 P.M. If there is a Committee meeting I will find out about it when I reach the market. We usually meet for about two hours between, say, 10 A.M. and 12 A.M. Sometimes we begin at 11 A.M. If I am at a meeting my neighbor takes care of my stall and sells to any customer who comes. By noon we are done and everyone returns to their business.

At lunch time I usually don't leave my stall. There's a restaurant called Hoteli wa Muongo[2] and they come around selling cooked food. So I might order some rice and they bring it to me. They cook maize and beans, rice, chapatis, muthokoi. . . . A plate of muthokoi, rice, or a chapati all cost Ksh.25. Maize and beans are Ksh.20, the dry ones that you can eat with your hand. That is called githeri [Kikuyu] like I gave Kilaya one time. They also serve chai [hot sweetened tea with milk]. But I don't drink their tea; it looks like water. It has very little tea or milk in it. I can't drink it; it's bad. When I get tired of eating this food, I go where they roast meat in that tall building at Gikomba and order a little meat; they put tomatoes and onions on it. They cut it up and put it on a plate with ugali [Kiswahili; cooked stiff maize dough]. Then I eat something good. That costs Ksh.80.

Sometimes Mbulwa and I eat together. I go call her and say, "Let's go for lunch." But if she tells me she has already eaten from the hotel on the back, then I go to eat alone. I tell her I want to eat good food. Or she comes to get me sometimes. She has a small stove and a small cooking pot at her stall. Sometimes by the time I go to get her I find she has food ready. Then she tells me to sit down to eat the food she has cooked. So if I eat there today, then I will ask her what we will eat tomorrow. She tells me and I buy the things and take them to her to cook on her stove. So, for example, meat we cook there. Or pumpkins, sweet potatoes. . . . The only thing we don't cook there is ugali so we might buy that. We eat the meat and drink the soup. Sometimes I tell her, I don't feel like githeri today. Why should I be eating bad food and I am working? Then we go to buy meat and put it in the pot to cook. Am I going to work so hard for other people while I keep my belt tightened? You have to eat properly and stay strong to work. People of my age who don't eat properly look so different.

In the afternoon I wait for customers. I don't yell much to attract customers, but I might say, "Mama, come see what I have!" It is mainly the stock

---

2. Anglicized Kiswahili meaning "hotel on the back" because the women hawkers carry the food in baskets or tins on their backs.

that attracts them. I don't bargain the prices but I might give someone a little more on top of the tin. There is often a lull around 2 P.M. when no customers come and it is really boring. Sometimes I sleep like this [lying sideways with one eye slightly open] so if someone comes I will see them and sit up. [Laughter.] I lie on the sacks with my eyes open and think about the customers coming. I think about my grandson talking about me being hungry. I think about Choma, my four-year-old grandson who is in nursery school and him whispering to me. I dream I will get money and go home and see the children; they climb all over me when I come bringing a large loaf of bread. They shout, "Our mother has come!" The customers tend to come at 2:30 or 3 P.M. or after. If God has planned for you to sell today you will sell from 9 A.M. to 4 P.M. and be sold out by 5. If not, you can be here all day and sell only two kilos. Business depends on God. Sometimes I can only make Ksh.300 per day. The food costs Ksh.100. So on a bad day the profit might be Ksh.200; on a good day maybe Ksh.3,000.

I usually close up around 5 P.M. because of the thugs. I like to go home early because there are other people on the road, but actually you can be robbed any time. I am old and can't afford to fight with people on the way at night. If I don't make money during the day, I won't be seeing it at night either. I take a *matatu* and buy food on the way home to have for dinner, like a fourth of a kilo of meat for Ksh.30, tomatoes for Ksh.10, potatoes for Ksh.5, *sukuma* for Ksh.5, and so on. I tell the sellers to cut them up for me which they do at no charge. I feel lazy and lie, saying I have no knife. I buy enough to satisfy me. I go home and cook on my paraffin stove, which goes slowly. While I do that people come and visit and I share the food with them. I sometimes ask Martha, "Why do all these people come here?" There are always a lot of them. One comes and sits and then another one. If you have cooked, can you refuse to serve them? She says I have become a healer and that they have come to consult me. These are mostly neighbors, both men and women. Sometimes I don't get to sleep until 11 P.M. I try to go to bed at 9 P.M. We talk and laugh. Martha says sometimes, "Mother, why do you have all these people here?" But I just answer, "Having people/friends is like having wealth. Never love money more than people." They will help you if you are sick. They carry water for me. I give them a jerry can to haul it in.

Some of them came to my *harambee*. We pray together too. Many came to the *harambee*. I gave the extra food from the *harambee* to my Biafra neighbors. We tell stories in the evening, recount the day's happenings. For example, one night they asked me, "Has your *mzungu* [European/white] left?" They wanted to know what she would eat at Kathonzweni. I told her she would eat whatever she found there. We pray together too. I might wash the dishes or the neighbors do it. If there aren't any visitors I might leave the dishes for the morning. Sometimes Martha does my laundry. When Martha came back from Kathonzweni and found my dirty clothes; she spent the whole day washing them. If Martha is not around I usually wash one dress in the evening but if I hang it out it will get stolen, so I hang it out in the morning. My landlady takes them in for me and Martha or the dry cleaner irons for me. You

Kathonzweni Market, 1997: The Pacers and the Bulls duke it out

take your already washed clothes to the *dhobi*,[3] who charges either Ksh.5 or 10 depending on the difficulty of ironing the item.

At my place I use a lantern if I want light at night. The ancestors said that you can't sew clothes at night so there's nothing else to do but sleep except if I am feeling low, in a bad mood, I sometimes go to Jane's or another neighbor's to watch TV. There are electricity and a latrine there too. I like to look at the flowers on TV and it makes me feel better. Especially now with all the bad things going on in Kenya I like to see other places. I go to see what people are doing, not to watch the news. I have a radio; I can listen to the news on that but I like to see what they are doing. I can see Italy, China, and so on. And sports in other countries. I might see some things about America but I can't be sure because I can't distinguish between white people. What I like about TV is that if I am feeling down or annoyed about something, when I watch and see other places or funny things that make me laugh, then I feel better. I see white people playing football; others swimming or jumping into the water; others swing from ropes up there. When there are competitions between black people and white people I can see who knows the game better. I have only seen one American who was black. A Maasai. I was told he is a university professor. He was in Maasai dress. He has three wives. I think about American black people that if I spoke to one of them, s/he would speak Kikamba or Kikuyu.

---

3. A Hindi term used in Nairobi to refer both to the laundryman and to the laundry.

I stay at Biafra out of necessity because there is no better place I can afford due to my problems. Under such conditions you lose shame and even have to pee in public sometimes. There is a big housing shortage in Nairobi and rents are high (Jane pays Ksh.1,500 per month for her room!).[4] I am better off than some others, who sleep in cardboard cartons. And I used to just sleep at a restaurant kiosk on a bench. Some think I am rich! I like staying at Kathonzweni better. If I could make money there I wouldn't come to Nairobi at all. I could stay there and supervise what the children are doing; now they just do what they want.

At Kathonzweni I wake up at about 7 A.M., or when my sleep is finished, and go to meet Ndambuki at his *thome*, his place where he makes a fire. Old men have such places.[5] Since Martin's wife is in the kitchen, which is very small, and since I am now old, I sit with Ndambuki so he won't be alone and will have someone to talk to. We are brought tea there by Emma and Monica's daughter, and maybe an egg or bread. We eat and then Ndambuki goes out with the cows. I don't do farm or household chores because I got tired of doing them when I was a child. Since I am a visitor I do no work. You know, my house there has five rooms, two are for sleeping and two for storage; one is a living room. I built it myself without any help from Ndambuki. I bought the bricks and the iron sheets for it. It is well painted, very beautiful. I go to see Elena or Elena comes over to see me. I look for something to take her that is available in Nairobi where there are more things, like potatoes, rice, and cabbages. I bring them from Gikomba. If I go there and she has already eaten, she will still ask for food to be prepared for me. They might kill a chicken for me. We talk about what is happening in Nairobi like with my business and politics. Elena tells me about what is happening there and how Martin and Emma are doing. We talk about the water problems; I need to build a tank since the well water has bacteria and is staining our teeth. She asks me if I am happy with the condition of my home; she says that she "holds the dog for me." If it is a Sunday Elena and I go to church together.

Ndambuki might drink instead of herding. He might get so drunk he falls down. There are big problems with alcoholism and unemployment at home. Lots of people do casual labor. They have forgotten their wives and don't care for them properly. They even beat them. But often women have no other choice so they stay with the husband, no matter how bad he is. The women workers use their money for their families, the men for drinking. Women are stronger in their minds than men are because women support their families. Men are stronger physically, though. Women are weaker because they were created from Adam's rib. Is Ndambuki stronger than I am? You saw when we went there. [Laughter.]

---

4. In 1998 Jane moved to two rooms with a bath close to her previous room at Biafra. The rent is Ksh.5,000 per month, or approximately $85, equivalent to about a fourth of the yearly income of most Kenyans.

5. Hobley described the *thome* as a gathering place for old men outside the village where women were not allowed to sit. At Berida's homestead its functions have clearly been widened. *Ethnology of A-Kamba*, p. 32.

Daily Nation editorial, 5 March 1998

No tangible action on women's issues

Assistant Minister Marere Wamwachai heads the delegation attending the 42nd Session of the United Nations Commission on the Status of Women. The meeting seeks to address . . . the progress of the member countries on the implementation of the recommendations of the Fourth World Conference on Women focusing on four critical areas of concern in the Beijing Plan of Action. These are violence against women, the girl-child [abuse], women and armed conflict and the human rights of women. Local non-governmental organisations with a bias for women's issues . . . [contend] . . . that these delegations have tended to be more of public relations missions than groups that present serious issues that face women in Kenya. . . . The assistant minister was to present a paper/report on Kenya's situation in the four mentioned areas but . . . a task force on laws relating to women has been in existence since 1993 . . . [and] . . . due to lack of resources, all the work has ground to a standstill. Kenya has ratified [but done nothing about] the Convention on the Rights of the Child . . . [and the] . . . Convention on the Elimination of all Forms of Discrimination Against Women. . . . We hope this is what Ms. Wamwachai puts before the New York meeting and that some tangible action will come out of it.

Letter to the Editor by W. Wabibi

It is interesting to read views in the Press on whether the newly created Ministry for Women and Youth Affairs should be headed by a man or a woman. In my opinion the gender of who heads this ministry is irrelevant. What is important is the logic behind the creation of such a ministry and what purpose it will serve. Are these two groups—women and youth—not part and parcel of the country's development today? Can't they be catered for like everybody else? This is nothing else but an additional and irrelevant ministry to spend taxpayers' painfully earned money. How absurd!

I might nap in the afternoon or go to the market, where I buy whatever we need, staples like flour, sugar, salt. I catch up with what the groups are doing. I am more interested in the activities of the groups than in business conditions there. I want to know about how people behave in the groups. We keep track of contributions and the collective labor in harvesting, etc. The neighbors help me with the harvest and I always make sure to be home then so I can help with the harvesting, even if I have stock here. I am also very interested in what they are doing about digging the pond and building the dam. I gave them permission to build on my property even though it was a good place to plant pumpkins and banana trees. It never dried up. If they succeed there will be more water and I will be able to plant more. I also try to be there for planting even if I have stock to sell here. If I go home they will have more direction in the work and I won't eat up all my profits in buying food for them here. I like meat and all food, really. I don't like stew without meat; that's like being in jail. If you work hard with your hands you will get the food you need. When I go home during the planting season and people help with the work I give them Ksh.100 to work a plot of land or for the women I give them old clothes. Some people won't help without pay. Some men have lost their land because they drink so much so they have to do casual labor for others. They beat their wives and don't even buy clothes for them. Can a drunk take care of anyone else? If you pay a woman she will use the money to feed her family, but his money goes for drink. Then he comes staggering home drunk and asks his wife for food. Where is that food supposed to come from? He already ate his.

In the evening Emma gives me dinner. Muthama brings food and Emma cooks it. Muthama's wife Rose also brings food and I give what is left over to the children. I eat whichever food comes first. I listen to the news on the radio. I pay no attention to Ndambuki's comings and goings. There are no thugs there. He eats food left in the cupboard for him, gropes around for it in the dark when he comes in. He eats only with the company of his drunkenness, talking to himself. I might sit with him if I am still awake or put on the lantern for him, but I go back to bed because his drunken words make no sense. It is the beer talking. I used to do wifely things with him like sharing a plate but his drinking has changed things. We even went down to the river together. He is very proud of me when he is sober, saying things like, "Berida is Ndam-buki's." Drinking has changed him. I have learned to eat earlier and faster to avoid him. He used to chase me around, once even with a sharpened *panga*. I used to hate the sight of him. Would you want to see someone who wants to kill you? So I stopped waiting for him. I listen for him to see how drunk he is to see if I should run away. I will hear his loud insulting voice, so I run to the farm or to one of the children's houses. I don't go to Elena's because I don't want Elena to know about his behavior. But she knows anyway. I ask him, "Who will you be left with because of your behavior?" "Why are you so violent when you are drunk?" I say when he is sober the next day. He replies, denying his bad behavior. I go to bed about 9 P.M. unless this happens, or maybe at 9:30 after we listen to the news.

We have big problems here in Kenya, especially with poverty. At Kathonzweni it seems like there is always a flood or a drought, and famine.[6] The worst famine was probably the one in the early 1960s called the Atta famine when we were brought food from America. That year there were floods and the roads were impassable. People drowned in the Kaiti River. The Kaiti River is even called that because of people drowning in it; it means strangling somebody [*kuita*; to strangle]. It's a big river and there was no bridge before; now there is one. People would start wading across thinking there wasn't much water. Then they would be swept away even with their plows if they had one. That river got its name in 1958 for killing so many people. We would light fires to make smoke and wave white scarves to show the pilots where we were so they could drop the food. Then in 1975 there was a terrible drought. Even in Kikuyuland bananas dried up. I went to Jane's home in Nyeri and saw banana trees dried up. They looked like someone had set them on fire. Cows were dying by the road. Normally even if there's drought in Ukambani there is always food in Kikuyuland. That's where we go to get it. But that time . . . everywhere was dry!

6. Jackson said that regional droughts were already common in Ukambani in the first half of the nineteenth century, but were relieved by buying food from Kikuyuland and temporary resettlement, often a retreat to the hills. But in the second half of the nineteenth century droughts became pervasive and happened once every five to eight years, a cycle that still seems to prevail. "An Ethnohistorical Study," p. 342.

Daily Nation, 16 January 1998, p. 1

CHAOS, AGONY IN TORRENTIAL RAINS

Many workers failed to report to work, hundreds of cars stalled as city roads were turned into waterways and homes in several estates flooded in the deluge that started on Thursday evening. . . . Most residents of the sprawling Buru Buru Estate woke up to find rain waters right at their doorsteps, as did those living in Jericho, Hamza, Madadara and Maringo estates. . . . Yesterday, most sections of Jogoo Road were submerged by the fast flowing waters. Motorists heading for the city centre drove at a snail's speed in a patience-shattering tailback. . . . [R]esidents of Greenfields estate phase six were unable to leave their houses in the morning because of the floods . . . [without wading through] waist deep water. . . . By 12 P.M. crowds of stranded school children, parents and other workers were still desperately waiting for transport. . . . Juja Road was cut off by a massive puddle near Mlango Kubwa. Hand cart owners charged a fee for those wishing to cross the road. At Jam City and Kasoito slum villages in Athi River, the makeshift structures were flattened. However, no rain-related deaths were reported in the place.

Daily Nation, 21 January 1998, p. 1

SHORTAGES LOOM AS ROADS COLLAPSE

[R]eports from various parts of the country indicated a widespread shortage of basic commodities and serious transport problems. . . . Public transport was still severely constrained and a spokesperson for Coast Line Safaris said none of their buses had left from either Mombasa or Nairobi yesterday. . . . The port received a consignment of humanitarian relief food for hundreds of people displaced by unprecedented floods in the region. The food imported by the World Food Programme includes maize, maizemeal, wheat and pulses. . . . Reports from Kilifi said the Government has started airlifting relief food and medical supplies to Ganze Division, which has been cut off for the past three months. . . . The managing director of M. A. Bayusuf Transporters, Mr. Mohammed Bayusuf, said . . . his company had introduced new charges to cover breakage, wear and tear of vehicles. He warned that shipping activities were likely to grind to a halt since none of the cargo being discharged was being transported. . . . [N]early 200 trucks transporting cargo for use in Kenya and the landlocked countries of East and Central Africa are still held up at various points along the highway. Some of them overturned, damaging the cargo. Attempts have also been made to loot some of the trailers and trucks. . . . Many tour companies have suspended visits to the Tsavo National Park . . . [so that] the game lodges . . . may be forced to close down. . . . Wote Town, the Makueni District headquarters, and its environs have been hit by an acute shortage of wheat flour, sugar and paraffin for the last three weeks because of the disruption of communication between Machakos, Emali and Wote. Most bridges leading to Wote from the Machakos/Nairobi main road have been washed away. The worst-hit areas are Kilala, Ukia, Nziu, Kaumoni, Kathonzweni and Kwa Matungu. Travellers from Emali to Wote are paying Ksh.1000 instead of the normal Ksh.180. . . . The Government donated 100 bags of maize to flood victims. . . . The Kenya Red Cross Society has also donated two lorry loads of clothes and food to the flood victims. . . . The Kenya Power and Lighting Company . . . said the heavy rains had wreaked havoc on the electricity supply system by instances of damages caused by trees falling on power line poles.

If it is not enough to have these things happen, we also have health problems. For example, let me talk about going to Kenyatta Hospital for treatment for my foot. Last week you took me, but normally I take a bus, Kenya Bus #18 from Gikomba which goes all the way there. When there is no [English] "jam" it takes a half hour, but it can take an hour to get there. I get up, pray, bathe, get dressed, and go to the hospital. We took along my cousin so he could show me to the doctor, another cousin, to look at my foot. That man is the son of

my mother's elder sister. When we found him he told them to take me to the
casualty unit. Then he went to his house. When he came back he asked me
what was wrong. I told him. He went and got a card. Without a card you won't
be treated.[7] To open a card cost Ksh.400. So the first time I opened a file. The
second time we waited in line and finally I was taken to X-ray. They took two
of them and saw that in my leg there was a vein that had been injured. The
X-ray cost Ksh.400. I had to buy medicines for Ksh.140 for the pain. They told
me to come back the next day; I was there all day from 8:30 to 4:00 P.M. to go
to the clinic. The fourth time is when I saw the doctor; I am supposed to go
back again. They are waiting to see if it gets better. They told me that if it
doesn't they will burn it with electricity. It is so painful and makes it really
difficult to walk!

And that time when I was in the hospital for nine months with tetanus!
They told me that the nail was rusty and could bring many diseases. My nails
and skin peeled off and my hair fell out. The only way I was able to know it was
night was because the lights would come on and in the morning they would
go off. I developed bedsores on my back. Today I look for the scars and wonder
where they went!

Long ago we had diseases like *ingola* [from *kingola*; to bend].[8] The only
symptom was that the sick person's neck would be twisted. You would just die
with your neck like that. I understand it was brought by rats. The sick person
would bite their tongue; the teeth would just grind together.[9] It killed a lot of
people. People in those days were foolish. They didn't know about medicines.

There was another disease that affected men's genitals. They passed pus and
blood with their urine. It is called *muluo* or *kisonono*. The men walk funny, like
this, with your legs spread far apart. If a woman sleeps with a man who has it
she will get it too and start passing pus with her urine. It can be cured with
medicine.[10]

Measles is a children's disease. There was no medicine for it, but you only
get it once. Before we would get some dirt from an anthill and mix it with a
little warm water, then apply the mud all over the child's body until he re-
sembled an anthill. As the child was sleeping some of the mud would rub off
and eventually you would notice that the rash was gone. Finally there would
not be the big scars left by the sores. Only the sores in the mouth were left.
There was also another remedy made from a tree root. We would pound the
root and squeeze the juice and give it to the child, who would get diarrhea. If
you gave a child cold milk or cold water, that's when a child died from measles. Or if they rubbed their eyes, their eyes got infected. Then the child would
start coughing. So we would take an egg and apply it to the eyes to prevent the
infection. Now people still get measles but when babies are born they are im-

---

7. In May 1998, we wanted to film Berida standing in line at Kenyatta Hospital but were not allowed to
enter by security personnel. The public relations director said that we could not enter without a card.

8. Berida's list of diseases bears comparison with Hobley's list in *Ethnology of A-Kamba*, p. 106.

9. These symptoms resemble lockjaw, or tetanus, more than bubonic plague.

10. Mbithe and I speculated that this is gonorrhea, which if untreated can cause yaws.

Daily Nation, Friday, 12 December 1997, p. 1

CITY CHOLERA TOLL INCREASES TO 29

The cholera toll in Nairobi over the past ten days rose to 29 yesterday, with 15 more deaths reported in the Korogocho slums [of eastern Nairobi]. The 15 deaths were recorded at the Provide International Centre, which caters for the poor in the slums. . . . Reports from Kitui [in Ukambani] indicated that cholera has killed 11 people in Kitui District in the last week. In Korogocho Mr. Kitheka said a child who was taken to hospital on Wednesday evening died yesterday morning. As the *Nation* interviewed Mr. Kitheka, another cholera victim was brought in on a handcart. Mr. Kitheka said the hospital was taking care of 20 cholera patients in two tents pitched in the compound while scores lay unattended in their homes. "The situation is deteriorating day after day, and, with the water shortage, the disease is spreading rapidly. . . ." Nairobi Town Clerk Zipporah Wandera said she did not know the cause of the shortage. . . . The Nairobi medical officer of health, Dr. Patrick Kirui, said, . . . "The most affected areas are Mathare, Korogocho and Mukuru." Dr. Kirui said that with the onset of the rains, the council had foreseen the outbreak of cholera and had set up a special committee to formulate control measures. The committee had gone round the city and isolated a few cases which council hospitals were handling until the nurses' strike started. He asked Nairobi residents to maintain high standards of hygiene and proper sanitation to avoid disease. Mr. Kitheka said they were finding it hard to cope with the swelling number of victims since desperate cases could not be referred to the Kenyatta National Hospital owing to the nurses' strike.

With their inadequate equipment, he said, nurses from his hospital and volunteers had been visiting the homes of victims to disinfect and advise relatives on preventive measures. "Eating places and butcheries in the slums are posing a health hazard since there is no water and the food is being handled by people already infected. Due to a shortage of beds at our hospital, cholera victims are sharing beds and out-patient victims are sharing houses with relatives," he said. Mr. Kitheka urged the city council to facilitate a free supply of water in Korogocho for some time, since many residents who cannot afford water sold by vendors are using contaminated water. . . . At Kaloleni [coast district] the area public health technician, Mr. John Karanja, . . . called on the women to help the health authorities to wipe out the epidemic. . . . He asked the women to identify cholera cases and seek assistance at the nearby mission hospital.

munized against it. So when they catch it it is not as serious. But those injections they give for it can be bad. You know that boy who spoke at my *harambee*? One of his arms is like this, all withered. He was given a measles shot badly and one of his arms became very weak. The child was sick and the mother didn't know whether it was measles or flu. He got a measles shot and his arm just swelled up. They had to suck out the medicine from his arm. The arm just withered.

Now a disease that is killing people is the chest disease, coughing. It is called TB. It kills whoever catches it.

But the worst thing now is that people are dying of *ndetema* [fever], with sores in the mouth, unable to swallow anything and complaining of headaches. They start vomiting and diarrhea follows. Then they die. You know the name of that disease [to Mbithe], even Jane knows it. It is called *ukimwi* [Kiswahili; AIDS] in Ukambani. The Kikuyu call it *mukingo* [neck]. A lot of men and women are dying from it. If you sleep with an infected man you will also catch it. That is why if you have a male friend you should stick to him;

don't go from one to another or you will die. It is everywhere, even at Kath-onzweni. I remember when that disease started. It was the year that there was a worldwide women's meeting in Nairobi. When was that? In 1985? Those women came from many different countries; among them some had the disease. Wherever there are women there will be some prostitutes. It wasn't here before in Kenya. Well, that is when Josephat Karanja [a prominent politician] died. After he died I started hearing rumors that PC Waiganjo was also suffering from that disease, and he died too [early 1990s]. After that is when I heard that the disease had spread.

So it came at that time. You could see a sick person and say, "Oh Lord!!!" You know, that person who jumped off of a building at Kenyatta Hospital the other day is better off! He had the disease. He had been examined and someone told him he had it, so he committed suicide. If you are told you have that disease, it is better to buy some drugs and commit suicide. You will never be cured. Kilaya, in your country is there a cure for AIDS? Here people cheat you. They say they will get you medicine for the disease if you give them Ksh.80,000. You can even pay Ksh.100,000 or 200,000. There is no medicine for Ksh.10. But you still die. People even have *harambees* to raise the money. But you still die. It is all useless. The best thing to avoid it is just to refuse to have sex, to not move around with many men, just stick with one partner. I feel so sad about the young people! I ask myself, why did I have my children?

My brother Antony [Moli] died from it, leaving seven children and two wives. I never really felt death, not even when my mother died. Her funeral was so big, with cars and choirs, that it felt like a wedding. I really didn't feel as if she had died. Only when Mutune and Antony died did I understand about death. Mutune died last year; he was sick with diabetes and terribly overweight. He just sickened for a long time and then he died. But Antony! I look at his picture and wonder why he had to die! He was so handsome and loved me so much. He used to call me "my sister." Before he died he gave me his watch at the hospital at Nairobi West and said, "My sister, take that watch." But that time he got better and was discharged. I didn't wear the watch, just kept it at home. After a short while I heard he was sick again and admitted to Kilimambogo [Ol Donyo Sabuk] Hospital on the way to Thika. He was head of the Post Office in Nairobi before he died. [Softly.] When he was dying I didn't feel like going there to visit him, so I called my nephew and gave him the fare to go and visit him. When he came back he told me that Antony had said I should go visit him, I shouldn't be afraid of him. I knew that if I went to see him I would just start crying. He had grown so thin! I saw people pitying him and I asked myself, "Why did I give birth?" But he got a little better and was discharged.

When he got home he asked Bernard to go get the priest to come and bless him [blessing for the sick]. The priest did so and said to him, "Antony, you have married a second wife."[11] But Antony said, "This is my wife whom I mar-

---

11. Polygyny has been a strongly contested subject in a number of churches. In this case Antony probably married his first wife by a customary ceremony rather than in a church.

AIDS

EXCERPTS FROM TAPE TRANSCRIPT
97-11-8-11

Berida: Ask her if in her country they have a cure for AIDS.

Mbithe: [Same]

Claire: All they have is a medicine that delays it. The average survival time has gone from a year to twenty months.

Mbithe: She is saying that there is no medicine to cure it. What the medicine does, before if you were told you had the disease you could live for a year, but now you can live twenty months, but a medicine to cure it completely is not available.

Berida: Do they have the disease in her country?

Mbithe: Back at home is there AIDS?

Claire: Yes.

Berida: But where did it come from originally? At least here I know it came during the women's conference.

Claire: We don't know. For a while Americans said it came from Africa. Now we don't think so. Does she know that its communication can be prevented if you use condoms, if you have protected sex? If you use condoms, you won't give it to people so often?

Berida: No, I know nothing about that. But since I won't go with anybody, I refuse to sleep with men.

Mbithe: She's saying, for her she can't even have sex with anybody. She can't agree.

Claire: But anybody who she is talking to, she should tell them to use condoms.

Mbithe: She's saying that even if you take care of yourself, when you are talking to others, you should tell them.

Berida: I have talked and talked and talked [see narrative], etc.

ried in a Christian ceremony." Then he was asked for the wedding certificate. His wife went to the cathedral in Masaku and got it. When the card was brought after a week he sent for the priest again to say a last mass for him. The priest came at about 4 P.M. They prayed and the mass was said. Then Antony said good-bye and go well to the priest. It was sundown. Somebody lit the lamp and Antony asked who had done it. He was told it was his daughter Mukonyo. Then he called his wives to come and lie down in the bed with him. He said his wife Priscilla should lie down on one side of him and his wife Wanzila[12] on the other. As soon as he said that, he died. [Strongly, with indignation.] People couldn't believe that he had died! Even his son said he only believed it when he saw the body at the mortuary. Even though my cousin who is a doctor at Kenyatta Hospital told us that Antony was going to die, we still didn't believe it. We just didn't think he was that sick. He was such a good man, so gentle, not one to annoy you. My Muthama takes after him. We have a saying, "The loss of one tooth can cause a person not to eat." [*Yeyo niyekukaa isyo ikaemea bisoni.*] After he died one of his sons was at the Polytechnic. My cousin the doctor at Kenyatta took in that son and said he would pay for his remaining education. Now he is selling dried staples at Gikomba.

You know my nephew, the one I came with to your house? That's Antony's son and his mother also has AIDS, Priscilla. I was just in Matuu to see her and she's not well at all. She has sores on her legs. That's why I was asking Kilaya if there is medicine in her country for it so she could send me drugs to help my sister-in-law. None of the children has it. I just look at her and bow my head. I say, "You'll be OK." Even at Gikomba, people are finished from it! I have talked and talked and talked to people about how to prevent it. I tell people like Jane, if you have a boyfriend who is not sick, stick with him.

---

12. This is a name given to a baby born suddenly by the road when the mother is walking somewhere.

Even if you meet a man with more money, don't get tempted. But men are worse than women about sleeping around. They have a lot of useless desire. But all women are alike. The way they are made is the same, whether they are black, Asian, or white. However, a man will see this one and think this one is different. Then he likes that one and wants to sleep with her. But as soon as he puts it there, he gets infected. I was told by my cousin at Kenyatta Hospital that a woman can have the disease for a long time without showing symptoms.

I have seen that with Antony's wife; it is four or five years since her husband died but Priscilla was looking so healthy and had put on weight. We were asking, if Antony died of AIDS, how come his wives don't seem to have it? But then she started complaining of having a fever, then headache and sore throat. She said she couldn't swallow; she had sores in her throat. She could only take milk or a little rice mixed with milk. [Softly.] I went to see her and came back here. When I got back, I called Antony's son, my nephew, and asked him, "Do you know what is the matter with your mother?" He said no. I asked him if he knew what his father had died of. I told him, "Your father gave you an education." (There are three of those kids; he is the only boy, the last-born is a girl married at Nakuru.) I told him, "Send for those people at Nakuru to bring your mother something to eat. She will soon be following her husband." I don't know how much longer she will live. Those who get good food usually survive longer than those without food. Those who have all the medicine will last longer. Priscilla is older than Wanzila and can't fight the disease; her blood is weaker. I was there on the first of June. I just looked at her [implication—couldn't believe what she was seeing]. And this was the same woman who, when she used to come to Gikomba people would just stare, she was so big! (You know, she belongs to Mbemba na Mboso.) Now she is so skinny. When I asked her how she was feeling she told me she had a fever. I asked her, "Is anything else bothering you?" She said, "No, just the fever." Her son went home yesterday. I told him to tell Priscilla that I would see her when Kilaya goes home. She has just sent a message asking why I don't go to see her. But I feel so bad just looking at her. [Softly.] She is being cared for by a maid employed by her son's wife, who is a teacher. Wanzila doesn't have the disease. She is in the cattle trade, buying and selling at Kabati and Masinga.

You can look at a person and know they have AIDS, not normal malaria. For example, my neighbor has it, my neighbor at Biafra. She's an old woman but she drinks. You hear her coming home late at night. She's my age. She is also very thin. People even ask me how I know people have it. The owner of the stall next to mine is always amazed because I am never wrong. If I say somebody has it, you just have to watch and see. I am always right. Last night my neighbor came and told me, "Berida, I feel like I have stomach ulcers. And I have sores in my mouth." I told her to go buy Vicks Kingo to suck on; it helped when I had sores in my mouth. She used to be very big but now she is so thin! Do you realize how bad that disease is? It is better to be run over by a car and die!

So many people are dying.[13] Mutune died a few years ago from the sugar disease [diabetes]. He was very big-bodied. He looked strong and he had money, but that didn't save him. Last April one of Mutune's sons died of malaria. He left a wife and three children. One of my cousins died recently, my uncle's daughter. She also died of AIDS. I used to go stay with her at her house and take care of her. I would take her to the hospital. The last time I took her one day; the next day Martha went to see her but she had died. Her employer has now hired her daughter, who has finished Form 4. That's good. I really worry about Mutinda, Martin's four-year-old. His legs aren't strong. He coughs and the sputum is black. I took him to Matuu with me and he was well fed and did better. When I am home I care for him and feed him well; there's only me to do that.

At least now we deal better with death. A long time ago, before Christianity came, a dead person used to be taken to the forest and thrown into the bushes to be eaten by hyenas. Everyone was treated the same way. If somebody was very sick and people knew he wouldn't recover, they used to take him to the forest to die and make a fire for him, leave food for him. That way he wouldn't come back to the village as a spirit [aimu[14]] after he died and get somebody else. If there was a person who was a fool in the family he would be taken to die in the forest so his spirit wouldn't come back so that no other child in the family would be ndia [foolish]. Even if a good person died, they didn't know how to bury people then. If an old person lived alone in a house and got deathly sick, they would just be left to die and decompose in their house. Everybody else moved out and the house was called a tomb. It was left to fall down. Wherever there was death people were scared of that home. They wouldn't go there for fear of catching death.[15]

The system we have now is better. We bury people in a nice way. We love our dead and so we show respect even when they are dead. Now a person is taken to the mortuary after they die. There are freezers there. Then announcements are made [on the radio] so that his people may know to come. Then we buy a coffin and remove the body from the mortuary and bury it. We lower the coffin with care into the grave and we don't throw the soil directly on it. We put a sheet of corrugated iron on top first. Also, the coffin is made of a kind

13. In December 1998 Berida's family was struck again by tragedy with the death of Berida's oldest surviving son, Dominic ("Jimmy"), from a combination of tuberculosis and typhoid. Berida then began an effort to pay the school fees for two of his children.

14. Lindblom called aimu "malicious" spirits, but they seem rather to have been ancestral spirits that could be malicious but were not always that way, the equivalent of ghosts. African religions frequently include a belief in the mediating role played by ancestral spirits with god/s. Veneration and respect for the aged is/was often connected to their proximity to the status of ancestral spirit. Lindblom, The Akamba in British East Africa, p. 35.

15. According to Hobley, the bodies of poor people and women were left in the bush, but chiefs merited a deep grave. Ethnology of A-Kamba, p. 66. Joseph Muthiani stated that "in former days" only men and the first wives of polygynists were buried, which may represent an intermediate stage. Akamba from Within, pp. 103–104. By the 1920s the government was forcing people to bury the deceased for health reasons. H. S. Mwaniki, The Living History of Embu and Mbeere to 1906 (Nairobi: East African Literature Bureau, 1973), p. 101.

of wood that won't be eaten by ants. Everybody does it that way, not just Christians. But the WaSwahili here in Majengo don't bury the dead in coffins. They just carry them on a stretcher and when they get to the grave, they just flip the body into it and cover it with soil.

When I look at the future I don't think about death. I have some goals I want to accomplish. What I want is to buy some land for my sons, but how to get the money is a problem. I really live at Kathonzweni and only visited Nairobi because my work was needed to pay the school fees. Last year was bad with no good rains. I want to stay at home in Kathonzweni and open a new shop that I will build along the tarmac when the paved road reaches there. I will build a kiosk the size of this table where I will sell provisions, cooking oil, sugar, salt, flour, etc. The schoolchildren will buy from it. Since there is no life in Nairobi, my life will be there, or maybe I will leave Martin in charge of it. I will train him; what else can I do with him? He's just staying at home with no job. I have already talked to the owner about purchasing the land for it. He wants Ksh.17,000 for it. That one Ndambuki won't take from me. I would like a peaceful home. I know God created me to be a peaceful person, but then I got a quarrelsome husband. I like to live with my children in peace. If as a family we can do things together, then we can get somewhere.

When I think about what I have accomplished, I know that I have done my best for my family. I have put effort into whatever I do. I have worked very hard. During my life I was happy until my husband started drinking beer. He loves me but drink turns him into a *bhang* user. Talk makes nothing; he talks nonsense like "Bitter water, bitter water like a tablecloth." Pray for us so we can overcome these things. What has made me happiest in my life is that God gave me my life for free and my children without my asking, so I feel contented with life. Aren't you grateful for your children, they are gifts from God? I asked God to give me the ability to support my children, since he gave me a husband who can't support them. We had nothing, not even a *sufuria* [Kiswahili; metal pot] in which to make tea. I used to make it in a clay pot. The children were naked. I would go home and find chaos sometimes; I turned around and came back to Nairobi so I wouldn't be beaten. When I look at my life, with all the problems I have had I could have committed suicide. I did not; I persevered. When I reached the point in my life where I could clothe and feed my children and they could look and dress like other people's children, then I was very happy.

I pray to God and ask for perseverance. I cross myself and pray for strength. Getting old is a terrible thing. I feel bad when I think about it. When one gets old, one becomes useless and even a matter for the curiosity of children. There are even some who come and watch me all the time at my room. In fact, I had rather die than get old. I have become a *mutumba,* a grandmother.

Are there lessons to be learned from my life? If there is a lesson from my life, it is that wives and husbands should live together in harmony, sit and eat together and build a home together. I would like to have a good family and not quarrel with Ndambuki all the time. I have told you all these stories, Kilaya, so that you will teach and maybe one of your students will hear them and emerge as a leader. My message to people in the U.S. is that you have helped us a lot and please continue the help. We have lots of problems; pray for us so we can overcome them.

Update and Analysis: 1999

In July 1999 I returned to Nairobi and found that, like Nairobi itself, whose skyline changes constantly with the addition of glossy skyscrapers built by corrupt government officials, Berida's life and family had also experienced a number of changes, generally not for the good. In Domitila's house in eastern Nairobi the conversation centered on the financial plight of Kenya and of the family, while a collection of nephews and sons were erecting a wall outside to improve security, an ever-increasing concern. The sudden death of Dominic in December 1998 had shocked everyone, including Ndambuki, who stopped drinking. Berida felt this was permanent, a change for the better but not a compensation for Dominic's death. However, Muthama had lost his job as a *matatu* conductor; his wife's teaching job now supports the family. Martin Wambua was in Mombasa looking for work. Angelina Ndinda had recovered physically from the severe beating by her (ex-?) husband but had gone into a severe mental depression verging on insanity. She moved back to Kathonzweni, leaving her three children to be cared for by Maggie in Nairobi, with the assistance of Mwenye, Monica's daughter. Maggie also recovered but then required surgery to remove a lump in her breast. The Kenyatta Hospital surgeon missed the lump on the first try so another surgery may be required, which she is putting off because she cannot afford it or the time away from her beauty salon job. Maggie is overwhelmed by the support of Angelina's children and Mwenye, and with helping Dominic's family. Dominic's wife earns no cash and his four children require school fees. Therefore, of Berida's nine surviving children, all adults, only two are helping the family with their earnings in 1999, Martha[1] and Maggie, no sons. In 1998 there were five earners.

The difference is catastrophic, added to by Berida's own retirement from business at age 63 due to problems with walking and her desire to stay at Kathonzweni. She spends as much time there as possible, leaving her Gikomba stall to Martha. Corruption in the NCC has resulted in publicly owned land at Gikomba being sold to developers. Berida predicts that when they try to build on it there will be bloodshed. The overt, shameless rapacity of high government officials sets the tone all down the line so that there is no expenditure on infrastructure like hospitals, roads, and schools. The economy is faltering severely and unemployment is pervasive. Even at banks small accounts are pillaged by employees, while officials and businessmen sell public school and market lands and pocket the profits. The chief challenge of development is outwitting extortionate government officials.

Kenya's strengths are a creative, energetic, and hardworking peasantry with its urban counterpart, as well as the persistent idealism and honesty of those

---

1. Martha's earnings go mainly to support her own children, however.

who work for constructive change. Its weaknesses are greed and dishonesty in pursuit of profit, the willingness at the highest levels to destroy the country's integrity and well-being for the purpose of self-enrichment, the victimization of those who at base keep the economy going, and the poverty caused by all of the above. In the last ten years there has been a seismic increase in the pervasive lack of responsible social conscience throughout the society. The struggles of Berida and her family become ever more difficult, materially worsened by a government that preys upon the people for whose benefit it should govern.

Claire Robertson
July 1999

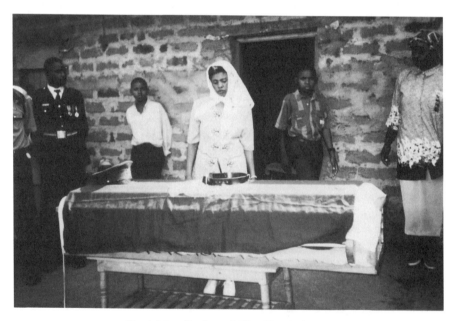

Dominic's police funeral: His widow and sons

Postscript

Our Relations: On Friendship and Cross-Cultural (Mis)understanding

Throughout the taping we often asked Berida if she had questions for us and she took the opportunity to ask some when they occurred to her. Below are excerpts from the transcripts of the longer exchanges that demonstrate her interests and our relationship very well. Berida's ability to pinpoint some of the irrationalities of U.S. life is noteworthy. Mbithe's input in the second excerpt also gives us the experiences and views of a Kenyan who has lived temporarily in the United States. Unlike what I have done in the rest of this narrative, I have put the excerpts in chronological order, which helps to demonstrate the reorganization involved in the editing. I have also included here as the first excerpt an example of a narrative that was relatively uninterrupted but that was too long (much longer than I included here) to be a sidebar. In order to create fluent conversation the tape transcriber in this case (and some others) omitted many translations of English to Kikamba and vice versa, despite instructions to the contrary.

Example of a Narrative Uninterrupted Except
for Translation and Occasional Questions

Excerpt from tape transcript 97-2-1-4 (included in text in chapter 3)

C. Today is the tenth of July, 1997, Thursday. Back to the cows. [We ran out of time the day before.]

M. Yesterday we talked about the cow being bought at Ksh.800, do you remember?

B. Yes, the one I took to Athi River was bought [from me] at Ksh.800; the one that was taken to Mombasa was condemned or rather rejected. It was bought at Ksh.4 yet it had been bought at Ksh.170. Even today I have never asked for the Ksh.4.

With the Ksh.800 I bought 3 more cows at Ksh.200 each. The other Ksh.200 I kept in my pocket. When I took those cows they were bought at Ksh.3,000.55. After that I went to a place called Simba and bought 10 cows at Ksh.900 and one of the cows died. I took the 9 cows to Mombasa and sold them at Ksh.15,000.

M. Which year was that?

B. In 1975. Then the drought ended and there was rain and so the Maasai stopped selling their cows. Now my house at home had collapsed, due to the rains. I went home to build a house. I arranged for bricks to be made and I used all the money in building. So I started farming. From my produce I got one bag of cowpeas [*thoroko*] which I came with to Gikomba. At that time the 2-kilogram tin of cowpeas was costing Ksh.2.50.

C/M. Were there other Kamba women who came to sell with her?

B. Yes.

M. Were you traveling with them in search of what to sell?

B. No, everyone went on their own; it was not group work.

M. Did you come alone?

B. Yes, and when I had sold the bag I got Ksh.250. Then I went back home with that money. I sold 3 bags of cowpeas and got Ksh.700. After that I heard that in Uganda the variety of bean called *rose coco* was being traded at sh.2 for the 2-kilogram tin in Malaba. So we went and brought the beans which we could sell at sh.28 for the 2-kilogram tin. Then I was approached by an Asian called Kalani [or Karani] who wanted to know whether I could do business on a large scale. I said if I had money I could do it. So he gave me Ksh.2,000 and I went and bought 19 bags of beans which included *rose coco, nyayo,* and *gathika.* Karani bought all 19 bags for Ksh.30,000. Then I went back to Malaba and then we were arrested because we did not have a permit to buy foodstuffs. Since we were many we decided to send a delegation to President Moi at his Kabarnet home so that he could assist us. We were not able to see him since his guards referred us back to Bungoma to see the Senior Superintendant of Police, by the name of Nzau. We went to see Nzau, who referred us to Mulu Mutisya [currently the Machakos KANU branch chairman. He is a veteran politician who has risen to the highest ranks in politics although he is illiterate. He is said to be a close ally of the President.] We went to look for Mulu Mutisya in Nairobi. We told him what our grievances were. Mulu requested his secretary to call the District Office (DO) of Busia. We waited at Mulu's office until 7 P.M. in the evening. I was called by Mulu Mutisya into his office when the telephone call came through. I listened as Mulu asked the DO why the people had been arrested while they were buying food to take to Ukambani where there is famine and hunger. Mulu instructed the DO that he should release the confiscated food to the traders. We were from many areas including Maasais, Kikuyus.

M. Had you gone there with these people?

B. No, everyone went on their own but we met there buying the food. There was drought and famine. Because that was where food was available. The DO agreed to release the food the following day at 9 A.M. on condition that we carry our identity cards with us to Malaba. Mulu was kind enough to request a bus to take us to Malaba overnight. A bus from the Akamba Public Road Services took us to Malaba and we got our food back. We sold the food and then we would go back for more. If one of us did not have their identity card they would borrow it from a friend to enable them to go buy the food. The demand for the food was very high indeed. We could arrive at 6 A.M. from Malaba and by 8 A.M. we had already sold all the food. People were coming from all over Ukambani to buy the food, also from Murang'a, Thika, and Kitui.

M. Where were you selling?

B. Just here at Gikomba.

C/M. Were you selling only beans or were there other foodstuffs?

B. We sold beans and some kind of Kikuyu peas which we referred to by their Ugandan name. We also sold green grams [mung beans]. We could also smuggle in clothes, shoes, especially *kitenge* type of clothes. For the shoes what we did was that one removed one's old shoes and crossed the border bare-footed, then bought the shoes and put them on and made several trips [across the border] if you needed more than one pair. Because the Kenyan government was not allowing goods from Uganda in. If you needed to buy *kangas* from Uganda then you could cross the border with no *kanga*, buy *kangas* in Uganda, and wrap them around yourself and pretend that they are yours. This is how we smuggled in the goods from Uganda. Once you have bought as much as you need then you can board a vehicle to Nairobi.

J. Where did you sell the Uganda wares?

B. At Gikomba also. By this time I had made some amount of money and I decided to go home.

C/M. What about the Ksh.2,000 you had been given by the Asian?

B. I refunded it to him when I brought the foodstuffs that I sold to him. He deducted his money. So I went home with money with the plan of building a shop and selling at home.

Excerpt from tape transcript 97-3-3-5

Berida: I don't get tired of talking because I spend the whole day talking at the market. [Laughter.] Since Kilaya sent Jane to me a while back to ask if I was willing to spend as much time as the research requires.

Berida [to Jane and Mbithe]: Let's talk about money later. Stick to business here.

[Interruption: tea is brought by church staff—a daily courtesy that was much appreciated.]

Berida: Why do you [Claire] not take milk in your tea?

Jane: She went and lived where there was no milk; after that she could not digest milk any more.

Berida: She should eat the food they are offering. Are there cows at your home? Are there farms? How do you cultivate?

Claire: Yes, there are cows and we have large farms and use tractors to cultivate.

Berida: Are there poor people?

Claire: Yes, many, very many. There are people who are homeless. Everywhere where there are big towns such people exist.

Berida: Why?

Claire: Because many people do not want to pay good wages or taxes to support the poor.

Berida: You mean there are people who sleep in the open?

Claire: Yes, that is true.

Berida: Is there space to build?

Claire: There are many buildings with no people in them even.

Berida: Then why don't those who sleep in the open sleep there?

Claire: Because the government has condemned [the buildings] and does not consider them fit for humans to live in. But the poor do break in and sleep inside, but it is dangerous.

Berida: Now, these homeless people, is it because they cannot use their hands and work and get money?

Claire: Many of them can't get employment because they have mental problems and were probably institutionalized and were released to go home when those hospitals were closed down. Some forgot to take their medicine that has been prescribed for them, and so they are crazy. The institutions which used to take care of them were closed down because people do not want to pay the taxes to support such projects. They believe that these people can simply take medicine while at their homes and support themselves.

Berida: Can these poor people farm?

Claire: It might not be possible because the farms are operated on a large scale and in many cases these people live in the urban areas. These poor people are not able to meet their needs and it is a very sad situation.

Berida: Is the cost of things very high there?

Claire: That is the problem. The cost of rent is very high. However, there were houses poor people could afford but sometimes the city planners pull down such houses and rebuild better ones which the poor cannot afford. So they are gradually pushed into homelessness, even whole families. And many of them even have jobs but those jobs don't pay enough to afford housing and child care.

Berida: Isn't there a government which can intervene to help these poor?

Claire: Well, the government is trying but not doing very well. Recently it has passed a new welfare bill that has raised a lot of criticism since it demands that anyone who is on welfare assistance must work, no matter what their condition. Many people think that this will cause a lot of misery and it is very sad. Many children won't have adequate child care.

Berida: But I hear that those people give birth to only two or three children.

Claire: Some people do have many children. Poor people sometimes have more children.

Berida: That is true; the poor have more children even in Kenya. The husband forces his wife to have sex.

Claire: Sometimes the government aid encourages people to have more children because you get more money that way.

Berida: Are there rich people?

Claire: Oh yes, many, but there are more who are in the middle.

Berida [to Mbithe and Jane]: Claire is very respected here, and people think that she is very rich.

Claire: Not really. But I think people should be respected regardless of whether they are rich or poor.

Berida: I personally also respect her, Kilaya, and consider her as my child; even at Gikomba the people usually tell me when they see her that "your child has come." [Laughter.]

Claire: Does she have any questions for us?

Berida: I have many questions about where she comes from. Do black people go there to their country?

Claire: Yes, there are many black people in the U.S.

Berida: I would like to go there too.

Claire: The problem that hurts black people in the U.S. is that their ancestors were taken there as slaves by white people.

Berida: You mean the slaves were taken to the U.S.? Then they must have become citizens there? In fact, there was a Maasai who came from the U.S. dressed like a Maasai with beads and ornaments. He was so huge, everybody at Gikomba just stopped what they were doing when they saw him, and he had three white wives. A university lecturer. Didn't any of you read about it in the newspapers?

Jane and Mbithe: No.

Claire: Because of the fact that blacks used to be slaves some white people look down on them as inferior. This makes it very difficult for the blacks to get good jobs. So actually in terms of proportion of the population, there are more black people who are poor. Blacks are about 11–12 percent of the population, but they form about 40 percent of the poor. So the proportion of blacks who are poor is large.

Berida: Do these slaves know English? Do they even know their homes?

Claire: Yes, they know English and they no longer are slaves. Most of them don't know where their ancestors came from in Africa but a few have done research and tried to trace their roots. Some of the earliest immigrants were black.

EXCERPT FROM TAPE TRANSCRIPT 97-4-13-15

Berida: When you were in the U.S. [to Mbithe] how was it?

Mbithe: It was nice.

Berida: How nice?

Mbithe: Just nice.

Berida: You know, somebody says it was nice—I saw this, I saw that compared to her home. Or you were not moving about?

Mbithe: What I can say is that the church people were very good and helpful. There were many people from different countries who had come to study [in California].

Berida: So you had gone to the church?

Mbithe: No, [my husband] had gone to study.

Claire: It can get very cold there.

Jane: Colder than it was yesterday?

Mbithe: Where you come from does it snow?

Claire: It can be below 0 degrees centigrade.

Jane [to Berida]: It is worse than the cold you felt at Namanga.

Berida: Until you have to wear socks?

Claire/Mbithe: Yes, you wear socks, boots, heavy coats which have feathers in them.

Berida: In the churches there do they have electricity?

Mbithe: Yes.

Berida: Where were you sleeping [to Mbithe]?

Mbithe: In a house.

Berida: How many tribes [Kiswahili; *kabila*] were there?

Mbithe: Many people from all over the world.

Berida: What were you eating?

Mbithe: There is rice, chicken. But things are very expensive. I was wishing I was at home and my mother would bring me some tomatoes from here. I used to send for millet flour and tea from Kenya by my father-in-law.

Berida: You mean things were expensive?

Claire/Mbithe: California is very expensive.

Berida: I know rice comes from there; there is yellow maize and what kind of greens?

Claire/Mbithe: Many people leave their countries to go to the U.S. to try to get rich. They may make a lot of money but they also spend a lot because of the cost of living.

Berida: Really?

Claire/Mbithe: So they become very angry because they are not getting rich.

Berida: People go to the U.S./abroad to get rich? Me, I would like to see the land.

Claire/Mbithe: Well, the maize plants are bigger than this [demonstration].

Berida: Yes, they are bigger and yellow.

Claire/Mbithe: The soil is very good but if you need to have a farm it should be over 360 acres.

Berida: [Whistles] One farm?

Mbithe: Yes, if you want to make a profit from farming.

Berida: Where would I get such a lot of land?

Claire: If you use tractors it won't cost so much to operate the farm. They are farmed using machines.

Berida: Who harvests the food?

Claire: Machines. If I get some photos showing machines harvesting I will bring them and show you. There is a machine that does most of the things. Well, you have a tractor, but you have different equipment that you attach to the tractor to do different tasks. First you have the plow, then the planter, then the cultivator, weeder, and harvester. The harvester knocks the corn down, takes the ears off, and shreds the corn off the ears and you have a truck alongside the machine. The machine has a big tube that comes out and the corn kernels come out of that tube into the truck. So in the end you have one machine that does everything.

Berida: The white man is clever.

Excerpt from tape transcript 97-13-1

Claire [to tape recorder]: Today is the eighteenth of July and we have here Jane, Berida, Mbithe, and myself. [Interrupted]

Berida: I am very grateful to her because she helped me with my money problem. I was not doing this work for her so she could give me money.

Claire: Also tell her that Jane's pay is because you [to Jane] helped me after I left; you wrote me and I asked you questions and you wrote back. So it will be the same this time. If I have a question I will send Jane to ask her. She is spending her time here. She can't sell her things.

Berida: I take Jane like my own daughter. I know she has a child to feed. And I don't work for Kilaya so that she can pay me money. She can give me whatever she wants when she leaves. God determined that we should meet and stop worrying about money.

EXCERPTS FROM TAPE TRANSCRIPT 97-16-1, 37-38

(IN THIS CASE THE TRANSCRIBER FOLLOWED INSTRUCTIONS
AND INDICATED THE LANGUAGE WHICH THE PERSON WAS SPEAKING)

Mbithe (E): She said, even if you look at the ladies who have aged, the ones who don't eat properly, they look older than you are.

Claire (E): I eat properly.

Mbithe (Ka): She says she eats properly.

Berida (Ka) Even in her country, people of her age who don't eat properly, if she looks at them she'll see that they are weak.

Mbithe (E): She's saying if you look back home at the people your age who don't eat properly, they are very weak.

Berida (Ka): If she looks at people in her country who don't eat well, their bodies are in bad shape and they look old.

Mbithe (E): The people who don't eat properly, their bodies are not good and they are weak.

Claire (E): That's right.

Berida (Ka): Are there people like that in her country?

Mbithe (Ka): Like what?

Berida (Ka): People without enough food to eat.

Mbithe (E): She is asking if in your country there are some people who don't have enough food?

Claire (E): Yeah [Sw] *Ndiyo.*

Mbithe (Ka): Yes, they are there.

Berida (Ka): You can see a person who is still young, but s/he looks like a [Sw] *gunia* [gunny sack].

Mbithe (E): She's saying they look like a sack.

• • •

Berida (Ka): Since she left her country to do this job, just like I travel to buy food and if I don't get what I am looking for then I'm unhappy, she must do the job that brought her here.

Claire (E): OK, I want to ask some stuff about names. Two things about it. When I write this book, does she want me to use the exact names of all the people? But a possibility is, I can give her another name to disguise whom we're talking of. It is her choice. I can disguise the place too.

Mbithe (Ka): She's saying there are two ways she can write the book. If you don't want people to know whose story this is, she can give you a different name and use different names for the children too. So nobody would know it's your story. Or she can use everyone's real names.

Berida (Ka): Will the book be used in her country or here?

Claire (E) Both places.

Mbithe (Ka): In her country and here. So if you want her to use different names you can tell her so.

Berida (Ka): You know, people will hear the story of Berida and Ndambuki. If he had become good, would I be talking about him like this?

Mbithe (Ka): So what do you want her to do?

Berida (Ka): Let her use our real names. If he hears about it he might even get ashamed and change.

Mbithe (E): She says use real names. Because Ndambuki might hear about the book and even change.

EXCERPT FROM TAPE TRANSCRIPT 98-1-43-48[1]

Berida: Are there cocks that crow at Kilaya's place?

Mbithe (E): Do you have any cocks that crow to tell you the time?

Claire: Yeah, but they are all in a place where no one hears them. [Laughter.]

Mbithe (Ka): All the cocks are kept in a place where they can't be heard by anybody.

Berida: Where are they kept?

Mbithe (Ka): They are kept on a very big farm.

Berida: No, she can't hear them crow.

Mbithe (Ka): They are not kept near where people live.

Berida: You mean she doesn't have any at home?

Mbithe (E): She is asking if you keep chickens at your home.

Claire: No, I don't have a farm.

Berida: What does she keep?

Mbithe (E): Which animals do you have there?

Claire: One dog.

Berida: Only one dog. [Laughter.]

Jane (E): She doesn't have a farm.

Mbithe (Ka): She doesn't have a farm.

Berida: She doesn't have a farm?

Mbithe (E): We are telling her you don't have a farm.

Berida: Do you live in a town?

Mbithe (E): Do you live in town?

Claire: Yes!

Berida: And when you need to go upcountry, where do you go?

Mbithe (E): And when you need to go upcountry where do you go?

Claire: I don't.

Mbithe (Ka): She doesn't go upcountry.

Claire: I may travel from one town to another.

Berida: But she told me they have farms.

Mbithe (E): She remembers that time you told her you have big farms.

Claire: We used to own a farm but we sold it.

---

1. In this transcription, unless otherwise specified Claire is speaking English and Berida is speaking Kikamba.

Mbithe (Ka): They used to have a farm but they sold it.

Berida: So they stay in town. What do they eat?

Mbithe (E): If you live in town, what do you eat?

Claire: The stuff we buy at the store.

Mbithe (Ka): They buy food from the shop. [Laughter.]

Berida: It must be expensive?

Mbithe (E): Is it expensive?

Claire: Yeah.

Mbithe (Ka): Yes, it is expensive.

Berida: At their place how much is one kilo of rice?

Mbithe (E): How much is a kilo of rice?

Claire: That is not expensive; it is one of the cheapest foods you can buy, but maybe not by Kenyan standards. It is about Ksh.120.

Mbithe (Ka): She says rice is among the cheapest foods and one kilo is about Ksh.120.

Berida: One kilo?

Mbithe (Ka): Yes.

Berida: Do they eat maize flour, Jogoo brand?

Mbithe (E): Do you use maize meal/cornmeal at home?

Claire: Yes, for making cornbread.

Mbithe (Ka): She says they use it to make something which is cooked using an oven.

Berida: What do they cook with the yellow maize?

Mbithe (E): What about the yellow corn? What do you cook with the yellow corn?

Claire: Cornbread.

Mbithe (Ka): They grind it into flour and make cornbread. I will bring some for you since I know how they make it. It looks like bread.

Berida: Is it made from the yellow maize?

Mbithe (Ka): Yes.

Berida: When they had brought us the yellow maize in 1963 we would pound it in a mortar and pestle and the covering would come off nicely. Then we would cook it with beans.

Mbithe (E): In 1963 when they got the corn from the U.S. they would pound it like *muthokoi* and then cook it the same way.

Berida: Then we knew that America was the one helping us.

Mbithe (E): That is when they knew Americans were the ones helping them.

Claire: Does she know how to swim?

Mbithe (Ka): Do you know how to swim in the water?

Berida: No, let her take us to Mombasa for a swim and let's go by airplane so that I can know how one feels when flying. [Laughter.]

Mbithe (E): She doesn't know how to swim and she is actually saying, "Why don't you fly us to Mombasa so that she can taste how one feels when flying?" [Laughter.]

Berida: I wanted to see her coming from the airplane.

Youngest son, Martin, presents gift to youngest son, Iain, 1998

Mbithe (E): She is saying actually yesterday what she wanted was to see you coming from the airplane.

Berida: I was looking very carefully as I thought that I would see her as she came from the plane.

Mbithe (E): She actually thought that as you would be coming from the plane she would be able to see you.

Claire: Actually, in most airports you can.

Mbithe (E): Yeah. Even here we used to long ago.

Berida: Let me ask her, do her parents stay in the same town?

Mbithe (E): She wonders if your Mom and Dad live in town.

Claire: They are dead.

Mbithe (Ka): Both have died.

Berida: She doesn't have parents?

Mbithe (E): Both of them?

Claire: Yes.

Berida: They are not there? But didn't they leave other children behind? Does Kilaya have brothers and sisters?

Mbithe (E): Do you have siblings?

Claire: Yes, two sisters.

Mbithe (Ka): She has two sisters.

Berida: Sisters?

Mbithe (Ka): Yes.

Berida: Where are they?

Mbithe (E): Where are they?

Claire: One is in Florida and one is in Paris.

Mbithe (Ka): One is in France and the other in America.

Berida: Was that where she was going in France?

Mbithe (E): Where you came through?

Claire: Yeah, that's right.

Berida: And now at her place do they have a place upcountry?

Mbithe (E): She says like Nairobi is a town while Kathonzweni is a reserve, in the country. In America do you have some people in town and others in a rural setting?

Claire: Yeah.

Mbithe (Ka): Yes, there are.

Claire: But usually you are not in a rural setting unless you own a farm.

Mbithe (Ka): She says there is no reserve if you don't have a farm. And you know, they don't have a farm.

Berida: Like on the card she sent me there was a picture of flowers. Are these flowers in the town or are they wild?

Mbithe (E): She says you sent a card to her with photographs of flowers. Were these flowers in town or in the forest?

Claire: Those are probably in town but there are flowers in the forest.

Mbithe (Ka): Those ones are in town but there are still others which are in the forest.

Berida: Are those the plants you have at home?

Mbithe (E): Are those the plants you have at home?

Claire: Yeah.

Berida: What do they call those plants in her language? [Laughter.]

Mbithe (E): What is the name of the species of flowers you sent to her?

Claire: I don't remember; I would have to see them.

Mbithe (Ka): She doesn't remember. She would have to look at them so that she can remember.

Claire: When she brings it.

Mbithe (Ka): Bring it then she will tell you.

Berida: Oh, I will bring it.

Mbithe (Ka): Have you finished your questions?

Berida (Ka): [laughing] Yes, let her ask me now but I haven't finished.

Mbithe (E): I am asking her if she will let you ask questions. She says yes but she hasn't finished her questions.

Claire: [Laughs.] It is fine.

EXCERPTS FROM TAPE TRANSCRIPT 98-2-1, 4

Berida: Ask her why she didn't bring the book she has written about me.

Mbithe (E): She is asking if you wrote a book about her, why haven't you brought the book to her?

Berida: So that somebody can be reading it for me.

Mbithe (E): So that somebody can be reading it for her. (Ka): The book is the one which made her come. It is this one. I will read it to you while she is here.

Berida: I saw another one when we began the first day; it is with Jane [the *Trouble* book].

Mbithe (E): She says she saw Jane with another book. Why didn't she get the first one so somebody can be reading it to her?

Berida: I saw myself there, even wearing another scarf I had worn during my mother's funeral.

Mbithe (E): She says she saw her photograph there which has the scarf she was using during her mother's funeral.

Berida: Is it that one?

Mbithe (Ka): Yes it is.

Berida: Aii! [unbelieving]

Mbithe (Ka): It is the one, see for yourself.

Berida: Bring it, I will see if it is the one [going through the book].

Claire: Can she find it?

Berida: Is it this one, Jane?

· · ·

Claire: Let me show her the photo. I know where it is.

Berida: Where is Berida in this book? [Claire finds picture and shows it to her.] Now, this is the scarf that was for my mother's funeral.

Mbithe (E): She is saying this is the scarf she used for her mother's funeral. (Ka): But when was this dress made?

Claire: I think that is a nice picture.

Jane (E): She is saying, when was the dress made?

Mbithe (Ka): When was this dress made?

Berida: It is very old.

Mbithe (E): She says that the dress is very old.

Berida: It used to be a cloth for sleeping on but it became so worn out and slippery that I could not sleep on it, so I took it and made a dress out of it. [Laughs.]

Mbithe (E): It was usually a sheet she used to sleep on but it was so slippery that she decided to make it into a dress, the dress she is wearing.

Claire: Oh yes, this one. [Laughs.]

Berida: When I came to Nairobi is when I bought it and it looked very beautiful.

Mbithe (E): She bought it when she came to Nairobi.

Berida: Don't close that page!

Mbithe (Ka): Give it to Claire! [Laughter, tug of war.]

Berida: Why should I give it to Kilaya? Which page was it? Don't I know these numbers?

EXCERPT FROM TAPE TRANSCRIPT 98-17-22

Mbithe (E): She said she was asked, Where did you find Kilaya so you could become friends? Then she answered it, Kilaya was brought to me by God. [Laughter.]

Berida: How did God bring her to me?

Mbithe (E): [Same]

Berida and Muthama present a *kyondo* to Claire at Gikomba, 1988

Domitila, Berida's sister, and Claire dance at Kathonzweni, 1998

Berida: I was sitting there, then I saw her standing there taking pictures.

Mbithe (E): She says she was sitting at her stall then she saw you standing somewhere taking a photograph.

Berida: She was with Jane.

Mbithe (E): You were with Jane.

Berida: So they left there and went walking around Gikomba then Jane marked me.

Mbithe (E): Then you and Jane went to walk around Gikomba and you told Jane, "Go and call that old lady for me, that mama."

Berida: When they went there near Akamba Arts, she asked Jane to come and call me.

Mbithe (E): You went to Akamba Arts; you stood there and you told Jane, "Go and call that mama for me."

Claire: I did?!!

Berida: Then I went. [Laughter.]

Claire: So I would never have called her an old lady because she is near my age.

Mbithe (Ka): She says she would never have called you an old mama because you are nearly age-mates.

Berida: Hey! This is a child!

Mbithe: She's saying that you are a child. [Laughter.]

Berida: This is a child, isn't she?

Mbithe (Ka): Yes.

Berida: Anyone seeing Kilaya. . . . I heard that she went back to her country where her skin was peeled. [Laughter.]

Mbithe (E): They are saying you actually went for a facial whereby they peeled off your top skin . . .

Claire: Hey! [Laughter.]

Mbithe (E): And had plastic surgery.

Berida: You are a smaller person than who was here.

Claire: It's because I changed my hair or something.

Mbithe (Ka): She says it's only the hair she changed.

Berida: And her head is satisfied?

Mbithe (Ka): She says she's satisfied.

Berida: She is looking good. People will look at her and not realize it is her.

Mbithe (E): People have said that they can't believe it's the same person!

Berida: That is why she decided to be injected with the drug that makes one thin. Yes.

Mbithe (E): [Laughter.] She's said that you went home and they gave you some injectable . . . [C. laughs] those injectables that make you become smaller. . . . And you look younger, you've just become a child. [Laughter.]

Jane (E): Where does she collect those stories and we're always with her and we drop her at home?

Mbithe (Ka): Where do you gather such stories and we're usually with you and drop you at home?

Berida: Like now, they will say, why don't you go and be given whatever it is by the white, you eat there.

Mbithe (E): Like now, she was coming then she was told, go and be given by the white person and you eat it there.

Berida: They would tell me to give them what I have been given by the white. I said, she gave me a pound (Ksh.20) and no, let's drink tea.

Mbithe (E): So they told her, give us what the white lady has given you. She said you had given her a pound. So she bought milk and you drank tea. [Laughter.]

Berida: I tell them the white lady can give me something when she is leaving but she can't give it to you.

Mbithe (E): She says that you give her something when you are going home but you don't give them anything.

Claire: If Berida can let me get a word in edgewise here? [Laughter.]

Mbithe (Ka): Let her talk.

Claire: We are at St. John's for the last time and you [transcriber] might want to translate every word she says. It's the 20th of May. Mbithe is here, Jane is here, I'm here, and Berida is here and this is the last day we are going to work on the manuscript. We're going to start to work on the manuscript after a couple of questions like, why does she think I'm doing this book? This is a good question Mbithe came up with.

Mbithe (Ka): Your first question is, why do you think Claire is writing this book?

Berida: I can't tell, maybe it's a book—teaching guide, or . . .

Mbithe (E): She says she doesn't really know why you are writing . . . [laughter] either you are writing for satisfaction or your reason for writing.

Claire: OK, I'll tell her my reason; I have several reasons.

Mbithe (Ka): She has many reasons to write.

Claire: OK, one is . . .

Berida [interrupts]: And what are they? She doesn't tell me.

Mbithe (Ka): She will tell you.

Berida: Ooh.

Claire: One reason is for instruction so that people can see, especially in American schools, and understand about the life of a Kenyan woman who is not a rich person but also not a desperately poor person. An ordinary Kenyan person, and see what her life is, and understand it, so those American children can become better people.

Mbithe (Ka): Her first reason is to teach children in America and show them not a rich and equally not a poor woman, but an ordinary person. When they learn that they will be better people.

Berida: I knew, I knew that she wanted a story [exultantly]. And I volunteered myself to give her what she wanted.

Mbithe (E): She says that she realized it's a story you wanted and she offered herself so she would help you in whatever you needed.

Claire: Well, she's done a very good job.

Mbithe (Ka): You have done well.

• • •

Claire: Well, [the book] can't be [sold] until it is done, until she has approved of it. . . . I can't . . .

Mbithe (Ka): She has to think twice. There's not going to be a book until you permit it.

Berida: My heart just liked her and I took her like my child, mother.

Mbithe (E): Her heart really liked you and she took you as her child.

Claire (E): Another reason why I'm doing it is because if there is any money from it, I want that money to help her.

Mbithe (Ka): Another reason for writing the book is if there is money that will come from it, then the money would be used in helping you. That's the second reason.

Berida: And it is the reason I did it . . . [laughter in the background] because the children one bears can drain a lot and my children don't have education. I knew, at least, let me give birth to a child in America.

Mbithe (E): She gave herself to tell the story because when you give birth to children, sometimes they go and change and within herself she decided to have a daughter in America. [Laughter.]

Berida: Because Kilaya was given to me by God and the God who created me and created her knew that at a certain time we would meet.

Mbithe (E): God looked for you. He brought you to her and the God who created you and created her, we usually say God gave birth, knew that one day you would meet and you saved her because her children don't have education.

Berida: And when she came to Kenya she saw a lot of women and she told me, the day she was brought by Jane, she told me to cook for her local beans and maize.

Mbithe (E): When you came to Kenya you saw many women, but the day you were brought to her by Jane, you told her to go and cook for you *kienyenji* [local maize and beans]. [Laughter.]

Claire: That's true.

Mbithe (Ka): It's true.

Berida: And I cooked and the Kikuyu cooked *nzave* and we took them.

Mbithe (E): She cooked and the Kikuyu cooked *njahe* and they took them.

EXCERPTS FROM TAPE TRANSCRIPT 98-12-10-12, 20-21, 26-28

Claire (E): Tell her another reason I wanted to do her story is that it is a good story and she is a good storyteller.

Mbithe (Ka): Claire says that the reason why she wanted to write this book is because it is a good story and you are a good storyteller.

Berida: God gave me the gift. Even in my village people love me for this. I do not know how to be angry; I do not love material things so much so that I am greedy, no, whatever God gives me, that is mine.

Mbithe (E): She says God created her like that—she does not know hatred and even where she is born, the people really love her. She says that she doesn't love material things so much that she stretches her neck [as she demonstrated] to desire more, but she decides what is mine, just give me what is mine.

Berida: Right now people have been telling me that this woman, this *mzungu,* is deceiving you.

Mbithe (E): Like now people keep telling her that you are being cheated by this white lady; this white lady is cheating you, she is cheating you.

Berida: There is a *mzungu* who comes to our place in Kitui and brings Ksh.50,000. I tell them I am not interested in money.[2]

Mbithe (E): They tell her that there is a white lady who goes to their place at Kitui and she brings 50,000 to those people, so Berida told them, as for her, she doesn't want money.

Claire: OK.

Berida: Do you remember that day on our way to Makueni when we reached a kiosk, a woman called Kilaya and told her she was a teacher at TumuTumu, please find me a client? She saw a chance to take Kilaya from me.

Mbithe (E): She's saying when we were going to Makueni, there was a lady who approached you and told you she used to be a teacher, can you look for clients for her so that you can be writing to each other? Berida is saying, she wanted to take you from her—right then and there.

Berida: These are jealous people.

Mbithe (E): She says these are the jealous people.

Berida: Jealous people are like that, and I don't like it.

Mbithe (E): When people are jealous they are like that. She doesn't like it.

Berida: You saw for yourself. That person was asking, where is she going with a fool who doesn't know how to read?

Mbithe (E): That person asked her, why is this person walking with this fool who does not know how to read?

Claire: Who asked her that?

Mbithe (Ka): Who asked her that?

Berida: That woman.

Mbithe (E): That lady who was talking to you.

Claire: So she was putting down Berida?[3]

Mbithe (E): Yeah, calling her a woman who is illiterate. But Berida says you were brought together by God.

Claire: And why would being literate make her story a better story?

Mbithe (Ka): What could make the story of an educated person be better?

Berida: Because s/he is clever.

Mbithe (E): Because s/he is clever.

Claire: Does she think people who are literate are smarter than those who aren't?

Mbithe (Ka): Do you think people who are educated are more clever than those who are not educated?

Berida: For example, you, Kilaya, and Jane can talk about me and I wouldn't know.

---

2. Berida received quite a bit more than that from her role in the project.

3. The woman in question approached Claire to ask if she could find her a penpal in the United States. Nothing else was said.

Mbithe (E): Actually, they are more clever because she's saying you and Jane and I can gossip about her and she wouldn't know what we are saying.

Claire: Yeah, but even if she can't write, she might still be able to speak a bunch of languages and speak a language that somebody else doesn't know who is literate, like me.

• • •

Claire: OK. Let's have a question of factual detail. We now have three different stories about having the daughters initiated. We have Martha's story telling us she was the last one. We have Berida's story telling us none of them were done and also Berida telling us half of them were done. So what's the true story here?

Mbithe (Ka): There's something she wants to know where the truth is. The story about your daughters being circumcised. Martha said she was the last to be circumcised. But you said half of your daughters were. Then you also said that none of them were done. She wants to know, of these three stories, which one is true?

Berida: Let me tell you the true one. Martha is the one who was circumcised, the only one. The others were never circumcised.

Claire: So why do we have all these different stories about this?

Mbithe (Ka): She wants to know why there are three stories about who is circumcised or not.

Berida: I don't know if I'm the one who said that or maybe I just thought I would lie to the *mzungu*. Because the truth is that only one of my daughters is circumcised. And it is bad to lie even before God.

Claire: So why the different stories?

Mbithe (Ka): And why are there three stories?

Berida: I just told you. Since I was seeing a *mzungu* for the first time,[4] maybe I thought I should lie to her. [Laughter.]

Claire: I'm going to ask Jane something, since she has known Berida for longer than you have. OK, Jane, what do you think Berida thinks about me?

Jane (E): Berida is not learned. But the way she behaves towards you, she behaves like a learned person. For one, she says that most women are scared of white people, but she's never scared, she's so courageous. And she is so cooperative, especially she regards you with another concern that she can tell you anything that you ask her. She tells us from her stories that she always regards you like her own daughter. She considers you most . . .

Claire: Most what?

Jane (E): She can't lie to you. She responds with . . . whenever you send me a letter to take to her, she always takes it with a lot of appreciation.

Claire: So do you think she likes me?

Jane (E): She likes you a lot.

Claire: I like her a lot. She's an unusual person, and she has been very helpful.

---

4. This was not our first encounter and Berida had seen many white people in Kathonzweni and at Nairobi.

Mbithe (Ka): She says she likes you a lot because you have helped her.

Berida: Let me ask you, Mbithe, when did you say you'll bring me the *dawa* [Kiswhahili; medicine, in this case pesticide]?

Mbithe (E): She had asked me for some pesticide for her beans and I forgot to bring it today.

Claire: Where's she going to put it?

Mbithe (E): They have got weevils. That's why she wants to use it.

Claire: She knows she has to be careful with it?

Mbithe (Ka): She is asking if you know you should be careful with that *dawa?*

Berida: Yes, I'm very careful. I put a mask on. They are saying a bad famine is coming. And we should preserve what we harvested with *dawa.* Even it can stay for three years.

Claire: Who says that?

Mbithe (Ka): Who says a famine is coming?

Berida: The radio has been saying it.

Mbithe (E): The radio, I wonder if it's the one they announced.

Claire: Because of the flood she's trying to preserve the stock, save the stock?

Mbithe (E): Yeah.

Bibliography

Bascom, William. "The Esusu: A Credit Institution of the Yoruba." *Journal of the Royal Anthropological Institute of Great Britain* 82, no. 1 (1952): 63–69.

Berman, Bruce, and John Lonsdale. *Unhappy Valley: Conflict in Kenya and Africa.* London: James Currey, 1992.

Brown, Elsa Barkley. "African-American Women's Quilting: A Framework for Conceptualizing and Teaching African-American Women's History." *Signs* 14, no. 4 (1989): 921–29.

Buss, Fran Leeper, ed. *Forged Under the Sun/Forjada baja el sol: The Life of Maria Elena Lucas.* Ann Arbor: University of Michigan Press, 1993.

Davison, Jean, and the Women of Mutira. *Voices from Mutira: Change in the Lives of Rural Gikuyu Women, 1910–1995.* Boulder: Lynn Rienner, 1996.

Dorkenoo, Efua. *Cutting the Rose: Female Genital Mutilation, the Practice and Its Prevention.* London: Minority Rights Group, 1994.

Geiger, Susan. "Women's Life Histories: Method and Content." *Signs* 11, no. 1 (1986): 334–51.

Gengenbach, Heidi. "Truth-Telling and the Politics of Women's Life History Research in Africa: A Reply to Kirk Hoppe." *International Journal of African Historical Studies* 27, no. 3 (1994): 619–27.

Gluck, Sherna Berger, and Daphne Patai, eds. *Women's Words: The Feminist Practice of Oral History.* New York: Routledge, 1991.

Hansen, Karen T. "Transnational Biographies and Local Meanings: Used Clothing Practices in Lusaka." *Journal of Southern African Studies* 12, no. 1 (1995): 131–45.

Hobley, C. W. *Ethnology of A-Kamba and Other East African Tribes.* 1910. Reprint, London: Frank Cass and Co., 1971.

Hoppe, Kirk. "Whose Life Is It, Anyway? Issues of Representation in Life Narrative Texts of African Women." *International Journal of African Historical Studies* 26, no. 3 (1993): 623–36.

International Labor Organization. *Employment, Income, and Equality: A Strategy for Increasing Productive Employment in Kenya.* Geneva: ILO, 1974

Jackson, Kennell A. "An Ethnohistorical Study of the Oral Traditions of the Akamba of Kenya." Ph.D. diss., University of California–Los Angeles, 1972.

Kanogo, Tabitha. *Squatters and the Roots of Mau Mau.* London: James Currey, 1987.

Kenya National Archives (Nairobi). File No. DC/MKS 10B/15/1 (includes *Muigwithania* I, 2, correspondence, petitions, memoranda).

Lamphear, John. "The Kamba and the Northern Mrima Coast." In *Precolonial African Trade,* edited by R. Gray and D. Birmingham, 75–86. London: Oxford University Press, 1970.

Likimani, Muthoni. *Passbook Number F.47927: Women and Mau Mau in Kenya.* London: MacMillan, 1985.

Lindblom, Gerhard. *The Akamba in British East Africa.* Uppsala: Appelbergs Boktrycheri Aktiebolag, 1920.

Munro, J. Forbes. *Colonial Rule and the Kamba: Social Change in the Kenya Highlands 1889–1939.* Oxford: Clarendon Press, 1975.

Muthiani, Joseph. *Akamba from Within: Egalitarianism in Social Relations.* New York: Exposition Press, 1973.

Mwaniki, H. S. Kabeca. *The Living History of Embu and Mbeere to 1906.* Nairobi: East African Literature Bureau, 1973.

Ndeti, K. *Elements of Akamba Life.* Nairobi: East African Publishing House, 1972.

Ngaiza, Magdalene K., and Bertha Koda, eds. *The Unsung Heroines.* Dar es Salaam, Tanzania: WRDP Publications, 1991.

Ngugi wa Thiong'o. "Foreword." In *Tell It to Women,* by Osonye Onwueme, 7–10. Detroit: Wayne State University Press, 1997.

Penwill, D. J. *Kamba Customary Law.* Nairobi: Kenya Literature Bureau, 1951.

Personal Narratives Group, eds. *Interpreting Women's Lives: Feminist Theory and Personal Narratives.* Bloomington: Indiana University Press, 1989.

Patai, Daphne. *Brazilian Women Speak: Contemporary Life Stories.* New Brunswick, N.J.: Rutgers University Press, 1988.

Robertson, Claire C. "Gender and Trade Relations in Central Kenya in the Late Nineteenth Century." *International Journal of African Historical Studies* 30, no. 1 (1997): 23–47.

———. "Grassroots in Kenya: Women, Genital Mutilation, and Collective Action, 1920–1990." *Signs* 21, no. 3 (Spring 1996): 615–42.

———. "Post-Proclamation Slavery in Accra: A Female Affair?" In *Women and Slavery in Africa,* edited by Claire C. Robertson and Martin A. Klein, 220–45. Madison: University of Wisconsin Press, 1983.

———. *Trouble Showed the Way: Women, Men, and Trade in the Nairobi Area, 1890–1990.* Bloomington: Indiana University Press, 1997.

Strobel, Margaret. *Muslim Women in Mombasa, 1890–1975.* New Haven: Yale University Press, 1979.

BERIDA NDAMBUKI has been living and working in Nairobi for almost thirty years while traveling back and forth to her home, Kathonzweni, in Ukambani, Kenya. Her work as a retailer of dried staples and a dealer in other commodities has taken her into Uganda and Tanzania as well as all over Kenya. She is married with nine surviving grown children and numerous grandchildren. She is a leader of women's groups in Kathonzweni and at Gikomba Market in Nairobi. This is her first literary endeavor.

CLAIRE ROBERTSON, Associate Professor in the departments of History and Women's Studies at The Ohio State University, has a Ph.D. in African History from the University of Wisconsin–Madison and has specialized in the study of African women, especially traders, for some twenty-five years. She has published numerous articles and four books, including *Sharing the Same Bowl: A Socio-economic History of Women and Trade in Accra, Ghana* (1984), which won the 1985 Herskovits Prize from the African Studies Association, and *Trouble Showed the Way: Women, Men, and Trade in the Nairobi Area, 1890–1990* (1997), during the research for which she became friends with Berida Ndambuki. Their collaboration produced this book.